the irish americans

Also by Andrew M. Greeley
THAT MOST DISTRESSFUL NATION

the
irish
americans
THE RISE TO MONEY
AND POWER

by
andrew m. greeley

HARPER & ROW, PUBLISHERS, New York

Cambridge, Philadelphia, San Francisco,
London, Mexico City, São Paulo, Sydney

FIRST EDITION

Designed by Sam Gantt

Library of Congress Cataloging in Publication Data

Greeley, Andrew M 1928–
  The Irish Americans.
  1. Irish Americans. I. Title.
E184.I6G72   1981   973′.049162   81-47353
ISBN 0–06–038001–2

---

81 82 83 84 85 10 9 8 7 6 5 4 3 2 1

Contents

Introductory Note

THE IRISH I WILL WRITE ABOUT IN THIS BOOK ARE THE IRISH CATHO-
lics, the approximately 5 percent of the American population who
give their ethnic group as Irish (their national background is Irish)
and their religious affiliation as Catholic. I exclude the marginally
larger than 5 percent who are Irish Protestants for two reasons.

First, Irish Protestants and Irish Catholics in the United States have
had very different cultural and historical experiences in American life,
live in different geographic settings, and, in most respects, are very
different from one another. It is also true that most of the prejudice,
most of the controversy, and most of the belligerent self-hating responses have dealt with the Irish Catholics.

Second, I do not know enough about Irish Protestants to write
intelligently about them. There exists little literature to guide research on them and there are no working hypotheses I can test.
Somebody who knows more than I do about the subject or who can
persuade an agency to fund research on Irish Protestants certainly
ought to write a book about them.

Unless otherwise indicated, the terms *the Irish, Irish Americans, Irish
Catholics,* and *American Irish* are used interchangeably throughout the
book to mean Irish Catholic Americans.

O N E

American–
But Still Irish!

LET US BEGIN WITH A NUMBER OF PROPOSITIONS ABOUT THE AMERICAN
Irish which everyone knows to be true:

1. Despite a long period in America, the Irish have not been occupa-
   tionally successful. They continue to be disproportionately working and lower-middle class in their occupational achievement.
   Nor are they successful in the educational and academic endeavors:
   they have failed to contribute their proportionate share of college
   graduates, scholars, and intellectuals.

2. Despite their membership in the Democratic Party (weakening
   with suburban integration), the Irish tend to be both conservative
   and racist.

3. Irish drinkers are more likely to have acute alcohol problems than
   are other Americans.

4. With Americanization in opposition to the liberal changes of the
   Second Vatican Council, Irish Catholics are beginning to drift
   away from their traditional Catholic faith.

5. While the Irish may still be a meaningful group politically, there is
   very little cultural difference between them and other Americans;

1

the link with the Irish cultural heritage is so tenuous as to be nonexistent.

6. Because of the Catholic insistence that the proper role of a woman is as wife and mother, Irish women have a decidedly second-class position in Irish family life.

7. Irish political leaders have rarely given more than lip service to liberal political causes because of their emphasis on pragmatic considerations and their concern about loyalty, and because of their propensity to political corruption.

One hardly need write a book to sustain such propositions. One need merely pick up an Irish-American novel like John Gregory Dunne's *True Confessions* or Tom McHale's *Farragan's Retreat,* or read Thomas J. O'Hanlon's *The Irish,* to see that the above propositions are well known, generally accepted, and incontrovertible.

They also happen to be untrue.

The preceding schematicized summary of the conventional wisdom about the American Irish is false in every detail:

1. In terms of education, income, and occupational achievement, Irish Catholics are the most successful gentile group in American society. Their college attendance rate (among all people of college age) crossed the national average in about 1907 and has remained substantially above it ever since. It is now roughly comparable to that of Episcopalians. Furthermore, of all the ethnic groups, only Jews are more likely at the present time to produce publishing academic scholars.

2. Politically and socially, the Irish are the most liberal non-Jewish ethnic group in America; the most likely to support integration; the most likely to support the legalization of marijuana; and also, astonishing enough, most liberal in a number of measures of attitudes about sexual promiscuity.

3. Among those who drink, there is no difference between Irish Americans and English Americans in the alcohol-problem rate. There is some evidence that alcohol-problem rates among the Irish are lower than they are among certain European groups, such as the Poles and the Slovenes.

4. Since the Second Vatican Council, the Irish are more relaxed in their approach to ecclesiastical discipline and practice than they

were during the immigrant era, but there is no appreciable sign of their departing the Catholic religion. (And, as we shall see later on, in choosing religious permissiveness contemporary American Irish are merely returning to the ancient Irish tradition.)

5. In some respects the Irish, one of the early immigrant groups of America, have unintentionally, and often despite themselves, maintained greater cultural diversity and greater cultural distinctiveness than groups that have come after them—in their family life, their attitudes toward achievement, their world view, their drinking behavior, and their political style. Irish distinctiveness continues unabated, with no sign that either generation in America or the decline of ethnic self-consciousness notably diminishes this distinctiveness.

6. Irish women hold more power in family relationships than women of most other ethnic groups. Indeed, in the old country the Irish are, according to a recent Common Market study, the most feminist of all nations in the EEC (Denmark being second).

7. Irish politics have indeed tended to be pragmatic. But there is a strong liberal strain in the Irish political heritage which can be ignored only by those who are uninformed on the history of urban America.

I submit the above counterpropositions not as a matter of personal opinion, conjecture, or surmise, but as documentable and indeed documented facts. This volume is not a "defense" of Irish Catholic Americans: if anything is being defended in this book it is objective reality. There is, I assert, an objective order of some sort in our society. Those who continue to deceive themselves about the condition of the American Irish are doing more harm to themselves by their ignorance than they are to the Irish.

I propose in this book to celebrate the success of the American Irish. As I will note many times, there are still considerable deficiencies in Irish Catholic life in America. Furthermore, the Irish Americans' success has been purchased at a heavy price. Nonetheless, the achievements of the American Irish deserve to be celebrated.

The self-hating and the defensive Irish Americans are arguing over the same question—Why aren't the Irish successful? The self-haters say, "The Irish can never really become successful Americans because of their problems with alcohol, their other-worldly religion, their anti-intellectualism"; the militant defenders say, "The Irish are as good Americans as anyone else; look at all the war heroes we have had, our great athletes, actors, and writers."

I deny the pertinence of the question about success. The empirical evidence establishes beyond any doubt that the Irish have become full-fledged participants in the educational and intellectual life of America and have not ceased to be Irish. The self-haters and the militant defenders accept the native American prejudice imposed on them in this country and Anglo-Saxon prejudice in the homeland.

The right question is, How can the Irish be American and still continue to be Irish?—that is the question to ask about any ethnic or religio-ethnic group in America. In this book I shall attempt to go a little bit beyond the beginning of an answer to the question, but we have only begun to understand how cultures get mixed and we know very little about how the subcultures of American pluralism inter-relate with the overarching national culture. Until very recently some scholars thought the question wasn't worth asking and others thought that it was even wrong to ask it.

What do I mean by success? What is the "money and power" which appear as the subtitle to this book? I do *not* mean merely that some Irishmen can be president of General Motors or editor of the *New York Daily News* or president of Columbia University or, even transiently, President of the United States. These and similar achieve-ments, however impressive, can be attributed to the special talents of extraordinary men—the admirals and the generals and the actors and the athletic heroes can be followed by the political and educational and corporate leaders without anything else being proven than, as they used to say of Joe Louis, "He is a credit to his race."

I mean something more than the individual success of a few gifted men. I assert that the Irish as a group—as a collectivity, to use the sociological term—have moved far beyond the average white Amer-ican in income, education, and occupation. Among Americans under forty, Irish Catholics earn three thousand dollars a year more than the average, have almost two years more of education, and are several grades higher on measures of occupational prestige. These advantages exist after one has taken into account the fact that the Irish are not heavily located in the South or in rural areas, where income is lower than in the rest of the country.

Not only are Irish Catholic Americans substantially above the average, they are at about the same level as Episcopalians and Pres-byterians and second only to the Jews in income, education, and occupation. It would be strictly and statistically true to say that Irish

Catholics are, in terms of annual income, now the most affluent gentile ethnic group in America and virtually tied with Episcopalians for being the most affluent non-Jewish religious group in America.

I am not making this assertion in any chauvinistic sense of bragging about Irish accomplishments and belittling the accomplishments of others. My point is rather that while in the nineteenth century the immigrant "Paddy" was portrayed in satirical cartoons as a large simian with a club in one hand and a bottle of ale in the other, and in the twentieth century such distinguished Irish-American writers as William Shannon and Daniel P. Moynihan have lamented the failure of the Irish to achieve economic success in America, the predictions of the cartoonists and the journalists and the professors in the nineteenth century about the Irish were wrong, as is the self-description of many of the twentieth-century Irish.

This fact must be respected as fact. It does not make the Irish better than others, nor does it make them worse. It merely puts them in their proper place in a description of American social stratification and raises two fascinating questions:

1. How did a group which was almost universally doomed to mere respectability in the nineteenth and early twentieth century happen to achieve great success in America?

2. Is the price of such achievement the loss of any identifiable Irish heritage?

The second question will prove relatively easy to answer; the first is more difficult to respond to because sociologists and social historians have yet to develop techniques and methods for studying the mobility of immigrant populations (and the Census Bureau, which refuses to recognize that European ethnic groups matter, doesn't ask the right questions—and in the absence of a religious question would not provide useful data in any case).

A number of comments must be made to dispel the kinds of responses one often hears to statements about Irish success. It is not the result of the Irish family having more wage earners than other families. Nor is it the statistical result of the fact that blacks and Hispanics are an underclass on which the Irish stand—not any more than is the higher income of any group statistically the result of low incomes in certain nonwhite populations. Although it is repeated frequently, this response makes no mathematical sense whatever because it seems to assume that a relative increase in the income of one group must be made at the cost of a relative decrease in the income of others. Finally, the success of the Irish is not the result of the emergence of a solid Irish middle class with very few rich and very few poor (a narrow standard deviation, in the terminology of statistics). Irish Catholics are overrepresented in the top 10 percent of the country in both income and education. The proportion of Irish Catholic Ph.D.'s is now above the national average, and Irish Catholic young people are as likely to go to college as Episcopalian young people.

When did this Irish Catholic success story begin to unfold? It seems to have happened almost overnight. Was it a phenomenon of the post-World War II economic expansion? Why wasn't it noticed until recently? Why indeed do some writers (like economist Thomas Sowell, who relies on census figures which mix Irish Catholics with Irish Protestants—who are less "successful" in quantifiable terms—and resolutely refuses to credit the fact that there are slightly more Irish Protestants—5.2 percent—than there are Irish Catholics in the United States—4.8 percent) refuse to admit that it has in fact occurred?

Actually, the Irish success story began long ago. In the first decade of the present century—when James T. Farrell's Studs Lonigan was enrolling in grammar school—the college attendance rate of Irish Catholics already exceeded the national average. Educational parity with the rest of the country was probably achieved throughout the Irish Catholic population by the 1930s (when the college attenders of the turn of the century would be in their fifties). Thus, the Irish success story seems to be forty years old at least. The economic disaster of the Great Depression probably masked the success, though by the late 1940s there ought to have been no doubt about it—long before Ambassador Shannon and Senator Moynihan wrote their books lamenting the Irish failure.

Leaving aside questions of prejudice and self-hatred, there are two reasons for misperceptions about Irish achievement in America. First of all, Boston is the intellectual capital of the nation and New York the cultural capital. Professors and media analysts have looked around themselves in these cities and seen an Irish population which seemed to have some wealthy folks—the Kennedys and the Murrays and the McDonnells—and a lot of solidly respectable clerks, cops, and foremen. That's the Irish, they have said to themselves and to the rest of the nation. As I will note later in the book, however, those in Boston and New York are not typical of the American Irish. The evidence available from contemporary surveys suggests that the Midwestern (north-central, to use the Census Bureau's term) Irish are more affluent, better educated, more devout, and more liberal than their East Coast relatives.

The second reason for misperceptions about the Irish is that there were no national data available to measure the upward mobility of immigrant groups until sample surveys began to ask questions about ethnicity and to do so over a number of years so a sufficiently large data base could be assembled to justify confident generalizations. From the late 1940s to the mid-1970s, the Irish success story in America went unmonitored.

In brief historical outline, the poor Irish of Mr. Dooley's Bridgeport were already sending their children to college at the national rate in the years before the First World War. Studs Lonigan was the son of an upwardly mobile independent entrepreneur (who would be wiped out in the Great Depression). During the 1920s my family could belong to a (Knights of Columbus) "country club" in Wisconsin. The Great Depression delayed and masked the progress that was occurring, but in the years after the Second World War a vast Irish business and professional class swarmed out of the universities and brought the Irish decisively into the ranks of the upper-middle class. Nineteen sixty marked the legitimation of all this with the election of John Kennedy and the much less noticed turning of the Irish toward the academy and to the ranks of the Ph.D.'s. In the 1970s the income gap between the Irish and the Jews was closing (although more Jews than Irish refuse to answer income questions). Among the Irish today, a Ph.D. degree is more common than was a high school diploma when my father graduated from high school in 1904.

Those who misunderstand the nature of statistical argument will often say in response, "Yes, but everyone's educational achievement has gone up in this century; the Irish haven't gone up more than anyone else, have they?" The answer is that if you mean the average number of years of school attended, the Irish average has indeed gone up more sharply than the national average; if you mean the rate of college attendance of young people of college age, the Irish rate has been *higher* than the white national average as far back as we have data (the first decade of the century).

Picture a relatively smooth line sloping upward from 1910 to 1970. The average represents the rate of college attendance of those who were college age for each decade (actually, the log of the odds ratio). There are two lines above the national slope—one for Irish Catholics and one for Jews. Both lines remain above the national slope throughout the sixty-year period. The lines for the Italians and the Poles, on the other hand, begin below the national slope but cut sharply upward in the mid-1940s and cross the national average in the 1960s.

To the question, then—Did the Irish benefit from the prosperity of the years after the Second World War?—the answer is yes but not disproportionately. Like everyone else they benefited absolutely, but unlike the Poles and the Italians, the prosperity and the G.I. Bill did not put the Irish in a position from which they could improve their relative situation, precisely because their relative situation (in terms of college attendance, at any rate) *was already above the national average.*

To move to the second half of my thesis, even though they've made it big, the *Irish are still identifiably Irish.* Just as the conventional wisdom once said that the Irish couldn't succeed in America, a new conventional wisdom is willing to admit that they have succeeded but are no longer Irish in any meaningful sense of the word. Two recent Irish-American writers—McCaffrey and Fallows—both propound this position, as do the typical St. Patrick's Day articles in American newspapers lamenting the passing of the "good old days."

Let me anticipate my discussion of Celtic culture for a moment and say that you will never be able to understand the Irish (should such a will-o'-the-wisp be your goal) unless you comprehend that their modified dualism forces them to oscillate on many emotional continua, including the one between self-pity and triumph. In any serious conversation about cultural survival, your typical Irish American will say first of all, "Ah, sure, they were great days and grand people and glorious times, but 'tis all over, finished, done, more's the pity." Long sigh and perhaps a sip of "the creature." "They'll not see our like again." Another very long sigh.

Ten minutes later some innocent may observe that Hugh Carey sits in Albany watching the world go by with melancholic black Irish wit and Daniel P. Moynihan sits on the banks of the Potomac lecturing the world with witty black Irish melancholy (or any other currently successful Irishmen or Irishwomen may be substituted ad libitum). The mick will wink his eye and grin at you: "Ah well, there's still a few of us around."

A reader unfamiliar with this cultural trait will be taken in by the Irishman who says that the old days are over. However, as the monsignor in the most affluent parish in Chicago once remarked, "The good old days are now."

In an earlier volume, called *That Most Distressful Nation: The Taming of the American Irish* (an occasional paragraph of which will turn up in this book), I committed the unpardonable offense of irony, noting that despite my title, the data (much more sketchy than those on which this book is based) suggest that the Irish haven't been tamed at all. The irony was missed, and reviewers reported that the Irish had indeed been assimilated and that the issue was whether it was a good thing or not. This time I avoid irony: the Irish have not been assimilated or acculturated or anything else like that. They have become American and are still Irish, not the way the Irish in Ireland are Irish perhaps (some ways less, some ways more), but still identifiably and probably irrevocably Irish.

What do I mean by becoming American and still being Irish? I mean that they have become the most successful educational, occupational, and economic gentile ethnic group in America while at the same time maintaining cultural patterns whose origins can be traced to their past and which do not seem to be eroding with education, generation in America, movement to the suburbs and, in some cases, intermarriage. Such patterns can be found in their family structure, their religious behavior, their political attitudes and participation style, their reaction to death, their attitudes toward family size and the role of women (larger families and support for feminism . . . and to hell with the seeming contradiction), their occupational choices, and their use and abuse of alcohol. In their politics, their family, their religion, their drinking, and their dying, the Irish are still Irish and show few signs of changing.

Are they like other Americans in many other ways? Of course they are. Different subcultures do not mean total cultural dissimilarity. Even the Irish in Ireland and the Italians in Italy are more like one another than they are different; both peoples belong to the same human race, the same Judaeo-Christian civilization, the same Catholic Church, the same Western world.

The areas of cultural dissimilarity on which I concentrate happen to be the ones which are available. As research goes on, we hope to explore more areas of subcultural diversity. So far, though, the evidence is that the Irish are and continue to be different . . . not completely different, but still different and not becoming appreciably less different.

My thesis about the survival of Irishness is frequently met with such objections as, "They don't identify as Irish anymore," or "They don't keep ethnic customs," or "They intermarry; there are no ethnic group boundaries." "They live like other Americans. How are they different?"

When my colleague William McCready and I were preparing our research on ethnicity and alcoholism, we were examining the standard scales used in the traditional alcohol research to measure "heavy" drinking. Professor McCready looked at me in surprise, "Almost everyone I know in the neighborhood either has given up drinking for his own good or is a heavy drinker according to these scales. How can you be a heavy drinker if you just have one drink before dinner every night?"

Precisely the behavior that could have been predicted two thousand years ago by someone who, studying the Celts, might have been asked what sort of drinking patterns one might expect from Celts should they survive another two millennia. Nor are drinking levels affected by education, generation in America, proportion of Irish in one's neighborhood, ethnic self-consciousness, and even ethnic intermarriage (not something of which this Celt—nor Professor McCready for that matter—feels inclination to be proud). The marginal increment in drinking caused by having two Irish parents is small: one parent is quite enough to pass on the heritage.

In addition, the Irish are (demonstrably, not anecdotally) the most politically active ethnic group in America. The same assertions that were made about drinking can be made about political activity. And these assertions could also have been readily predicted by a "sociologist" two thousand years ago.

Those who refuse to believe in the durability of residual behavior among ethnic subcultures seem to have "blank slate" models of human behavior. After one generation or two in America, they seem to believe, the immigrant groups have all their cultural uniqueness wiped out and are ready to be written on by the fresh new chalk of American society. Furthermore, each child is assumed to go off to the (public) schools without any previous influence of family culture, to be shaped into a good little American who is utterly unaffected by his family's past.

Yet we know, for example, that black children speak a dialect of English heavily influenced by West African forms and that Jewish children have a high achievement motivation passed on through their heritage (and a low propensity to alcohol, too). Why would not behavior patterns of other subcultures also survive for centuries? Or is it possible that those who assert that the Irish subculture has vanished don't think it ought to survive? Might it not be that some ethnic subcultures are good and others are bad? Could it be that it is the bad ones which are said to have vanished because the wisest people in the country wish to heaven that they would vanish and the sooner the better?

In our research on drinking, my colleagues and I have demonstrated that many important ethnically linked traits are transmitted in early childhood without any conscious intention on the part of the parents to transmit an explicitly ethnic characteristic. The example of parents, the behavior of the other members of the subculture of which the family is a part (neighbors, friends, relatives), the values to which the parents commit themselves, the relationship of parents to one another and to the children—all these subtle but powerful influences insure that, let us say, Irish and Jewish subcultural approaches to politics and drinking, for example, get transmitted from generation to generation no matter what happens in school or what is seen in the mass media or even whom one marries.

My sister the theologian tells the story of a student named Tony who, with characteristic Italian hand gestures, objected to her course on the Theology of Ethnic Pluralism on the ground that his background was Italian but he was as American as anyone else. Said sibling, having read one of my books, asked Tony how often he went home to visit his mother (Italians have the highest rate of parent/child interaction of any ethnic group in America). Hands still waving, Tony replied that he went home at least every weekend and sometimes more often. He was astonished at the laughter of the other students. "What's the matter? Don't you love your mothers? Aren't you good Americans? All good Americans see their family as often as they can." Only then did it dawn on him that behavior which he took to be typical of all good offspring was in fact ethnically linked.

*   *   *

In the next chapter I will make a number of predictions about what one might expect about Irish Americans on the basis of what one knows about ancient Celtic culture and the history of Ireland. The predictions all can *and will* be sustained by empirical evidence. The hand of history is upon the Irish, I suggest, just like it is on everyone else—perhaps more heavily on the Irish, because there has been so much glory and so much sadness in their history.

I don't want to claim too much. Irish Catholic Americans have

more in common with Italian Catholic Americans than either have
with their ancestors in the time of Julius Caesar. Yet there are differences in, let us say, their drinking and their politicking which would
be expected by those who have studied the lands of their origins, and
these differences are not going away.

The marriage relationships of Jewish Americans and Italian Americans will be, of course, heavily influenced by the culture of contemporary America, but they still have different average attitudes about
the role of women, differences which, again, would have been perfectly predictable to a social scientist two thousand years ago who
knew only about Celtic and Mediterranean cultures.

Some critics of research on ethnicity, such as Harvard Professor
Orlando Patterson, complain that ethnicity is "imprisoning." Perhaps
it is. Heritages transmit liabilities as well as assets. But no useful
purpose is served by supposing that the heavy hands of heritage will
go away if only we would not talk about them.

It is utterly beyond my power in the present book to show how,
for example, the Irish attitude on the role of women (pro-feminist in
both this country and Ireland) has been handed down through the
centuries. I can merely call attention to the parallels among the ancient Irish brehon laws as to the rights of women, the response of the
Irish to a Common Market study on the role of women, and the
Irish-American response to questions on feminism in the National
Opinion Research Center's (NORC) General Social Survey. The
heritage, I will be content to contend, is a useful model for ordering
data about the present—more useful than any other available to us.
Irish Americans are not totally explained by their heritage, but understanding the heritage will help one understand the American Irish
and may even help them understand themselves.

Thus, I will devote several chapters to discussing the history of that
heritage before trying to assess its place in contemporary America.
Chapters Two and Three will be about the Celtic heritage (from
prehistoric times to roughly the twelfth century) and the painful
(and still unresolved, perhaps unresolvable) cultural clash that resulted from the English invasions of Ireland. Chapters Four and Five
will look at two of the formative experiences of the Irish in the
United States—the immigrant trauma itself and the now all but forgotten political nationalism with which the American Irish tried to
achieve respectability for themselves by working for, conspiring for,
contributing to, and occasionally even fighting for a free Ireland

(characteristically, they achieved partial freedom for Ireland and political power if not respectability for themselves). In subsequent chapters, I will discuss the present condition of Irish Catholics in America—a condition which, if it leaves something to be desired, is a hell of a lot better than any our ancestors could have dreamed of.

TWO

The Celtic Inheritance

LET US IMAGINE YOU HAVE COME UPON A GROUP OF PEOPLE WHO TALK a lot, enjoy puns and word games, sing songs, tell stories, write verse, are addicted to politics, drink too much, give considerable power to their womenfolk, are rather quick to lose their tempers, become contentious at the drop of a single word, seem to have a special mystical link with nature, are given to long journeys, and look at the world with a curious mixture of melancholy, fatalism, and grotesque hopefulness. You will see them as characters in an O'Faillon short story, or perhaps as personages in a James T. Farrell novel, or maybe as members of any one of a score of Irish Catholic parishes on the southwest side of Chicago or its adjoining suburbs.

Well, not exactly. Listen to Roman author Strabo describing mysterious Celts who lived out beyond the fringe of the Roman Empire at the time of Caesar.

Relying upon the work of a predecessor called Posidonius, Strabo says this of the Celts:

To the frankness and high-spiritedness of their temperament must be added the traits of childish boastfulness and love of decoration. They wear ornaments of gold, torques on their necks, and bracelets on their arms and wrists, while people of high rank wear dyed garments be-

14

sprinkled with gold. It is this vanity which makes them unbearable in victory and so completely downcast in defeat. In addition to their witlessness they possess a trait of barbarous savagery which is especially peculiar to the northern peoples, for when they are leaving the battle-field, they fasten to the necks of their horses the heads of their enemies, and on arriving home they nail up this spectacle at the entrances to their houses. Posidonius says that he saw this sight in many places, and was at first disgusted by it, but afterwards, becoming used to it, could bear it with equanimity.

And Diodorus, apparently a student of Posidonius, too, has a few things to say about the culture of the Celtic inhabitants of Gaul.

Physically the Gauls are terrifying in appearance, with deep-sounding and very harsh voices. In conversation they use few words and speak in riddles, for the most part hinting at things and leaving a great deal to be understood. They frequently exaggerate with the aim of extol-ling themselves and diminishing the status of others. They are boasters and threateners and given to bombastic self-dramatization, and yet they are quick of mind and with good natural ability for learning. They have also lyric poets whom they call Bards. They sing to the accompaniment of instruments resembling lyres, sometimes a eulogy and sometimes a satire. They have also certain philosophers and theo-logians who are treated with special honour, whom they call Druids.

Not all that much has changed, it seems, though a number of invading tribes have come—the Norsemen, the Normans, different waves of English—and there have been certain geographic changes from the County Kerry to the County Queens and from the County Mayo to the County Cook.

For our purposes, though, invasion, Christianization in a number of different forms, emigration, and even Americanization have left their marks, and some of the Celtic cultural characteristics have been muted. Strabo would not be all that surprised observing the modern Celts at a place like, say, Beverly Country Club in Chicago; he would hazard the guess that they still probably rule the province in which they live. He would be right, of course.

The Celtic heritage then is alive and well and most of the time unrecognized. One of my Irish-American friends commented after reading a book of ancient Irish poems of whose existence she had been unaware, "Those people think like I do." Yet, one is surprised; how can a submerged cultural heritage last so long? Is it possible that this generation of Irish growing up in the cities of the United States is still affected by the drinking, politicking, word-spinning, fatalistic, hopeful style that is a result of the heavy hand of a cultural heritage that has been almost wiped out at least six times since the Danes sacked Clonmacnoise?

One answer would be, Why wouldn't the Celtic heritage survive? No one is surprised that Hispanic heritage survived in Mexico, French heritage in Canada, Jewish heritage wherever there is a Jewish community in the world. Why ought the ancient Celtic heritage vanish? Why alone should descendents of the Celts come into life as a cultural tabula rasa, without any trace of influence of the great deeds of the mighty folk who, even before Patrick, walked the green hills of Ireland?

The mechanics and dynamics of cultural transmission and the survival of cultural heritage are not matters to which social scientists pay much attention, since they are more often interested in discontinuity than continuity, and in the elimination of old cultures rather than their persistence. My colleagues and I have been able to account for the durability among the Irish of religious world view, political style, and drinking behavior with an explanation that relies mostly on early childhood influences. Five generations in the United States have not notably affected Irish drinking, politicking, or praying; why should the invasions of the English or the Normans or the Norsemen or even the Christian monks of previous generations have made Celtic cultural influence inoperative?

Today's American Irish are very different in many respects from their Celtic predecessors. We have one wife at the most, we don't believe in reincarnation, we don't habitually send our children to foster homes—though we do believe strongly in human survival, we give women far more power and opportunity for personal achievement in our families (or maybe they simply take far more power), and we have much stronger sibling rivalries than do most other ethnic groups. A young woman who writes in her autobiographical statement for Harvard admission "I'm an Irish Catholic Democrat from Chicago and proud of it" would not surprise Strabo. How much of that opening line can be accounted for by ancient cultural influence is problematical. Presumably it will not explain a large part of the variance, as my social scientist colleagues would say. But yet it would also presumably not be completely unimportant.

To take exactly the opposite position, we must not expect inhabitants of Great Ireland to be similar in every respect to the inhabitants of Old Ireland.*

Most of the families from which contemporary Irish Americans are descended came to the United States more than a century ago—before Parnell and Archbishop Croke and Walsh evolved the great national compromise that produced the modern Irish nation; before the Easter Rising and the Irish Civil War; before the various land reform laws that gave the Irish peasants their own farms; before the Celtic literary revival at the turn of the century; before the Irish Republican Brotherhood; and before partition and the emergence of the country which has been successively called the Irish Free State, Eire, and the Republic of Ireland.

Sophisticated university students coming from Warsaw to the United States are dismayed by the polka-dancing peasants on the northwest side of Chicago, and the sophisticated Parisian intellectual doesn't know what to make of Quebec. Neither, in truth, does a professor at Trinity College feel much at ease at an Irish-American St. Patrick's Day party. Leaving aside questions of inferiority or superiority, cultural traditions change when they cross an ocean. Those people who cross the ocean and their descendents add one set of experiences to the ancient heritage while those who stay behind add another set of experiences.

The new heritages which emerge from this division may be first cousins, but they are often suspicious first cousins. "What rights do you Yanks have to think of yourselves as Irish?" asks the Old Irelander angrily. "You ought to be Yanks." To which the Great Irelander replies,."What the hell do you mean, Yanks?" To paraphrase Bernard Shaw slightly, Old Ireland and Great Ireland (and there are more of us than there are of them) are two people divided by a common heritage.

Which of the two cousins is more committed to the glories of the past? The wise man would be prudent not to judge. The Irish Americans are living in a pluralistic society where heritage has suddenly become important again. The Old Irelander is repelled by what he thinks is artificial Irishness; dismayed by the cultural stagnation of the De Valera years, he is frequently interested in minimizing his Irishness, emphasizing the fact that the Irish are Europeans. "There is no

---

* In one of the tales, Eric the Red, that noble Icelander (at least half Irish himself), sails beyond Greenland to a large body of land already settled by Irish monks which he calls Great Ireland, God forgive him, comparing it to Little Ireland on the other side of the Atlantic. Great Ireland was probably Labrador or Newfoundland.

particular need to be Irish," one perceptive Dublin sociologist said to me, "when everyone else around you is Irish." To which the Great Irelander is likely to reply, "Why in the hell would anyone want to be European when he can be Irish?"

Tolerance, an occasional Irish virtue, suggests that in their respective contexts both sides might be right. Anyway, it would appear that the Old Irelanders politick as much as we do, are as much a mixture of fatalism and hope, and oddly enough drink rather less than we do.

★   ★   ★

One place to begin a discussion on the Celtic heritage is with an old folk tale. In Jean Markale's *Women of the Celts,* we find "The Adventures of Art, Son of Conn," which appears to be one of the versions of the Quest for the Grail. The theme of the perilous cup is interwoven with that of tasks to be overcome before reaching the goal of the journey, the chosen woman who represents sovereignty. Art also needs her to fight the influence of a *geis* that is affecting the kingdom of Ireland and is clearly analogous to the spell affecting the desolate Land of the Grail.

> Because King Conn of the Hundred Battles had taken as concubine Becuna Cneisgel, a woman of the Tuatha De Danann exiled from the Land of Promise for some mysterious crime, Ireland was struck by infertility. The people tried sacrificing a child, for which a cow was substituted. But because the king could not send away his concubine, for he was bound to her by a *geis,* he still lacked a third of Ireland's harvest. One day, Becuna Cneisgel won a game of chess against Conn's son Art and forced him with another *geis* to bring back and marry a mysterious Delbachem, the daughter of Morgan, who was on a distant island. Art left and had to overcome fantastic trials in his search for the fortress in which Delbachem had taken refuge. He was received by her mother, who made him drink the contents of a cup; he had to choose between two, one full of poison, the other of wine, each held by a woman. Forewarned by a fairy queen, Art chose the right cup and then all he had to do was cut the head off his lady-love's mother, seize all the treasure in the castle, and take Delbachem back to Ireland. Then Becuna Cneisgel gave up and left Ireland, which immediately returned to its former prosperity.

Note that the pivot in every stage of this story is a woman. A woman imposes the tasks upon Art; another is the object of his search; yet another, a mysterious queen comparable to Peredur's Empress, who might well be just another face of Delbachem, helps Art in his ordeal. An *evil* woman is responsible for Ireland's infertility through her relationship with the king; this had shaken the natural balance he controlled, just as the forbidden amorous adventure of the Fisher-King had rendered him impotent and his land barren. Finally, a woman holds the cup through which Art finds victory, for it contains the wine he drinks to give him the courage and strength to fulfill his quest.

The story has a familiar ring to it: you have heard something like it somewhere before. Small wonder; it is an early version of the legend of the Holy Grail, an abbreviated version of a complex ritual and mythological cycle common to all the ancient Celtic people, an outline of the cycle scholars can now reconstruct from the traces which are available in the various surviving Celtic heritages. It was a spring ritual dealing with fertility (as spring rituals usually do) involving in some as yet unfathomed fashion a reference to blood as a source of life, linking both the magic cup and the magic woman to the deity. Seeking both vessels, the mythological cycle seems to have been saying, man also seeks God.

In the pre-Christian Irish version, the story has a rather different ending than does the version which has come down to us. The Irish Lancelot of the Lake gets the girl and the Grail, and the flesh is denied for Lancelot and his cousins Parsifal and Tristan, and so is the quest for happiness. The poor ancient Irish slob who was their predecessor managed to come home with both. Instead of losing forever his true love, he gets her and then has to work out the inevitable conflicts. But life and love and the flesh are not denied; on the contrary, they are affirmed. The medieval French can have their tragedies if they want them. The pre-Christian Irish preferred comedy when it came to telling a story about what life means. It would seem the Irish, even in those ancient days, were a difficult and contentious people who thought they knew more than others.

*   *   *

There was a profound strain of fatalism in the ancient Celtic culture. When it was written for you to die, you would die and there was nothing you could do about it. Warriors went charging wildly into battle quite unafraid. If they were supposed to survive, they would survive, if they were supposed to die, they would die and that was that. On the other hand, there was hope too. The warriors would not die permanently but would be born again (since the Celts believed in reincarnation), if not in this world then in the land of promise (also called the multicolored land) in the West.

The gods of the Celtic myths—Dagda and Lug, for example—were on the whole much more benign and pleasant folks than their counterparts on Olympus, although occasionally their triune female deity could become a bit bitchy. Later it was relatively easy for Dagda to become the Father in Heaven and Lug to become Jesus. Any number of the feminine deities might have become Mary; the one chosen was Bride, patroness of spring, new life, and poetry. She kept her shrine, her secret fire at Kildare, and reemerged as St. Brigid, who was also known as the "Mary of the Gaels." Many of the Irish believed Bride to be the Blessed Mother reincarnate. Although Mary and Brigid were of course sharply distinguished in the official religious tradition, the Brigid cross still pleads for warmth during the winter months over the fireplaces in western Ireland. The cross is the ancient Indo-European sun symbol, the spokes of the wheel representing the sacred disc wheeling back and forth across the sky. For the Christian Irish it came to symbolize Christ, the Light of the World, but remained a sun symbol. Similarly, the so-called Celtic cross is an Indo-European symbol of intercourse between the male and the female. It was transformed into a Christian cross representing Jesus and Mary. The Christian monks were skilled at converting the symbol without destroying its fundamental meaning.

In earlier ages, such transformations were known as the "baptism" of paganism. Today, understanding as we do the continuity of religious symbols, we would say much more benignly that Patrick and his followers had an instinctive understanding of the history of religion and saw that the mixture of hope and resignation at the core of the Celtic world view could be readily adapted for Christian use. Why not apprehend Lug as a prefigure of Jesus and Brigid a prefigure of Mary?

In a number of different studies using quite different measures, my colleagues and I have found that this unique blend of fatalism and hope persists two and a half millennia after that first trace of Celtic religious culture. In a study of all the American ethnic groups, the Irish have the highest scores on hope and also the highest on fatalism—measures which are negatively correlated for everyone else but positively correlated for the Irish. In another study done by my colleague William McCready, the Irish are rarely either "pessimistic" or "optimistic" in their world view; they are either "hopeful" or "fatalistic." King Art and the magic Princess Delbachem are still alive and well living on the southwest side of Chicago—which is more than you could say for Guinevere and Lancelot and that crowd of cultists of the unhappy ending.

*   *   *

Who were the Celts? They were a people, more appropriately a collection of people, who diverged very early in Central Europe from the primal Indo-European horde and swept westward in the millennium before the rise of the Roman Empire and the coming of Jesus of Nazareth. From Gibraltar to the Faroes and from the Rhine to the Danube (and if we are to believe Harvard scholar Barry Fell, to the forests of North America), the Celts dominated the Western world until they were pushed back to its fringes by the Romans and later the Anglo-Saxons. A distinctive culture survived only in Ireland, Scottish Ireland, Wales, the Isle of Man, and Brittany (where the British survivors of the Anglo-Saxon conquest settled—a conquest delayed perhaps for a hundred years of Celtic revival in Britain by the historical Arthur).

Clinging to the bays and the peninsulas and the rocky mountains and the twilight lands, the Celts managed to endure and ever flourish to the present (each generation, one suspects, characteristically asserts, "They will not see our like again"—a line made famous in Maurice O'Sullivan's book *The Islander,* a story of growing up on the islands just west of the Dingle peninsula, and mercilessly but brilliantly satirized by Flann O'Brien in his *The Poor Mouth: A Bad Tale about Hard Times).*

We know a good deal about Celtic culture, though much less than we do about contemporary Mediterranean culture since the Celts developed writing only late in their classical age. Most of our knowledge comes either from archaeological excavations—the most important in Switzerland and Austria—or from tales written down by monks in early Christian monasteries. (Of course there is still much to be learned about the Celts, particularly from archaeology. Hundreds, perhaps even thousands, of potential finds are lurking underneath Irish farmers' fields, and it is not at all unlikely that in the years immediately ahead there will be several revolutions in our knowledge of Celtic antiquity.)

At the risk of considerable oversimplification (and from a drastic

summarization of a fascinating literature), one can make the following observations about ancient Celtic culture with no sharp dividing
line between its pre-Christian and Christian manifestations:

The Celts were very sensitive to the rhythm of nature. Their poetry,
both Christian and pre-Christian, is filled with birds, fields, trees,
skies, rocks, and stars. The Celts were a mystical people, but their
mysticism was not of a world-denying variety. They established contact with the Ultimate not by cutting themselves off from nature, but
by immersing themselves in it. Most archaic cultures were acutely
observant of nature since life depends on the natural forces. The
Celtic sensitivity to nature has, in addition, an affectionate respect for
its forces, particularly the sacred land from which all life comes (the
Irish king was expected, metaphorically, to sleep with the goddess
Maive—or Queen Maive—who was supposed to be a sacred fertile
land of Ireland). Celtic culture and Celtic mysticism were "in communion" with nature.

Early Irish Catholicism was similarly "incarnational" in its religious perspective. It emphasized the sacred goodness of the land, of
the natural forces, and of the ordinary events of human life in a way
that the platonic Mediterranean Catholicism did not. Perhaps the
most noble expression of this "nature" Catholicism is in the famous
poem attributed to St. Brigid in which she pictured God the Father as
an Irish king striding through the bogs on a wet and rainy day with a
band of warriors. Arriving at the rath (hill fort) of another king,
eager for food and the singing of songs and the telling of tales:

> *I should like to have a great pool of ale for the King*
> *of Kings; I should like the heavenly Host to be*
> *drinking it for all eternity.*

> *I should like to have the fruit of Faith, of pure*
> *devotion; I should like to have the couches of*
> *Holiness in my house.*

> *I should like to have the man of Heaven in my own*
> *dwelling; I should like the vats of Long-Suffering*
> *to be at their disposal.*

> *I should like to have vessels of Charity to dispense;*
> *I should like to have the pitchers of Mercy for*
> *their company.*

*I should like there to be cheerfulness for their
    sake; I should like Jesus to be there too.*

*I should like to have the Three Marys of glorious
    renown; I should like to have the people of
    Heaven from every side.*

*I should like to be a vassal to the Lord, if I should
    suffer distress he would grant me a good blessing.*

I must confess that I am deeply moved every time I read the verses.
The poet, in bold image, wants the party to be a good party so that
God will enjoy it—and would like to have Jesus there too.

The image is impeccably Christian, but only the Celtic heritage
would be so dazzlingly reckless to use it. If Jesus could come to the
marriage feast of Cana and change water into wine to keep the party
going, one has to say that God would enjoy a good party. Nonetheless, only the Irish poets have said it.

The world view of the Celts is a "modified dualism." There is this
world of the fields and the flowers, the roads and the hedges, the
rocks and the rain, the billowing clouds, the soggy bogs: it is the real
world and not an illusion. The pleasures of the real world—food,
drink, farm, stories, the body of the beloved—are all to be enjoyed;
"There's nothing wrong with them at all!" But there is also another
world, peopled by gods and goddesses plus fairy folk and various
characters, such as leprechauns and pooka or banshees or angels and
saints or even Jesus and Mary, who have the habit of turning up at
unexpected places (just as did Lug and Morrigan and Dagda and
Bride before them).

This multicolored land is also real and more important than the
world of everyday; but it is not completely distinct from the material
world. On the contrary, the two interact and coexist. You never can
tell who might be lurking out there in the bogs or what creature—
good or evil or both or something in between—might be clumping
down the road in the mist. Bless yourself or say a prayer just to make
sure that the Good Folks are around and know that you are on their
side.

The Celtic world view does not have the sharp dualism of that of
the Greeks, which drew a firm, hard line between matter and spirit.
Neither is it like the animism of nature religions that knows no

distinction between matter and spirit. One lives in the world of the profane and enjoys it; but one is always prepared for the sacred to appear benignly or malignly (more often the former than the latter) without warning at the most astonishing times and places.

The modified dualism of the Celtic world view produces the peculiar oscillation of the Celt, ancient and modern, between puritanism and hedonism, between mortification and orgy. The mythological Irish hero would go through long periods of fasting and self-discipline and then engage in prodigious feats of eating, drinking, and wenching, as though there were no particular contradiction between the two kinds of activities. The penitential practice of the Irish monastery before 800 A.D. was the most severe that one can find in the annals of Western Christiandom (though it is not clear how often penitentials were used and how much they were written to persuade the Roman Church—with which the Celtic Church was in bitter rivalry—that the Celts were better Christians than anyone else). In one of O'Faillon's contemporary short stories, two adulterous lovers mortify their flesh by crawling up the rugged mountain of Corghpatrick on their knees and then decamp to the Salt Hill resort outside of Galway for several drinks, a good dinner, and a reassuring night together in bed.

If Irish Catholicism can fairly be charged with puritanical tendencies, it can also be fairly charged with libertine propensities. The Celtic heritage sees no contradiction between being a libertine and a puritan, or indeed, in moving rapidly from one modality of existence to another. On the contrary, if you have a modified dualistic world view (even if you don't know that is what your world view is), the pilgrimage from pleasure to penance and back again might make a great deal of sense.

Yet another element in the Celtic heritage is the comic tradition. Vivian Mercier argues (in *The Irish Comic Tradition*) that the Irish comic inheritance is archaic, that it is in direct touch with its primitive roots in the preliterate past, that it is more archaic than any modern Western literary tradition. It is precisely the archaism which gives the Irish comic tradition its strength and its interesting combination of absurdity and playfulness.

. . . like Homer or Aristophanes, he [the Gaelic writer] seems to believe in myth and magic with one half of his being, while with the other half he delights in their absurdity.

This play-spirit is characterized by two elements: the fantastic and the grotesque. "The humour of other cultures besides the Irish displays one or the other of these emphases, but I doubt whether both types of humour have been simultaneously fostered to the same degree by any other people." The fantastic, while it is often wild and occasionally sublime, is usually one step away from parody and fun-poking. "Behind the bards and the hagiographers, who endlessly strive to outdo each other in their accounts of heroic deeds and saintly miracles, there lurks the figure of the sceptic and/or parodist. Anyone who knows the contradictions of the Irish mind may come to suspect the sceptical parodist is but the bard or the hagiographer himself in a different mood."

> . . . and Cuchulain said: "I swear by the god by whom the Ulstermen swear, unless a man is found to fight with me, I will shed the blood of everyone who is in the fort."
>
> "Naked women to meet him!" said Conchobar.
>
> Then the women of Emain go to meet him with Mugain, the wife of Conchobar Mac Nessa, and bare their breasts before him.
>
> "These are the warriors who will meet you today," said Mugain.
>
> He covers his face; then the heroes of Emain seize him and throw him into a vessel of cold water. That vessel bursts round him. The second vessel into which he was thrown boiled with bubbles as big as the fist therefrom. The third vessel into which he went, he warmed it so that its heat and its cold were rightly tempered.

One can hear the howls of obscene laughter around the peat fire at that one, and the voices saying (in Gaelic, of course), "Good enough for him! Two pots boiling? Sure, he must have been a hot one!"

Nor are the "holy saints" immune from mockery, as is evidenced by the many versions of the famous dialogue between St. Brendan and the monk Scothian. To test his virtue, the monk habitually slept between two beautiful girls. Mercier recounts the story:

> Now two maidens with pointed breasts used to lie with him every night, that the battle with the Devil might be the greater for him. And it was proposed to accuse him on that account. So Brenainn came to test him, and Scothin said: "Let the cleric lie in my bed tonight," saith he. So when he reached the hour of resting the girls came into the house wherein was Brenainn, with their lapfuls of glowing embers in their chasubles; and the fire burnt them not, and they spill the embers in front of Brenainn, and go into the bed with him. "What is

this?" asks Brenainn. "Thus it is that we do every night," say the girls. They lie down with Brenainn, and no-wise could he sleep with long- ing. "That is imperfect, O cleric," say the girls; "he who is here every night feels nothing at all. Why goest thou not, O cleric, into the tub of cold water if it be easier for thee? 'Tis often that the cleric, even Scothin, visits it." "Well," says Brenainn, "it is wrong for us to make this test, for he is better than we are." Thereafter they make their union and their covenant, and they part *feliciter*.

The grotesque and macabre components of the play-spirit are also strongly sexual. The "wake games"—those bizarre forms of jolliness with which the Irish celebrated death—involved kissing, mock mar- riages, and gross phallic symbolism as well as "playing tricks on the corpse." Similarly, ridicule of marriage and sex ran through much of the wedding celebrations. Weddings were frequented by masked *crossans* (cross bearers) with grotesque bellies and phalluses as part of their costumes. The clergy managed to clean up the wakes and wed- dings—more or less—but, as one can tell from an occasional Clancy Brothers' ballad, the Irish are still laughing behind the back of the priest at the absurdity of both sexual union and death. If one lives very close to the forces of life and death, maybe laughing at them is one way to survive.

Irish comedy is savage. There was no fate worse than having the poets turned loose on you. The bards were satirists and parodists who ridiculed and attacked even the highest in the land. They delighted in stirring up trouble and making things difficult for any king who was reluctant to defend his honor in battle. Mercier says, "The bardic system throve on a constant diet of tribal warfare and cattle raids."

The poets loved to play with words, to deliver neat and witty epigrams, to engage in wild flights of fantasy; but they were testy, easily angered men, and when they turned their fury on you, you were in great trouble indeed. The later masters of Irish wit and parody and satire, such as Swift, Joyce, and O'Casey, came by their savagery legitimately.

So no matter how serious or grotesque their lives were, they must still laugh at them, and the joke might be scatological and obscene, perhaps, but a joke it remained. This is a dangerous and frequently barbaric perspective, but it is still one that helps man keep his sanity— and one that curiously enough can easily coexist with Christian faith.

Did the comic tradition cross the Atlantic? In some of the Irish-

American writers there can be no doubt that it remained alive. Edwin O'Connor's *The Last Hurrah* is as fantastic a book as one could imagine, and James Michael Curley's reply, *I'd Do It Again,* is even more fantastic. The not sufficiently noticed works of Edward R. F. Sheehan are models of pure Celtic fantasy—combined with the sexuality that apparently got lost when the tradition went into English (though not for Joyce). Flannery O'Connor is an unquestioned master at showing the macabre and grotesque that can exist alongside profound faith. J. F. Powers's Father Urban may not be Irish but his "mort" is not dissimilar from the fate of poor Cuchulain. Young Tom McHale, in his *Farragan's Retreat,* serves up a gross mixture of the fantastic, the grotesque, the blasphemous, the satirical, and the tragic, which indicates that even the younger generation is not immune from the tradition.

Another component of Celtic modified dualism is the strange propensity of the Celts to deal with death by defying it. Just as one responds to one's human enemies by ridiculing them, so the Celt responds to the ultimate enemy of all of us by laughing at it. Vivian Mercier insists that the grotesque humor which is a central element in Irish comedy is in fact the result of the Irish preoccupation with ridiculing death—and not infrequently ridiculing it by life-affirming sexual activity. The corpse is in the house, the mourners are singing and dancing and drinking and telling stories, and out in the fields lovers are having intercourse. "Fuck death," says the Celtic comic.

Is the defiant ridicule of death a healthy response, religiously or psychologically? Church authorities have not thought so and hence that millennium-long and ultimately successful battle to eliminate the wake (almost nonexistent now in Ireland): it is simply not "respectful" to be "carrying on" in the presence of death.

Psychologists might be somewhat less certain than an ecclesiastical authority. They, too, wonder about the violent intensity with which the Celt asserts that he is stronger than death, that he intends to follow Dylan Thomas's advice and not go silently off into that good night.

To tell you the truth, I don't know what to think—even of this propensity in my own personality. I'm not sure whether it's religious hopefulness, pagan repression, or some complex unanalyzable mixture of the two. The Irish reaction to death is perhaps the most intricate combination of our pagan past and our Christian faith. It is never very clear at any given moment in the Celt as an individual or the Celts as a group whether the Christian or the pagan attitude toward death is the more dominant. As fatalists, we acknowledge the inevitability of death; hopers, we keep our fingers crossed. We know we don't want to give up the good world in which we live. We are in terror of the sacred, be it good or be it evil, which is likely to intrude in our life just when we don't want it and demand of us that we give up our life. So we ridicule death, laugh at the sacred—and cross our fingers once again.

Whatever else it may be, the Irish reaction to death is surely not your simple Christian faith in resurrection. But neither does it preclude the resurrection of faith; it may in some imperfect and perhaps half Christian way include it.

The Celts were given to great voyages. Indeed, the voyage was often the link between the world of the flesh and the world of the spirit, between the profane and the sacred, between this land and the many-colored lands. Brendan did not sail through the west to find gold but rather to find the land of the promise—"Paradise." The body of the dying King Arthur is loaded onto a ship and borne off to Avalon whence someday it will return at last and the Celts will rise again in England.

With Ireland an island with many harbors and rivers and lakes, it is not surprising that the Irish would become seafolk and wanderers. Actual voyages, legendary voyages, and religious voyages could easily be confused with one another. For the Christian Irish, the *peregrinatio* was the ultimate religious act short of martyrdom (and there were no martyrdoms in Ireland until the English came). To found monasteries in England, France, Switzerland, the Rhineland, northern Italy and Austria, with neither missionary work nor the preservation of culture as a goal, was the primary intent. One rather went into self-imposed exile as a religious act, an act by which one sacrificed the thing which meant only less than life itself—the sacred land of Ireland. St. Columcille on the rocky shores of Iona, looking across the sea at his native country (from which he was allegedly banned for stirring up conflict between two branches of the royal O'Neill family), lamented for his homeland just over the horizon:

> *Delightful I think it to be in the bosom of an isle, on the*
> *peak of a rock, that I might often see there the calm*
> *of the sea.*

That I might see its heavy waves over the glittering ocean,
*   as they chant a melody to their Father on their*
*   eternal course.*

That I might see its smooth strand of clear headlands,
*   no gloomy thing; that I might hear the voice of the*
*   wondrous birds, a joyful course.*

That I might hear the sound of the shallow waves against
*   the rocks; that I might hear the cry by the grave*
*   yard, the noise of the sea.*

That I might see its splendid flocks of birds over the
*   full-watered ocean; that I might see its mighty*
*   whales, greatest of wonders.*

That I might see its ebb- and its flood-tide in their
*   flow; that this may be my name, a secret I tell,*
*   "He who turned his back on Ireland."*

That contrition of heart should come upon me as I
*   watch it; that I might bewail my many sins,*
*   difficult to declare.*

That I might bless the Lord who has power over all,
*   Heaven with its pure host of angels, earth, ebb-,*
*   flood-tide.*

That I might pore on one of my books, good for my
*   soul; a while kneeling for beloved Heaven, a*
*   while at psalms.*

A while gathering dulse from the rock, a while fish-
*   ing, a while giving good to the poor, a while in my*
*   cell.*

A while meditating upon the Kingdom of Heaven,
*   holy is the redemption; a while at labour not too*
*   heavy; it would be delightful!*

A century later St. Donatus, an Irish monk and Bishop of Fiesole, the town overlooking modern Florence, would write of the same country:

The noblest share of earth is the far western world
Whose name is written scotia in the ancient books

Rich in goods, in silver, jewels, cloth and gold,
Benign to the body, in air and mellow soil
With honey and with milk flow Ireland's lovely plains
With silk and arms, abundant fruit, strong women and men
Worthy are the Irish to dwell in this their land,
A race of men renowned in war; in peace, in faith.

Donatus is buried in the old white Romanesque cathedral, in Fiesole. Across the street one can look down into the Arno valley and the Duomo of Florence.

Barry Fell would have us believe—on the basis of evidence I am not competent to evaluate—that before the Romans wiped out their ocean-going fleets, the Celts had established an extensive kingdom in North America whose people would be absorbed into or perhaps more precisely constitute the eastern Algonquian tribe. However controversial such a novel theory may be and how many legends may have slipped into the *Navagatio* of St. Brendan, it is clear that by the time that tale was set down, Irish navigators had a fairly accurate picture of the North Atlantic basin.

Later, the Irish would have to be immigrants to all the nations in the English-speaking world and to many other countries besides. They left Ireland as reluctantly as did Columcille and Donatus and yet settled relatively easily into their new environment, perhaps because the tradition of the voyage was so powerful with them. Even today, Irish priests and nuns turn up in most nations of the globe and yet never quite leave Ireland behind.

The Celts were devoted to learning. Although it would appear that they developed writing only just before the pre-Christian era, the druids were careful students of the cycles of nature. (Some scholars suspect that the druids had developed a script for their own use long before anyone else found out about it.) Indeed, the druid may well have been more of a magus or "practical scholar" than he was a priest or a religious leader; he was certainly eager to understand the how and the why of the working of things. His Christian successor, the monk in the monastery, was also profoundly committed to learning, even if learning involved little more than the preservation of past knowledge and wisdom and not the creation of anything new.

The vocation of learning came easily from the pagan past to Celtic

Christianity and is beautifully symbolized by the poem of a monk to the best known cat who has ever lived, a certain Pangur Ban:

I and Pangur Ban my cat,
'Tis a like task we are at:
Hunting mice is his delight,
Hunting words I sit all night.

Better far than praise of men
'Tis to sit with book and pen;
Pangur bears me no ill will,
He too plies his simple skill.

'Tis a merry thing to see
At our tasks how glad are we,
When at home we sit and find
Entertainment to our mind.

Oftentimes a mouse will stray
In the hero Pangur's way;
Oftentimes my keen thought set
Takes a meaning in its net.

'Gainst the wall he sets his eye
Full and fierce and sharp and sly;
'Gainst the wall of knowledge I
All my little wisdom try.

When a mouse darts from its den
O how glad is Pangur then!
O what gladness do I prove
When I solve the doubts I love!

So in peace our tasks we ply,
Pangur Ban, my cat, and I;
In our arts we find our bliss,
I have mine and he has his.

Practice every day has made
Pangur perfect in his trade;
I get wisdom day and night
Turning darkness into light.

Irish Catholicism has often been accused of being anti-intellectual; the charge is perhaps more valid of the stripped down, hyperactive, immigrant American-Irish Catholicism than it is of the Catholicism of Old Ireland. It must also be said, however, that when you are under occupation by a foreign army, deprived of all political and civil rights, and threatened every decade or two by famine, it is hard to develop much in the way of intellectualism.

The Irish pilgrim monks preserved much of the learning of the Western world throughout the Dark Ages in monasteries like Clonmacnoise and Kells in Ireland and in their establishments all over Western Europe. The American Irish of my generation were brought up to believe that at one time Ireland was the land of saints and scholars—to compensate no doubt the fact that in the thirties and forties of this century we had precious few of either. Most Irish in the eighth and ninth centuries were neither saints nor scholars, though there certainly were more scholars there than anywhere else in Europe, and perhaps more saints too. There are scholars today both in Old Ireland and Great Ireland, indeed an impressive collection of first-rate young scholars in Great Ireland.

Perhaps because they developed a written language so late, the Celts were forced to rely heavily on the oral transmission of law, customs, religion, and philosophy. Poetry was a useful mnemonic device for transmitting oral tradition. Indeed, the brehon laws were in verse form; in the early stage in Celtic culture the poets and the lawyers were the same people. Poetry, therefore, was an obsession with Celts.

The ancient heroes of the mythological cycle—Finn MacCool and Cuchulain—were clearly in love with the sound of their own voices (and such legendary womenfolk as Dierdre, Grainne, and Maede conceded nothing to their male counterparts in their abilities to spin out long, complicated, and well-prepared poetic statements even at the most critical times). Like the Irish politician, the Irish priest, and the Irish paterfamilias of a later era, the ancient Celt did not know when to stop talking. Indeed, playing with language then and now becomes often not a means of communication. It is more of an amusement and entertainment, not infrequently self-entertainment (I am convinced that Jimmy Joyce's *Finnegans Wake* is a secret joke— himself laughing all the time—at scholars who would labor over dim dissertations trying to explain it).

It would appear that archaic people all over the world have not only more elaborate language structures (conjugations, moods, and the like) but also more extensive vocabularies than do modern people—perhaps because a spoken language needs greater flexibility and nuance than a written language. The vocabulary of the Irish speaker in western Ireland is half again as extensive as the vocabulary of the well-educated English speaker of London. Furthermore, as one approaches the *Gaeltacht,* or Irish-speaking regions in the west, the vocabulary of English speakers increases.

The modern Irish delight in ridicule, elaborate obscenity, scatology (there are available massive books of limericks and not a single one could be repeated on television), puns, riddles, and other such word games apparently abounded in ancient Celtic Ireland.

In a world of modified dualism, the transitions or turning points between times were especially sacred and especially dangerous. Twilight (between day and night), dew (which is neither rain nor sea water), the turning points between the seasons, the states which were neither life nor death (in which both Cuchulain and Arthur still sleep—once and future kings) are all examples of what Victor Turner calls liminality: situations when the ordinary structures of human society and the physical cosmos dissolve and almost anything can happen.

Wakes, baptisms, and weddings are also regarded as transitional times when the primordial chaos threatens to rush in, bringing with it both good and evil spirits and heaven only knows what else. The most important of Irish feasts are Samhain, on November 1; Imbolc, on February 1; Beltaine, on May 1; and Lugsnada, on August 1, each of them representing a change of season (winter, spring, summer, and autumn, the seasons being determined by the planting and harvesting and not by solstices and equinoxes). At the beginning of winter, Samhain is thought to be the most dangerous of the transitional periods because it is the feast of the dead. Imbolc is critical because between February and the middle of March is the time when the seeds must be planted and evil spirits can rush in to affect the crop. Beltaine, the spring turning to summer, is a happy, lighthearted fertility festival in which the coming of the harvest is celebrated. Lugsnada in August was the harvest and vintage festival with orgiastic celebrations and gratitude for fertility.

These festivals reappear in the Christian calendar as Halloween; the feast of St. Brigid (the presentation of Jesus in the temple on February 2); Easter in April (an anticipation of May Day); and Lady Day and harvest time in August. Pagan content survives in rural Ireland but in the United States has been reduced to such harmless pastimes as trick-or-treat or the Easter parade. The last generation of Irish Americans may have, like my mother, sprinkled holy water about the house when there were thunderstorms, but it was mainly concerned with medals, rosaries, relics, and other religious objects. The Irish today, one might argue, are no more superstitious than anyone else—though in an era of astrology and other such practices that may still be pretty superstitious. Amazingly enough, in a survey of young Americans, Irish young people are more likely than others to take astrology seriously.

Rulers of transitional times, the Irish goddesses were frequently connected with rivers. The Marne, the Seine, the Neckar, the Main, the Lahn, the Ruhr, the Lippay, the Seddern, the Cylde, the Shannon (the Goddess Sioana), and the Boyne (Boanna) all have names that are Celtic in origin. Sources of the sacred rivers were "womb openings." The rivers were the source of life and sacred not only because they were water but because they were flowing and rushing waters.

Many of the goddesses came in triads: Morrigan, Mecha, and Badh representing a maiden goddess, a bride goddess, and a crone goddess. Robert Graves thinks that the single line flowing into three concentric circles which is the famous decoration of the ancient burial monument at New Grange in Ireland represents the ancient White Goddess who is simultaneously maiden, bride, and crone at different stages of the life cycle. The interpretation is plausible, but New Grange was built long before the Celts came. No one can say with any degree of confidence what are the symbolisms or decorations.

The social and political cement that held the Celts together was loyalty. The brehon laws comprised a customary law without any formal enforcement. Social structure was little more than a loose and endlessly shifting confederation of petty chieftains. To the extent that he had any power at all, the high king was more a religious than a political leader. Effective political unity came to Ireland, and then only to a part of Ireland, in 1921. Personal commitment, one's pledged word, family responsibilities, elaborate systems of fealty, and equally elaborate systems of grudges were all that were required to hold society, such as it was, together.

I know of no study that would enable us to say whether loyalty was more important in archaic Ireland than in other archaic societies. Certainly it did not prevent war and bloodshed, though it perhaps minimized the impact of armed conflict. The Celtic system of loyalty was no match for the iron discipline in the Roman legions which facilitated the brilliantly controlled tactics of the Roman military commanders; nor was it any match for the superior social organization of feudal Normans or the rationalized ruthlessness of the English armies from Cromwell on. All one can say is that in both Great Ireland and Old Ireland, loyalty seems to be a more important social bond than it is in most other places in the modern world.

Eoin MacNeill, the great historian of Irish culture (and one of the leaders of the Easter Rising), has insisted that the term *tribal* is not an accurate one to describe Irish social structure, but as D. A. Binchy notes, *tribe* is just about the only word we have available in English to translate the Irish *tuath,* "a very small area, roughly corresponding to the modern barony" under the rule of a king or *ri* (from the same Indo-European root as the Latin *rex*).

In addition to ruling his tiny kingdom, the king might be an "over king," which meant that other leaders gave him hostages and paid him tribute. While the over kings ruled subordinate kings, they had no direct power over the lesser kings' subjects. In his turn, the over king would be subordinate to the highest king known to the laws, the king of a province. Occasionally some provincial king would claim to be "high king" *(ard ri)* of the whole country, but there was little ground in the laws and not much hope in practice of his exercising authority over the whole country.

Under the king were the nobility, who owned the land collectively as families, not individuals. Indeed, the extended family was the basic social unit; individual rights came from membership in the family, which consisted of "the descendents of a common great grandfather, four generations. . . . It was the normal property-owning unity, and it was also the unit for the purpose of dynastic succession."

Beneath the nobles in the pyramid were the "professional men"—the brehons who interpreted the law, the druids who were religious leaders, the "prophets" who foretold the future (the Irish word is *faith,* which is from the same root as the Latin *vates*), and the poets, who were apparently of two groups—the popular bards and the more scholarly *fili*. It was into this "professional class" that the Christian clergy were later to fit as replacement for the druids and the prophets—a fit that was not always a comfortable one, as Binchy remarks.

Finally came the common man, who was most likely to be free (slavery was rare), with his rights clearly specified by law. In Binchy's words:

> Then, as always, he did the chores: he tilled the soil, paid his taxes in the shape of food rent to the king, and usually stood in a quasi

contractual relation known as clientship to a neighboring nobleman, who in return, for a fixed render of provisions and a certain amount of boon work (or unpaid labor), advanced him stock to graze his land and guaranteed him a limited protection against the violence of other powerful neighbors.

There was no such thing as cities in Celtic society; indeed, there were not even towns. It was from the ninth-century Danish savages that the Irish learned about towns, and even then they tended to be centers for the Danes and later the Normans and the Anglo-Irish. The Irish kept to the countryside. (Even now they will tell you in the west that Dublin is not Ireland and that Cork really isn't either. Only the western cities of Limerick and Galway have some claim to the title. For the purists, only the Irish-speaking countryside—the so-called *Gaeltacht*—is *really* Irish.)

Thus, Celtic Ireland was "at once tribal, rural, hierarchical, and familiar."

There was little scope for the development of those political, administrative and judicial institutions which characterize the state as we know it today. The *tuath* was a small unity both in extent and population, hence there was no need for any intermediate bodies between the ruler and his subjects. Further, it contained no cities or walled towns, and it is a commonplace of history that the structure of our modern society is based on the city and the marketplace; the very words we use—politics, civilization, and so on—are a reminder of the urban roots of the society we live in.

But the most striking phenomenon in Irish society—and one that has important implications for an understanding of the American Irish and their political style—is that ancient Ireland had, as Sean O'Connor has put it to me, a system of law without law enforcement. The legal structure was entirely customary. In Kathleen Hughes's words:

How, then, was order maintained? Law was based on custom, and was declared through a special class of legal specialists, but, with one or two exceptions where the king had authority to execute it in special cases, it was privately enforced. There were no crimes against the state, only injuries to private persons, which must be met by compensation adjudged according to the injury received and the status of the injured party. Irish law had a well-developed surety system. Guarantors were taken to ensure the performance of customary obligations: each kin-group had, for example, its representative who guaranteed the duties to which his kinsmen were bound, and the king kept a "man of pledge for base clients" permanently in his household. When a man made an extraordinary contract he gave some treasure in pledge for its fulfillment, and if it was of major importance he also took guarantors who pledged themselves to see that the contract was maintained. If anyone failed to fulfil his contract his guarantors were liable, and failure meant loss of status with its rights to compensation and other privileges. The man who did not keep faith was degraded and lost his honour-price.

The king was not interested in law enforcement; there was only the most rudimentary form of state, and one obtained one's rights ultimately by force or threat of force. But it does not follow that either law or lawyers were lacking. On the contrary, there was an elaborate and detailed structure of laws and a powerful and learned legal class—the brehons. In Binchy's words:

> The main interest of Irish law for the student of early institutions is that it shows how a legal system based not on state sanctions but on the power of traditional custom, formulated and applied by a learned professional caste, could function and command obedience. . . . They showed remarkable ingenuity in devising methods of procedure which would compel the average citizen of the *tuath* to keep the rules. Perhaps, indeed, their very success hindered the evolution of public justice by diminishing the need for it.

One of the methods for keeping order was the combination of surety and honor described by Kathleen Hughes. If worse came to worst and the decisions of the brehons were not honored, the lawyers could turn to their allies, the bards, whose acid-tongued ridicule could bring even the most recalcitrant *ri* into line.

The Irish, of course, had no monopoly on either customary law or legal masters, but unlike common law, the brehon laws never had a chance to develop into a modern, state-enforced legal system. A foreign law was imposed and the Irish customary law was relegated to the bogs. (Yet even in modern Ireland there persists a profound suspicion of the formal, state-enforced legal system.)

It is tempting to make the obvious comparisons between the picture of Celtic Ireland that we have outlined and the political and legal behavior of the American Irish. Personal loyalty; informal arrangements; tight family structures; ridicule; boycott; and great love of legal learning combined frequently with little concern for the enforcement of the letter of the law; a fondness for legal contention and argument; suspicion of formal governmental regulations; indirect and circuitous ways of accomplishing one's purposes—all these are characteristic both of the American Irish and the ancient Celts.

Obviously, the relationship is a complicated one. The skills described above would have been necessary to survive a thousand years of foreign rule even if they were not part of the tradition. They also happened to be the skills that were appropriate for British parliamentary politics when the Irish Catholics began entering such politics in the early nineteenth century. At this stage in the development of our understanding, it is probably enough to say that much can be found in the Celtic tradition that is consonant with the behavior of the contemporary American Irish.

Women had an extraordinary amount of power in the ancient Celtic world. They could own property, choose or reject a husband, institute a divorce and recapture their dowry, take the sexual initiative, enter "trial" marriages of a year and a day, and even fight in battle. They were not the complete equals of men by any means, but their rights were carefully guarded by law, and in the relaxed sexual environment of the ancient Celts they enjoyed more personal status and more right to sexual pleasure than did women in the Mediterranean cultures. The relative equality of women is still part of Irish culture.

As Jean Markale notes in *Women of the Celts:* "This sexual freedom to a large extent explains the importance of women in Celtic society . . . it was full of archaism largely gathered and integrated from the original habitance of Western Europe. It was halfway between the patriarchal type of society, which is agricultural and based on the ownership of the land by the father of the family, and matriarchal societies, in which the mother, or women in general, remained the basic link in the family and the symbol of fertility."

One may have reservations about Markale's vision of ancient societies as matriarchal and patriarchal; nonetheless, Celtic women were remarkably independent. "She could become head of the family, rule, be a prophetess, enchantress, or educator, marry or remain a virgin (which meant refrain from marriage), and could inherit part of her father's or mother's property."

Two millennia later, the British Gallup organization did a survey for the European Economic Community of attitudes toward the role of women in nine European societies. The second most "feminist" society was Denmark and the most "feminist," Ireland. The Danes and the Irish ranked first or second in virtually all the indicators. The Gallup study went completely unnoticed in the Irish media and indeed was unknown at the Irish University until a wandering American sociologist showed up in Dublin with it.

Despite what American anthropologists have observed, the wife has enormous power on the peasant farms in western Ireland (apparently even more in the cities of Ireland and England). The husband works the land ("Ah, the man is a good worker!" is the highest compliment his wife can pay). But the woman keeps the books and manages the money, educates the children, and frequently even determines whether and when the property is going to be sold. She also seems to do most of the talking to visitors.

I will say more about Irish-American family life in a subsequent chapter. Here it suffices to note that both historically and at present the Irish woman is scarcely the poor battered victim of her husband and the Church that some Irish and Irish-American intellectuals have attempted to portray her as. Celtic women, for a couple of millennia, have been a hardy bunch. The truth is, I suspect, that many of their menfolk like them that way. I sure do.

★   ★   ★

Nature mystic, modified dualist, pilgrim, part puritan, part libertine, fatalist, hoper, ridiculer of death, scholar, loyalist, admirer of strong women—the ancient Celt is a little more complicated than Strabo's wild drinker and manic warrior. In both Old Ireland and Great Ireland, there have been additions, subtractions, changes, developments, overlays, modifications, regressions, depressions, continuities, discontinuities, contradictions, and surprises. Yet somehow much remains. Strabo would still recognize them at Beverly Country Club, especially as the night wears on and "the creature" begins to flow.

THREE

The English
Invasions

THE KEY FACT OF IRISH HISTORY IS THAT SINCE 1169 IRELAND HAS BEEN occupied partially or totally by an English army. The occupying army never subdued the Irish; neither have the Irish been able to get rid of the occupying army.

There have been five different waves of English invasions: the Normans in 1169; the Tudors in 1534; the Stuarts and the unspeakable Oliver Cromwell during most of the seventeenth century; the Protestant Union of the two parliaments in 1800; and finally, the establishment of the gerrymandered, truncated province of Ulster in 1921.

There have been ten major rebellions against English rule: that of Silken Thomas, the Earl of Cabir, in 1537; the Ulster rebellions of the various members of the O'Neill clan in 1595, 1641, and 1649; the revolt of Patrick Sarsfield in 1689. A century later Wolfe Tone and the United Irishmen launched the first of a series of risings which culminated in the merging of the English and Irish Parliaments in the Act of Union in 1800 and ended with the abortive rebellion of Robert Emmet in 1803. During the Great Famine it was the Young Ireland rising of 1848, and after it, the Fenian rising of 1857. Finally, after the failure of the parliamentary approach to home rule in Ireland, there came the Easter Rising of 1916 and the independence of twenty of Ireland's twenty-six counties in 1921. Since then, the permanent revolution has endeavored to drive the British out of Ulster.

Until the seventeenth century the invasions and revolutions were minor affairs, involving small armies and handfuls of leaders. The ordinary people of Ireland went about their lives more or less indifferent to the nationality of the particular lord who happened to rule them, an indifference that was reinforced by the fact that the lord himself might not be altogether sure.

With the coming of the Reformation, political war turned into religious war and Oliver Cromwell won his place in history as the first modern practitioner of genocide. During his decade-long invasion of Ireland, more than half of the population of the country died—about three-quarters of a million people—and in the two centuries that followed, Ireland went through an era of rebellion, atrocity, repression, misery, famine, punitive legislation, sullen resentment, and then the whole new cycle all over again—the Great Famine of 1848-49, in which the population of Ireland was again cut in half, from eight million to four million, by death and migration. There were at least four major famines in the two hundred years between Cromwell and 1848 during which tens of thousands, perhaps hundreds of thousands, of people died. But these other famines are remembered infrequently, being overshadowed by the Great Famine, which was the worst holocaust the world was to see before the one conducted in the Nazi concentration camps in the early 1940s. The Great Famine, however, was not the last famine; it was merely the worst. There would be a later one in the 1870s, precipitating the so-called "land league" war and a new wave of immigration to the United States (perhaps the largest of the emigration waves).

The nation's political and cultural elites were wiped out not once but several times. Lands were devastated, forests destroyed, populations ravaged repeatedly. The marvel is that anything that was Irish survived at all. Beginning with the reign of Elizabeth, the government's policy was to replace the Irish population with Scotch Presbyterians who would found "plantations," just as the "Plymouth plantation" and the "Baltimore plantation" were founded by colonists sent to North America to replace the savage and inferior American Indians. There were some "plantations" in and near the city of Cork, but most of them were located in Ulster, the northern Irish province where there had been the greatest resistance to English domination. The native Irish who were not won away from their superstitious papist ways by the Penal Laws were physically replaced by Presbyterian immigrants. Today we would call such a scheme genocide.

The plan was gradually abandoned when more easygoing and lackadaisical monarchs sat on the English throne. The English imperialist vision preoccupied only the Protestants of the earth. The Irish survived because of their own stubbornness and English inattention, but often they barely survived.

The picture is complicated by the fact that one wave of invaders became the next wave of revolutionaries. The Fitzgeralds who, from their citadel in Kildare, resisted the Tudors were themselves descendents of the Norman invaders who had come several centuries before. Many of the allies and leaders of the O'Neills were "Old English" Catholics, residents for several generations in Ireland, making common cause with the Irish against English Protestantism. Wolfe Tone and Robert Emmet were Protestant Anglo-Irishmen, as were some of the Young Irishmen of 1848. Parnell, the great Irish parliamentary leader at the end of the nineteenth century, was also a descendent of the Anglo-Irish. Many leaders of early twentieth-century Irish nationalism, such as the famous Maude Gonne and Erskine Childers, were English Protestants.

Sending English armies to Ireland was a risky business for the English crown. The descendents of each new invading army rapidly became more Irish than the Irish, many of them because they could not stand idly by and watch the horrible effects of the policies that the sober, responsible men in England had calmly imposed on the occupied land.

Nancy Cardozo, in her biography of Maude Gonne, tells of that high-spirited young woman's experience when riding with friends in western Ireland in the late 1890s. She came upon an English landlord expelling a tenant family. When told by the bailiff that the woman of the house was dying, the landlord replied, "Let her die; we must teach these people a lesson!" A fitting description of long years of English imperialism in Ireland.

*   *   *

Ireland was made to be invaded. The Celts themselves had come in invading waves for centuries, the Danes came, and the Norman English came after the Danes. Indeed, the Norsemen and the Normans were ethnic cousins, the first coming directly to Ireland, the second coming via France and England. They did battle with one another in the twelfth century, and the Normans (who had some of the native

Irish on their side) routed the Norse king of Dublin (who had others of the native Irish on his side). Both groups, of course, settled down to become thoroughly Irish and indistinguishable from the rest of the population save by their names and by their cultural contributions—the Norsemen brought seaports and roads, the Normans, towns and cities, then Gothic cathedrals.

Given its long seacoast and hundreds of miles of navigable rivers, Ireland was certain to be invaded whenever hunger or population pressures or greed led to new stirrings among the mobile tribes on the continent of Europe. These invasions did not represent much in the way of a change for the countryside. It is true that in the ninth century the Danes sacked the great monastery at Clonmacnoise and raided the treasury of sacred vessels. However, twelve pious Irish kings had also sacked Clonmacnoise before the Danes got there. Armed bands had wandered around the countryside fighting one another as long as anyone could remember. New invaders fought those who had come before them but also made alliances with them.

In retrospect, who the "good guys" were and who the "bad guys" were seems to have been of little significance to the peasants of Ireland. There was very little sense of nationhood, as the high king who ruled in Tara was more a religious than a political figure. Rarely did he exercise much power over the rest of Ireland. High kings ruled only when they had the military power to enforce their rules, so political chaos and confusion were as natural as the bogs and the green grass. At the famed battle at Clontarf, when Brien Borou and the native Irish routed the Danes, there were as many Irish allied with the Danish king (by now a Christian) as there were fighting on the "Irish" side. For several hundred years the invading English found Irish leaders who were quite willing to make common cause against their own local enemies according to the not unreasonable strategy that once you got rid of your neighbors you could take care of the English one way or another.

Irish historians concede that English involvement in Ireland was historically inevitable. Such historians say the chaotic nature of Irish polity created a power vacuum into which ambitious feudal lords and then monarchs were irresistibly drawn. Ireland was close, disorganized, available, potentially profitable, and also, if every other justification failed, a marvelous potential base for an attacking enemy. During the War of the Roses, Ireland was the base for the House of York against the House of Lancaster. Later on, it would be a base for Spaniards against the English crown and a minor base for Germans against Great Britain. This nervousness about Ireland as a potential threat eventually became a self-fulfilling prophecy.

In the years before Henry VIII, the ebb and flow of English advance and Irish retreat, Gaelic resurgence and English reaction did little to destroy Irish culture or make Irish political life more chaotic than it had been. There were two sets of laws, ancient brehon laws of Ireland and the Anglo-Saxon and Norman legal system of England; two sets of nobility, the Irish kingships and the more recent English Norman counties and earldoms (with the most noble persons holding titles from the two systems); two approaches to religion, Gaelic monastic and English diocesan (both Catholic, of course); two systems of land holdings, Irish tribal and English feudal; two systems of political alliance, loyalty to the English king and loyalty to relatives, friends, and tribal allies. While these two conflicting and competing cultural systems were obviously at odds with one another, sometimes bloodily so, and while ideally the English had the vague hope that their cultural system would eventually triumph, in practice the English lords in Ireland were indistinguishable from their Irish counterparts.

In fact, the most vigorous of all the Gaelic resurgences was led by the Norman English nobles of Kildare, the Fitzgeralds. Garrick More Fitzgerald, the most powerful of the clan, was imprisoned for a time by Henry VII in the Tower of London, but was sent back as the king's deputy in Ireland (and virtually uncrowned king) with Henry's rueful comment, "All Ireland cannot rule this man; this man must rule all Ireland."

Until the time of Henry VIII, then, Ireland was as likely to absorb the English invaders just as effectively as it had absorbed the Danes, and the Celts before the Danes. The change started, not unsurprisingly given Irish culture, with the wandering eye of a woman.

During the middle of the twelfth century two Irish warrior kings, Dermot MacMurrough and Tirenan O'Rourke, fought with one another, as Irish warrior kings had been doing for at least a millennium, with raids and counterraids, bravery and brutality, resentment and counterresentment, and finally, MacMurrough kidnapped O'Rourke's wife, Derborgille.

The abduction was an abduction in name only, proof of the old Irish adage that a man chases a woman until she catches him, and Irish and Norman historians agree that Ms. O'Rourke arranged her own abduction: she informed MacMurrough where she would be, then rode off on horseback with him—weeping and screaming that she was being taken against her will. As one Irish historian remarks, neither of them could be accused of acting in the folly of youth, he being forty-two and she forty-four.

O'Rourke got his wife back the following year, but he never forgave MacMurrough. Finally in 1166, MacMurrough went into exile and sought the help of the French-speaking king of England, Henry II. A decade before, the English pope, Adrian IV (the only English pope in history), troubled by the religious chaos in Ireland, commissioned Henry to take over that country and straighten it out. The king had then been and still was too busy, but he encouraged some of his restless and impatient Norman knights to support Dermot, the chief of them being Richard Fitzgilbert de Clare (his nickname was Strongbow). Note the names: de Clare of course is French, Strongbow is Anglo-Saxon. (Clare would become not only an Irish name but the name of an Irish county.)

In what was almost a casual invasion, the Norman knights came to Ireland in support of Dermot, routed both O'Rourke and his ally, Rorie O'Connor, and Norse king of Dublin, Hasculf, established Strongbow (who married Dermot's daughter Eva) as the king of Leinster and of Dublin. The Normans, brave and resourceful warriors, within a century "conquered" Ireland and offered it in vague feudal submission to the still preoccupied English kings.

In the process, however, they became mostly Irish themselves. While they changed the culture of Ireland, Ireland also changed their culture. The names the Normans left become indistinguishable in Irish history from the Danish and Celtic names before them—Fitzhenry, Fitzgerald, Barry, Prendergast, Fleming, Roche, Evers, Synott, Coogan. As Irish historian Father Frances Xavier Martin remarks, "The tragedy of the Norman invasion was not the conquest of Ireland—for that never took place—but the half conquest. The Normans never came in sufficient numbers to complete the conquest. If the conquest had been complete as in Normandy, England and Sicily, a new nation would have emerged, binding the qualities of both peoples. Instead, by the year 1300, it was a drawn battle, with the Normans controlling most of the country but the tide was already beginning to turn against them. The Irish question had become part of the heritage of Ireland and of England." *

Martin's point is well taken. There was nothing inherently wrong

---

* "The Anglo-Norman Invasion," in *The Course of Irish History,* T. W. Moody and F. X. Martin, eds. Dublin and Cork: Mercier Press, 1967.

about the tribal chaos of the Irish polity. Kings like MacMurrough and O'Rourke had fought each other for centuries, not infrequently even stealing each others' wives. Little harm had been done to the culture or the people of the land; feudalism as a step in nation building would have been useful to Ireland since it was near another land that had embarked on a path that began with feudalism and would end with a centralized modern state. Internally, Ireland didn't need a centralizing feudal organization, but it had to fight other countries who were organized that way. If the Normans had been successful in feudalizing Ireland, it would have been a land much better able to fight off England. The Normans were good at cultural synthesis: in France they had become French, in England they had become English, in Ireland they became Irish. In France and England they had succeeded in imposing their own social order; in Ireland they were never strong enough to do that and were instead absorbed by the prefeudal tribal structure of the old Gaelic civilization. The cultural synthesis was not complete; Ireland was never really organized feudally and was indeed culturally inferior to England to the extent that it seemed unable to organize and fight dramatic wars of invasion and defense.

Until the time of Henry VII (approximately 1500), in other words, the fundamental misfortune of the English invasion of Ireland was not that Ireland had absorbed too much of what English feudal culture had to offer, but that it had not absorbed enough to be able to resist the powerful English crown.

With the coming of the House of Tudor, England left behind the feudal ages for a strong monarchy well equipped to embark on an imperialistic venture. Ireland was still politically disorganized and was very ill-equipped to resist English imperialism. To make matters worse, the conflict between the centralized English government and a decentralized Irish nation coincided with the Reformation. Political wars do not lead to human and cultural genocide; religious wars do.

The policy of genocide did not emerge at once. Henry VIII was determined to impose his new church on Ireland, to break the power of Norman Irish lords, to bring the restless Gaelic countryside under centralized control. He proceeded about these goals with characteristic ruthlessness; but he had no intention of destroying Irish aristocracy (Gaelic or Norman), much less of wiping out the Irish culture and the Irish people.

His daughter, Elizabeth, went a step further down the line toward genocide. She began her "plantations" in Ulster, replacing the unreliable "natives" in the most militant part of the island with sturdy, reliable Protestant lowlanders. But it was only with the coming of the Puritans that the destruction of Ireland as a people and as a nation became a matter of implicit and then virtually explicit English policy.

In the century and a half between Cromwell and the Act of Union in 1800, genocide—though hardly by that name—was the theoretical policy of the English crown in Ireland, though the policy was not vigorously enforced during the second half of that era. After 1800, there was a shift away from the Penal Laws, and in 1832, under the influence of Daniel O'Connell, came the legal "emancipation" of Irish Catholics. Nonetheless, even after O'Connell the country was kept in political and economic dependency, a province ruled by the central government in Westminster for another century in which there would be famine, cruelty, betrayal, and murder as British imperialism became ever more efficient in its techniques, more arrogant in its assumptions, and ever more insensitive in its responses until it gradually lost its grip on its Irish colony.

It was during the "colonial period," then, from Cromwell to David Lloyd George, 1650–1920, that the terrible harm was done to the Irish nation and Irish culture. The Irish language, which had survived the onslaughts of the English language from the time of Strongbow, succumbed, for all practical purposes, only in the second half of the nineteenth century, and the historical Irish heritage was virtually destroyed.

★   ★   ★

The Penal Laws began in Elizabethan times, were reinforced during the reign of Cromwell, and developed to their fullest after the triumph of William of Orange at the Battle of Boyne in 1691. They represent the most savage, repressive legislation that the modern world has ever seen. Land was confiscated from the Catholics: between the time of Elizabeth I and William of Orange, the British government took twelve million acres out of a total of fifteen million cultivatable acres in Ireland. Catholics, four-fifths of the population, were left with one-seventh of the land.

By 1704, Catholics owned but 14 percent of the land in the country (even though they constituted about 80 percent of the population), and by 1778 only 5 percent of the land was in Catholic hands. The remaining Catholic landlords went over to the established church to protect their property. The proprietors owned sixty thousand pounds a year of the total rental of Ireland, which was calculated at that time at four million pounds a year.

The Catholics got a subsistence living from the land, giving much of the fruit of their labors to the landlords while trying to feed an increasing population with a decreasing income. They were excluded from trade and business, and although northern Ireland entered the industrial age, the Catholic south was held in virtual agricultural slavery. Jonathan Swift in 1729 published "A Modest Proposal," a savage satire in which he proposed a solution to the Irish question "by killing off seven-year-old children," whose flesh, he suggested, would make "a most delicious, nourishing and wholesome food." There is no evidence that British public opinion was much stirred by Swift's satire.

In the early 1700s, the most repressive of the Penal Laws were enacted. All priests were required to register their names and their parishes under penalty of being branded with a red-hot iron; they were required then to swear allegiance to the House of Stuart or suffer banishment. Unregistered priests were to be castrated, though the Dublin government refused to go along with this barbarism. In 1719, all bishops were banished from Ireland under penalty of being hanged, drawn, and quartered; friars and monks were also banished. Public crosses, which were widely venerated by the Irish people, were destroyed. Catholic chapels were not permitted to have belfries, towers, or steeples. Catholic pilgrimages were banned under pain of flogging. Catholics were forbidden to sit in Parliament, to vote for members of Parliament, and to be members of grand juries (the local government bodies). They were forbidden to send their children abroad for education or to have schools of their own. A reward of ten pounds was promised for the apprehension of Catholic schoolmasters. Education at Trinity College in Dublin was reserved for Protestants. Catholics were forbidden to marry Protestants, and death was decreed for any priest who performed such a marriage. All marriages were civilly invalid unless they were performed by a minister of the Church of Ireland. Catholics were excluded from the legal profession; they could not be barristers, solicitors, magistrates, or judges. They could not be members of municipal corporations. They could not serve in the army or the navy; they could not bear arms; they could not wear swords on ceremonial occasions. They could not own a horse worth more than five pounds; any Protestant seeing a Catholic with a more valuable horse could compel him to sell it for five pounds. Catholics might not acquire land from Protestants; a Catholic landowner could not deed his estate as a whole; no Catholic could hold a lease for more than thirty years, but a Catholic who became a Protestant could inherit his father's whole estate.

Lord Chancellor Bowes summarized the whole thing beautifully when he said, "The law does not suppose any such person to exist as an Irish Roman Catholic." His successor, John Fitzgibbon, the earl of Clare, called Catholics "the scum of the earth." Wolfe Tone, the Protestant revolutionary, described the Penal Laws as "that execrable and infamous code, framed with the art and the malice of demons, to plunder and degrade and brutalize the Catholics."

Dean Swift, no lover of the Catholics by any means, commented, "The rise of our rents is squeezed out of the very blood, and vitals, and clothes, and dwellings of the tenants, who live worse than English beggars." Bishop George Berkeley commented that the Irish peasant was "more destitute than savages, and more abject than negroes. . . . The very savages of America are better clad and better lodged than the Irish cottagers throughout the fertile counties of Limerick and Tipperary."

There was no restraint of any sort on the landlords' power to get the highest rents possible. Resulting from the increase of population, the shortage of land was acute, and rents constantly moved up. Even though he paid his rent, the peasant had no guarantee against eviction to make room for another willing to pay more. As much as they hated the "rack-renting," they hated the tithes even more. The peasants' tithes provided vast sums of money for the Protestant Church of Ireland, which served very few people. In 1753, for example, out of sixty-seven Protestant parishes in County Clare, sixty-two had no Protestant church and most had no parson or curate; nonetheless, the peasants contributed to the support of those parishes.

There were still more Penal Laws. No Catholic was permitted to have more than two apprentices. No Catholic was permitted to manufacture or sell books or newspapers, or to grant mortgages. No Catholic priest, even if he was registered, was allowed to move one step outside his parish. A Catholic wife who became a Protestant was permitted to live apart from her husband and make him support her. Catholic orphans were brought up as Protestants. Protestants were forbidden to take Catholic apprentices. A Protestant landowner lost his civil rights if he married a Catholic, and a Protestant heiress who married a Catholic forfeited her inheritance.

Writing in 1780, Arthur Young observed:

> The cottages of the Irish, which are all called cabins, are the most miserable looking hovels that can well be conceived. . . . A landlord in Ireland can scarcely invent an order which a servant, labourer, or cottier dares to refuse to execute. . . . Disrespect, or anything tending towards sauciness, he may punish with his cane or his horsewhip with the most perfect security. A poor man would have his bones broken if he offered to lift a hand in his own defense.*

And Edward Wakefield noted, "Landlords of consequence have assured me that many of their cottier's would think themselves honoured to have their wives and daughters sent for to the bed of their master—a mark of slavery which proves the oppression under which such people must live." **

In other words, the state of the Irish in the 1700s was not very much different from that of the slaves in the southern part of the United States at the same time. The survival of the Irish under such circumstances is quite surprising. They must have astonished their British and Anglo-Irish overlords, who thought that the "final solution" to the Irish problem shouldn't have taken so long.

Interestingly enough, much of the Penal legislation also affected the Ulster Presbyterians, who were as ready to join revolts as their Irish Catholic enemies well into the nineteenth century. The rising of the United Irishmen in 1798, for example, was a truly national affair, with the Presbyterian farmers of the north, the Catholic peasants of the south led by their priests, and the Anglo-Protestant disciples of the French Revolution, such as Wolfe Tone in Dublin, banding together in common cause against England. By the late nineteenth century, however, while the alliance between the left-wing Protestants and the southern Catholics continued, the Ulster Presbyterians had opted out of the coalition.

There are many different ways to survive under such a repressive regime.

---

* Biovanni Costigan, *A History of Modern Ireland*. New York: Pegasus, 1970, p. 94.
** Ibid.

Among the more interesting phenomena of Penal Ireland were the "hedge schools," illegal and informal schools in which teachers and students met, frequently out of doors, so that some sort of education would be imparted to Irish Catholic children. The hierarchy, clergy, and laity of Ireland feared that the official school system was nothing more than an attempt on the part of the ascendancy to convert the children of Irish Catholics. This unquestionably helped to shape the mentality that led to a separate parochial school system in the United States.

The Irish Catholics, like the blacks of the American South, proved adept at developing modes of accommodation while retaining an independence of spirit. The propensity of the Irish to answer a question by asking one may be a product of the Penal times. It is plausible that the informal, roundabout, casual, and frequently implicit and unspoken Irish political style is a legacy from those Penal times, too. The fundamental distrust of official structures and disregard for official laws that allegedly characterize so many Irish politicians (and which unquestionably, in fact, has characterized such worthies as Mayor Hague of Jersey City and Alderman Prendergast of Kansas City) likewise may be traced to behavior patterns acquired during the Penal times.

Many of the Penal Laws were unenforceable, and no serious attempts were made to enforce others. Nevertheless, the Irish Catholics spent their lives in a country where it was presumed that they had no right to exist.

While there were no organized revolts between the enactment of the Penal Laws at the beginning of the 1700s and "the '98," there was, nonetheless, "agrarian revolt," as Irish Catholic vigilante groups rose up to protect what little was left to their countrymen. The White-boys began as a protest against tithing; the Oakboys against forced labor on the roads; the Steelboys to fight against evictions; and after them came the Ridgeboys, the Peep o'Day Boys, the Thrashers, Caravats, Shanavests, Rockites, Ribbonmen, and the Defenders.

Most of these secret vigilante groups were relatively harmless. Few people were killed, but houses were destroyed, hayracks burned, and cattle killed. Since these groups were secret societies, they were officially condemned by the Catholic Church; members were excommunicated, though it is unlikely that the parish priests were very opposed to their activities. The Mollie Maguires, who appeared in the coal fields of Pennsylvania, must certainly be viewed as an adaptation on the American scene of the Whiteboys and similar groups of the eighteenth century.

A final means of adaption to the Penal Laws was emigration to France and Spain to fight in the army, and to America to begin a new life. Those most likely to migrate to America before 1800, however, were not Irish Catholics but Ulstermen, who disliked the Anglican ascendancy in Dublin as much as the Catholics. Perhaps as many as a half million Ulstermen migrated to the United States and became an implacable enemy to British rule in the colonies.

These Ulster migrants defined themselves as Irish and used the term *Scotch-Irish* (which was given to them by others in America) only to distinguish themselves from the *Famine Irish,* who came after 1848. Also in this prerevolutionary migration were some south-of-Ireland Protestants, mostly of Celtic rather than Anglo-Saxon ancestry. Most of them were shopkeepers and artisans who had become Protestants during the Penal years; they were in good enough financial condition to emigrate during the earlier famines of the eighteenth century. Periodically, the Irish Catholic leadership lamented the fact that the Protestants, be they Ulstermen or converts, were better able to take advantage of the opportunity to migrate than the Irish Catholics; but of course they also had more opportunity to develop the self-confidence necessary even to begin to think about changing their situation than did the oppressed and miserable Irish Catholics. It was only the incredible crisis of the Great Famine that forced migration on many of them as the only alternative to death.

Beginning with the campaign of Daniel O'Connell and the resultant first Catholic Emancipation Act of 1829, the British government slowly and reluctantly repealed the Penal Laws, though it was only with the Wyndham Act of 1903 that the last laws against Irish Catholic land ownership were eliminated. A measure of the reluctance of the British government to remove the Penal legislation was that the price set for Catholic emancipation in 1829 was that O'Connell agree that the property qualification for voting be raised from forty shillings to ten pounds. Potential Catholic voters were thereby reduced from two hundred thousand to less than 10 percent of that.

With such a history of extreme repression, it is indeed surprising not that the Irish hated the English, but that after their final liberation in the 1920s the hatred died so quickly. While it is presumably unwise to say so publicly in modern Ireland, an occasional Irishman will lament the fact that the British made such an absolute mess of the Union of 1800. Some sort of federation of independent states in the British Isles might have made a good deal of economic, social, and political sense, of benefit to all concerned. But both the Anglo-Irish ascendancy in Dublin and the British public and government in London were absolutely assured of the moral and religious superiority of Protestant rule; that freedom be given to Irish Catholics was as inconceivable to the English voter from Dublin Castle to Westminster as was freedom for blacks in the American South.

★　★　★

Perhaps three-quarters of a million Catholics died in the famine of the mid-seventeenth century; 1741 was called by the Irish "the year of the slaughter," with over four hundred thousand deaths from famine. But these were minor events compared to the Great Famine at the end of the 1840s. In 1841, the population of Ireland was over 8 million; by 1851, at the normal rate of increase, it should have been over 9 million; in fact, it was only 6.5 million. In the space of a decade Ireland lost 2.5 million people, probably less than half by migration. In other words, between 1847 and 1850 somewhere between 1 and 1.5 million Irish Catholics died while the British government barely lifted a finger to save them. Indeed, it continued to export agricultural products from Ireland and to clear tenants off the land. The Potato Famine, then, was one of the great disasters of modern Western Europe.

It is estimated that the population of Ireland was about four million in 1800, which meant that in the years between 1800 and 1840 the population had more than doubled, and some British observers described Ireland as the most densely populated country in Europe. These people lived always on the edge of famine, depending on the success of one highly unpredictable crop, the potato, for their existence. When the crop prospered, there was work and food aplenty (or at least enough); but when it failed, disaster was almost inevitable. The British government did not create the blight that destroyed the potato crop in the 1840s, certainly, but it did force upon Ireland the kind of political and economic subjection that made some sort of disaster practically inevitable.

The state of pre-Famine Ireland was described sympathetically by three Frenchmen: Gustave de Beaumont, his friend Alexis de Tocqueville, and Duvergier de Hauranne.

De Beaumont:

> I have seen the Indian in his forests and the Negro in his chains, and thought, as I contemplated their pitiable condition, that I saw the very extreme of human wretchedness; but I did not then know the condition of unfortunate Ireland. There is no doubt that the most miserable of English paupers is better fed and clothed than the most prosperous of Irish laborers.

De Tocqueville remarked that the wrongs done the people in Clare are retained "with a terrifying exactitude of local memory."

> Whatever one does, the memory of the great persecutions is not forgotten. Who sows injustice must sooner or later reap the fruits. . . . All the rich Protestants whom I saw in Dublin speak of the Catholics with extraordinary hatred and scorn. The latter, they say, are savages . . . and fanatics led into all sorts of disorders by their priests.

Duvergier de Hauranne wrote that there were in Ireland "two nations."

> There is nothing between the master and the slave, between the cabin and the palace. There is nothing between all the luxuries of existence and the last degree of human wretchedness.*

The fact that there existed within Ireland two nations, one the oppressor and the other oppressed, is clear when one ponders that between 1845 and 1850, when more than a million Irishmen were dying, two million quarters of wheat a year were shipped out of Ireland. In the Poor Law Act of 1847 it was stipulated that no peasant with a holding of a quarter-acre or more was eligible for relief—thus forcing people to sell their land. Lord John Russell, the prime minister of England, responding to an appeal from Lord Clarendon, viceroy in Ireland, wrote: "The state of Ireland for the next few months must be one of great suffering. Unhappily the agitation for Repeal

---

* The three Frenchmen are quoted in Costigan, op. cit., pp. 91, 103, 105.

[of the Penal Laws] has contrived to destroy nearly all sympathy in this country." Later, Clarendon told Russell, "I don't think there is another legislature in Europe that would disregard such suffering as now exists in the west of Ireland, or coldly persist in the policy of extermination."

The permanent head of the Treasury, Sir Charles Trevelyan, observed smugly: "The poorest and most ignorant Irish peasant must, I think, by this time have become sensible of the advantage of belonging to a powerful community like that of the United Kingdom, the establishments and pecuniary resources of which are at all times ready to be employed for his benefit." At another point he wrote, "The Irish problem [referring to overpopulation] being altogether beyond the power of man, the cure had been applied by the direct stroke of an all-wise Providence in a manner as unexpected and as unthought of as it is likely to be effectual." Finally, when a million people were dead, Sir Charles was moved to some compassion: "It is hard upon the poor people that they should be deprived of knowing that they are suffering from an affliction of God's providence."

Sir Charles Wood, Chancellor of the Exchequer and Trevelyan's boss, wrote to an Irish landlord: "I am not at all appalled by your tenantry going. That seems to me a necessary part of the process. . . . We must not complain of what we really want to obtain." And Sir Robert Peel benignly observed, "The time has come when it is not any longer necessary to pet Ireland. We only spoil her by undeserved flattery and by treating her to everything for which she herself ought to pay." Nassau Senior, Professor of Economics at Oxford, on whom the governmental leaders depended for economic advice, was quoted as saying that he feared the famine of 1848 would not kill more than a million people, and that would scarcely be enough to do much good. The London *Times* rejoiced at the thought that soon the native Irishman would be "as rare on the banks of the Liffey as a red man on the banks of the Manhatten." *

The Irish landlords (most of them Protestant) were facing financial ruin even if, unlike the peasants, they were not dying from hunger. What is more, they were also obligated to pay taxes for their tenants, who were paying less than four pounds a year rent. Most of

---

* Sir Robert Peel, Sir Charles Trevelyan, and Sir Charles Wood are quoted in Costigan, op. cit., pp. 185–187.

these people had not been able to pay rent for years, the landlords in effect being required to pay taxes for income they weren't getting. The only solution to their problem was to get rid of their tenants. That meant clearing tenants off the fields in which they and their ancestors had labored for generations. Whole villages were destroyed and their inhabitants driven away. An Irish officer, Sir William Butler, described what he had seen as a boy:

> One day I was taken by my father to the scene of an eviction. On one side of the road was a ruined church; on the other side stood some dozen houses which were to be pulled down, and their *denizens* evicted. At this time the weakening effects of the famine were still painfully evident in the people, and the spirit of opposition which, in after years was to become so strong, was not in being. The sheriff, a strong body of police, and above all the crowbar brigade—a group composed of the lowest and most *debauched* ruffians—were present.
>
> At a signal from the sheriff the work began. The miserable inmates of the cabins were dragged out upon the road; the thatched roofs were torn down and the earthen walls battered in by crowbars; the screaming women, the half-naked children, the paralysed grandmother and the tottering grandfather were hauled out. I was twelve years old at that time; but I think if a loaded gun had been put into my hands I would have fired into that crowd of villains, as they plied their horrid trade by the ruined church of Tampul-da-voun.*

To make matters worse, Asiatic cholera entered the country through Belfast and swept the island, causing tens of thousands of deaths. Eviction, starvation, emigration, disease—the British government had to do something: Lord Clarendon had a marvelous idea. The queen should visit Ireland. The city of Dublin would spend a thousand pounds in banquets for her majesty when two shillings would keep a family of five alive for a week. Despite some protests, the queen and her family came. There was a royal levee in which two thousand people were presented to the queen and a parade of inspection was held in which a thousand troops participated. Neither famine nor disease nor emigration were the least affected by this brave gesture of English imperialism.

---

* P. F. Speed, *The Potato Famine and the Irish Emigrants.* London: Longman Group, 1976.

All through the Famine, according to Cecil Woodham-Smith, cartoons were published "week after week depicting the Irishman as a filthy, brutal creature, an assassin and a murderer, begging for money, under a pretence of buying food, to spend on weapons." *

And Lord Tennyson, that darling of Victorian poetry, commented, "The Kelts are all made furious fools. They live in a horrible island and have no history of their own worth the least notice. Could not anyone blow up that horrible island with dynamite and carry it off in pieces—a long way off?" **

The island was not carried a long way off, but many of its people were; and not all of them made it safely to other shores. Thousands, perhaps tens of thousands, died either on the passage from Ireland or shortly after arriving in the New World. At Grosse Isle, near Detroit, for example, there is a plaque which reads, "In this secluded spot lie the mortal remains of 5,294 persons who, flying from pestilence and famine in Ireland in the year 1847, found in America but a grave." The North Atlantic crossing of the Irish emigrants was not as bad as the middle passage by which black slaves were brought to the United States, but it was bad enough, and those who survived could only look to a slight improvement. In Mrs. Woodham-Smith's words:

> The Irish famine emigration is unlike most other emigrations because it was of a less-civilized and less-skilled people into a more-civilized and more-skilled community. Other immigrations have been of the independent and the sturdy in search of wider horizons, and such emigrants usually brought with them knowledge and technical accomplishment which the inhabitants of the country in which they settled did not possess. The Irish, from their absymal poverty, brought nothing, and this poverty had forced them to become habituated to standards of living which the populations amongst whom they came considered unfit for human beings. Cellar dwellings, whether in English towns or the cities of North America, were almost invariably occupied by the Irish. Poverty, ignorance and bewilderment brought them there, but it must not be forgotten that cellar dwellings resembled the dark, mud-floored cabins in which over half the population of Ireland had been accustomed to live under British rule.***

---

* Cecil Woodham-Smith, *The Great Hunger*. New York: Harper & Row, 1963.
** Costigan, op. cit., pp. 185–187.
*** Cecil Woodham-Smith, op. cit., p. 207.

Many of the ships were called "coffin ships," not inappropriately. For example, the bark *Elizabeth and Sarah* was a small craft of 330 tons and carried 276 people to the promised land across the ocean. It was supposed to have carried twelve thousand gallons of water, but it had only a little more than eight thousand, in leaky casks. The captain was required by law to distribute seven pounds of food to each passenger weekly, but no distribution was ever made. There were thirty-six berths, thirty-two of which were to be shared among the 276 passengers; there was no sanitary convenience of any kind. The trip took eight weeks, and forty-two persons died during the voyage.

The Grosse Isle way station in Canada was an incredible center of human misery.

> On May 26 thirty vessels, with 10,000 emigrants on board, were waiting at Grosse Isle; by the 29th there were thirty-six vessels, with 13,000 emigrants. And "in all these vessels cases of fever and dysentery had occurred," wrote Dr. Douglas (medical officer in charge of the station)—the dysentery seems to have been infectious, and was probably bacillary dysentery. On May 31 forty vessels were waiting, extending in a line two miles down the St. Lawrence; about 1,100 cases of fever were on Grosse Isle in shed, tents, and laid in rows in the little church; an equal number were on board the ships, waiting to be taken off; and a further 45,000 emigrants at least were expected.*

One ship, the *Agnes*, arrived at Grosse Isle with 427 passengers, of whom only 150 were alive after the fifteen-day quarantine. After the quarantine the emigrants were crammed into steamers for transportation to Montreal, a trip of two or three days during which death often claimed half those aboard.

In 1847, one hundred thousand emigrants left Ireland for Canada. Seventeen thousand, it is estimated, died en route and at least fifty thousand more died in Canada itself. Thousands more died in the United States, but the disaster there was less severe.

It took perhaps a century for Ireland to recover from the effects of the Great Famine. By the early 1860s the population of the country was close to its 1800 level of four million. Through a combination of late marriage and continued emigration, the population was con-

---

* Ibid., p. 220.

tained at that level, with only marginal increases or decreases, for another century. It was only with the economic gains and development plans of the 1960s that sustained population increase began.

The descriptions of the Great Famine recorded by contemporary observers—corpses lying in the fields; the streets "black with funeral processions"; tenant farmers being packed into ships so that the lords would not have to pay poor taxes on them; emaciated men, women, and children struggling down the lanes on their way to death; frantic riots for food, occasional murders of the gentry, and (heaven save us) even a splendid state visit from Queen Victoria—can only begin to give a picture of the unspeakable horrors of such a disaster, one which the British political leadership viewed with some complacency because it helped to solve the problem of overpopulation in Ireland.

Was England guilty of genocide in the 1840s? Surely not in quite the way Adolf Hitler was; the British government did not directly execute the victims of starvation and fever. But British political and economic policies allowed an agricultural disaster to assume catastrophic proportions. British leadership viewed the sufferings of the Irish people with little compassion, and in some cases satisfaction.

There is another important difference, too. Those who managed to live through the extermination camps were hailed as heroes and given courage by a world that acknowledged the inhumanity of what had happened to them. There was no such solace for the survivors in Ireland or for those who immigrated abroad. The Irish immigrants were unwelcome, unwanted, and despised. Worse than that, their sufferings were tucked under the rug of world history, to be forgotten even by their own descendents.

When Cecil Woodham-Smith's *The Great Hunger* was published, the critical reaction was callous. No one, of course, denied the truth of her story or tried to defend the policies of the British government, but precious few reviewers seemed to be aware that there was in the United States a substantial population descended from those who fled for their lives at the time of the Great Famine. It is not that Mrs. Woodham-Smith ignores the connection:

> It is a matter of history that the Irish political record has some black spots. Irish emigrants, especially of the famine years, became, with rare exceptions, what their transatlantic environment made them, children of the slums, rebuffed, scorned by respectable citizens and exploited by the less respectable. The Irish were the most unfortunate emigrants

and the poorest, they took longest to be accepted, longest to become genuinely assimilated, they waited longest before the opportunities the United States offers were freely available to them.

The story of the Irish in the New World is not a romantic story of liberty and success, but the history of a bitter struggle, as bitter, as painful, though not as long-drawn-out, as the struggle by which the Irish at last won the right to be a nation.*

There seems to be a grudging reluctance on the part of American intellectuals to face the horrors of the Great Famine, the perils of the North Atlantic crossing, and the inhuman experiences of the immigrant Irish. Indeed, one finds precious little compassion for the Irish either in contemporary accounts of the early years of immigration or in present reflections upon those years. I am unaware of a single American intellectual who ever bothered to try to understand the present state of the American Irish in terms of their past experiences. The Irish have never been an approved object of sympathy or understanding in the American republic.

That is perhaps just as well, because at this point in time we are capable of declaring ourselves able to do without the compassion, sympathy, and understanding of certain liberal intellectuals; we made it in spite of generations of hatred and oppression. There lurks in the Irish psyche a profound skepticism about fashionable compassion. We are inclined to think such compassions are just a bit phony, and we wonder where those who proclaim them were when we needed their help. We also find it just a bit ironic when they demand that we feel guilty for what their ancestors did to the blacks and the American Indians. They do not seem to display much guilt for what happened to us at the hands of their ancestors here and in Europe.

However deeply felt and generally widespread is this skepticism among the Irish toward liberals, any recollection of the Great Famine exists, if at all, deep in the unconscious of the American Irish themselves. Many of us had grandparents, many more of us had great-grandparents who fled during those years or shortly thereafter. The story of the Great Famine, the crossing of the Atlantic and the fever on board ship, and the misery of the slum tenements of New York and Boston are neither part of our family traditions nor of the history we are taught—certainly not in the public schools, nor in the paro-

---

* Ibid., p. 269.

chial schools either. That the rest of the world would want to forget is understandable, but the Irish have cooperated, one might almost say enthusiastically, in blotting out the memory of the Great Famine. Perhaps it is too horrible to remember; perhaps we were so eager to become Americans that we quickly shed the memories of a non-American past; perhaps we so wanted to prove ourselves capable of respectability that we thought it expedient to dismiss the injustices that had been visited upon our predecessors. Maybe part of the price of acceptance into American society was that we forget the past. In any case, we have forgotten it.

That does not mean that its effects do not linger with us. No one would argue that the effects of the slave trade and slavery could be overlooked in an effort to understand American blacks—not even if blacks themselves wanted to forget. There is little difference in the history of the blacks in America and the Irish in Ireland until the 1860s. Both lived in abject misery, the victims of political oppression and economic exploitation. The principal difference is that the Irish, having white skins, were eventually given a chance to "earn a place" in American society; the blacks were not permitted to do so. Just as no reasonable student of American blacks thinks that their contemporary situation can be understood merely in terms of what happened since 1865, neither should any serious student of the American Irish assume that their history began when they arrived in this country.*

★   ★   ★

The Great Famine, for all practical purposes, destroyed Old Ireland. After it, there would only be cultural stasis and disintegration. Emigration creamed off the surplus population and many, if not most, of the more gifted and talented younger generation until the 1960s. The Irish language was forced into *Gaeltachts* on the western fringes of the island. The culture and tradition of the Irish would be reduced to folklore, their religion would be reformed (by Cardinal Paul Cullen of Dublin) to a new "devotional" Catholicism which combined French piety with English administration.**

---

* A monumental history of Irish Catholicism is being prepared under the direction of Patrick A. Corish of St. Patrick's College, Maynooth, Ireland.

** Emmet Larkin points out that intensely devotional Irish Catholicism as we know it isn't traditional at all, but an artifact of the Cullen years. Cullen in effect replaced the dying Irish language and culture by an intensely pious Catholicism as the focus of what little was

The sexual and family lives of the Irish were also profoundly affected. Marriages were delayed until people were well into their middle thirties, until the father was prepared to give up his farm to his first-born son, who only then could marry and bring his wife into the family house (exiling the mother and the father to the front room of the house). The other children migrated to the cities of England or America never to be seen again (American wakes were held when young people left for the States, because they were not expected to return). The late marriage and the transfer of property to the first-born kept the family holdings intact and minimized the possibility of another famine—and in the process another population explosion. However, the cost in sexual frustration and family tension was enormous and still haunts the Irish in both Ireland and the United States today.

The Church has been blamed by Catholics and non-Catholics alike for the late age of marriage in Ireland—in keeping with the practice of blaming the Church for the things that the English government had in fact caused. However, as Robert Kennedy points out, the Church bitterly opposed delayed marriages. Kennedy demonstrates that agricultural innovation (something as simple as a new kind of hoe) led to higher age at marriage. If there was a chance of ever so slight an escape from poverty, the Irish farmer would wait even longer to marry, hoping somehow to improve conditions for the children he somehow still expected to have.

The delay of marriage and the resulting sexual frustration and puritanism were not the result of Catholic teaching. The traditional Celtic Catholicism had always been tolerant if not lax on sexual matters—as it was of the economic, social, and political policy deliberately imposed on Ireland by the occupying power.

The struggle for political freedom went on, however. The distinctive Irish Parliament—the last relic of the fiction that Ireland was not a colony but indeed a separate nation united with the British crown—was eliminated in 1800. That backfired, however, because now there were Irish Catholic parliamentarians in London, often holding the balance of power between the Liberals and the Tories.

In the nineteenth century, particularly under the leadership of

---

left of Irish Catholic life in the country. In terms of regular religious practice, devotional Catholicism is doubtless superior to what went before, but most of the richness of the old religious tradition was lost—though some has been recovered in the Irish church-music revival in the years since the Second Vatican Council.

Gladstone, the previous British policy was reversed. Penal Laws were gradually repealed, home-rule legislation was pushed (though not passed until 1914 and then suspended), and Irish peasants were given increased rights over their land and eventually accorded something like ownership in the 1880s. So satisfied were the English with the land reform and the consequent relative prosperity for the Irish peasants that they were astonished when the Irish still insisted on rebelling in the first part of the twentieth century. George V, a humane and sympathetic man, was absolutely astonished at the Easter Rising, because he thought land reform had permanently settled "the Irish question."

There were three basic strains that characterized the Irish nationalist organizations in the nineteenth century after Daniel O'Connell: the parliamentary group, seeking constitutional home rule toward the end of the century under the leadership of Charles Parnell; the land reformers, such as Michael Davitt's Land League; and the secret revolutionary organizations, such as the Fenians and the Irish Republican Brotherhood (IRB).

These groups sometimes cooperated and sometimes squabbled with one another. The Sinn Fein, which was the political base of the revolt of 1916–23, stood somewhere between Parnell on the one hand and the IRB on the other. The founder of the Sinn Fein, Arthur Griffith, conceived of the union of Ireland and Great Britain much like the dual monarchy of Austria-Hungary. But after the events of the Easter Rising, the Sinn Fein and the Irish Volunteers became the Irish Republican Army and were swept irresistibly toward open revolt. The IRB, a small secret society, had written the scenario for revolt before 1900, and the stupidity of the British government in thinking that land reform would ultimately placate the militant minority that the IRB represented seems, in retrospect, quite incredible.

Even more stupid, however, was the bloody suppression of the Easter Rising in 1916, which drove the overwhelming majority of the Irish people—who had in the relative prosperity of the first decade and a half of the twentieth century little taste for armed revolt—into the arms of the IRB. These events, stirring, complicated, tragic, and often futile, took place in Ireland after its emigrants had arrived on the shores of the United States. As a matter of fact, one can say that instead of being shaped by the post-Famine political events, the American Irish helped shape the events. Without the financial and political support of the American Irish, it is questionable whether the revolt which began in 1916 would have been successful. Eamon De Valera, after all, was born in Brooklyn.

The Irish question was of course insoluble, for the English were absolutely convinced that their rule of Ireland was legitimate both legally and morally, and the Irish were equally convinced that it was both legally and morally illegitimate.

How can one explain the rebelliousness of the Irish? H. B. C. Pollard, an English police chief in Ireland during the Civil War, characterized only somewhat the fundamental English Protestant conviction that Irish Catholics were an inferior breed.

> Whether revolutionaries are aware of it or not, their morbid discontent with existing society, and their perfect willingness to embark on a course of action which will bring death and ruin to thousands, and even to themselves, in pursuit of a grand experiment or an inner vision, is not a wonderful self-sacrifice but merely a perverted form of self-gratification. The communist who talks glibly of shooting down the bourgeoisie is gratifying a perverted instinct with the prospect of a wholesale blood bath. The visionary who rushes to martyrdom for a cause gratifies once and for ever his masochistic propensity.
>
> It has been said that the Irish derive keen pleasure from the woes with which they cause themselves to be afflicted; and pleasure in pain is typical—significantly typical—of many of the conditions which I have outlined above. And when it is understood in its true bearing on the psychology of revolution and of revolutionaries, it must destroy the fine illusions and the glamour that, to some minds, hung about the leaders of "the murder gangs." There is nothing particularly fine about a group of moral decadents leading a superstitious minority into an epidemic of murder and violent crime; yet this is what has happened of recent years in Ireland, it is what has happened time and again in the past, and it is what will happen again in the future; for the Irish problem is a problem of the Irish race, and is neither a by-product of politics nor of environment, but is rooted in the racial characteristics of the people themselves.*

The cycle of revolt, strife, and depression was such that culture, learning, science, and technology had little opportunity to develop in Ireland. There had been a great culture in the monasteries between the time of St. Patrick and the invasion of the Danes in the ninth

---

* H. B. C. Pollard, *Secret Societies of Ireland.* London: Philip Alan and Co., 1922.

century, and there always was a folk culture; but generation after generation of Catholic aristocracy was either destroyed in battle or fled the country in the wake of unsuccessful rebellion. The Protestant aristocracy (in later days called "the Ascendancy"), cultivated as it may have been on occasion, had little influence on the rest of the country. Only in Belfast was there any industrial development, and the Act of Union cut short the economic and industrial development beginning in the south of Ireland. The Penal Laws with their victimization of Catholics, the repeated famines, and the devotion of the best resources of the most gifted people to rebellion were all factors that guaranteed Ireland would exist in a state of disorganized chaos while most of the rest of Europe was making an eventful entry into the modern world.

The myth of the slovenly, irresponsible, happy-go-lucky, and carefree Irish has caused most of us to assume that Ireland really did not have what it took to become a successful modern industrial nation. The Irish were seen as too busy with their dreams and their drink, with their poetry and their feuding, to ever become an effective modern state. What this stereotype overlooks is the fact that the Irish who migrated to the United States yielded nothing to anybody—save perhaps the Jews—in their striving for achievement, and that the Irish Republic, for all its problems, has been one of the most successful revolutionary countries of the twentieth century.

There are two important points that need to be made about the Republic. First of all, despite the intense factionalization of the period before the establishment of the Irish Republic, true democratic principles were established and maintained by the new government. The pro-Free State faction, led by William Cosgrave, accepted dominion status with Britain and finally prevailed over the anti-Free State faction led by Eamon De Valera. During the civil war these two factions killed each other off in much greater numbers than the English had, yet De Valera and Cosgrave proved sufficiently adroit as politicians to keep extremists in line and to build a civilized and responsible democratic system. The former prime minister Jack Lynch continued that tradition of political astuteness by his adamant refusal to get involved in the Ulster conflict.

Michael Collins and the IRA defeated the British in the Black and Tan War of 1921 through the tactics of terror, and the IRA has not abandoned these tactics since. Ironically, the IRA was probably responsible for Collins's death when he agreed to the compromise of the

Irish Free State and the partition of the island. In the bloody civil war that followed, the "Free Staters" and the IRA killed each other with as much enthusiasm as they had previously displayed against the Black and Tans. In the middle 1920s, Eamon De Valera, who had been allied with the IRA, decided that he could accomplish by electoral politics what the IRA could not accomplish by force of arms. He broke with the IRA, took the "oath" (with a mental reservation that only an Irishman could understand), and proceeded to end most of the ties with England that the IRA found objectionable.*

The uneasy truce between the "legion of the rearguard" (the irreconcilables) and "Dev" was finally broken, and the IRA turned once again to its tactics of guerrilla terror, even though it ought to have been clear that it was not 1916 and that they did not have the active sympathy of most Irishmen. For four decades the IRA continued to struggle, raiding Ulster police posts, stealing large supplies of guns, bombing buildings, and robbing banks in both England and Ulster. The failure of the Ulster and British governments to respond to moderate Catholic elements in Ulster (such as those represented by Bernadette Devlin who, for all her socialist rhetoric, is hardly a terrorist) gave the IRA a new lease on life.

J. Bowyer Bell traces in meticulous detail the persistence of the IRA and makes two general conclusions:

1. Even though its tactics lost all hope of effectiveness fifty years ago, the IRA has stubbornly persisted in the style of the Easter Rising and the Black and Tan War.

2. No defeat, however shattering, has prevented the IRA from returning to the battle.**

However violent the IRA, it still can be said that with the possible exception of India, Ireland is the only revolutionary country of the twentieth century that has been able to permit political opposition. More than that, when De Valera finally ousted Cosgrave in an election, the event was, so far as I know, the only time in modern history that a revolutionary government has been pushed from power by a peaceful, democratic election. De Valera's party has remained in con-

---

* He thus earned a reputation for "cuteness," by which is meant not attractiveness but deviousness. Prime Minister Jack Lynch is also said to be "cute."

** J. Bowyer Bell, *The Secret Army—the IRA, 1916-1970.* New York: John Day, 1971, p. 378.

trol for most of the last four decades. However, on three occasions the opposition party has formed governments, and once, in a paradoxical twist that only the Irish could accomplish, the Fine Gael, the legitimate successor of the Free State Party, proclaimed the existence of the Republic of Ireland, something which De Valera, ardent republican that he was, never quite managed.

Ireland was part of the first generation of modern revolutionary countries, along with Turkey and Mexico. It can be said with no exaggeration that Ireland was the most successful of the revolutionary nations. Unlike the others, it did not have a population problem, owing to that peculiar method of birth control, the late marriage, and the fact that its surplus population could migrate to England and the United States. Nevertheless, the ability of the Irish Republic to produce political democracy and economic prosperity in a relatively short period of time after independence suggests that Ireland could have been one of the great and strong nations of the modern world if it had achieved its freedom, say, one hundred years earlier. The question is of course academic, but it still must be conceded that prosperity (along with, it must be confessed, a certain dullness) came rather quickly and almost anticlimactically after half a millennium of strife and misery.

It also must be remembered that most of the Irish immigrants to America fled for their lives from a nation that had been oppressed for almost a thousand years. They had virtually no political or legal rights; abject poverty was a matter of course for them, conflict and rebellion were endemic, and education and industrial development were effectively prohibited. The very fact that they were Irish Catholic meant they were marked as permanently inferior. Their cultural traditions, including their language, were systematically extirpated, and their most gifted leaders were hanged, shot, imprisoned, or exiled.

The memories of these events may have faded from the minds of the American Irish. (Which of my American Irish readers, for example, ever even heard of Owen Roe O'Neill, or how many know what happened to Parnell, or how many are aware that there was another Michael Collins besides the astronaut?) But the results of such a tragic heritage are not easily eliminated. To lament, as some Catholic self-critics have, that the Irish in the United States have not produced as impressive a cultural and intellectual presence as the Jews, let us say, is to forget completely what the history of Ireland has been since that generous English pope presented it to his friend Henry II. What ought to be surprising about the American Irish is not that they have not been quite as socially and financially successful as the Jews, but that they have been successful at all. And what is astonishing is not that their intellectual and cultural contributions are limited, but that they have any time for the arts at all. Nor is it surprising that the Irish political style is pragmatic and suspicious of ideology; under the circumstances, it is astonishing that there is enough trust remaining from their heritage that they are capable of politics at all.

We can conclude this sketchy account of the history of Ireland by saying that whatever comparisons might or might not be made to other groups, the Irish came to this country with a history of a thousand years of misery, suffering, oppression, violence, exploitation, atrocity, and genocide. Their country was given no opportunity to develop intellectually or economically. Their aristocracy was repeatedly liquidated or exiled. Their culture and even their language were systematically eliminated. They were thought of as an inferior people and, like all oppressed people, began to half believe it themselves. Like all such people, they were torn between the desire for respectability and savage resentment of their oppressors. If anyone thinks that the twin themes of respectability and resentment are not part of the heritage of the American Irish, he simply does not know the American Irish very well.

FOUR

Immigration

AT THE END OF THE SIDE ROAD, JUST NORTH OF THE TOWN OF BAL-
lyhaunis in County Mayo, Ireland, there is a trim, neatly painted
white cottage with a corrugated iron roof, flower boxes and pots in
front, and a dazzling flower garden behind. The house is clean, with a
well-swept barn. A few more houses cluster just a short distance
away. In the distance one can see a river and some swamp land.

The little hamlet is called Ballendrehid—the house by the bridge.
Most of the land was once a shallow lake and was reclaimed at some
unspecified time in the past for a new draining system—one suspects
in the late 1700s or early 1800s, when the English knew an exuberant
burst of hydraulic enthusiasm and built canals and draining systems
which changed (mostly for the better) the topography of both England and Ireland. (Not far from Ballyhaunis is the town of Cong—
famous for its Ashford Castle Hotel—where the British built a canal
between Lough Corribe and Lough Mask to extend deep into the
heart of Mayo a navigable waterway. The construction of the canal
provided desperately needed income for many Mayo peasants during
the time of the Great Famine. Unfortunately, as one of the guide-
books puts it, limestone rock, out of which the canal was hollowed, is
too porous to hold water. Even at times of flood, the waters of Lough

Mask rarely flow more than halfway through the canal toward
Lough Corribe before they sink back through the ground into the
underground river which joined the two lakes for centuries, and rise
again mysteriously and almost magically just outside of Cong. The
English were superb hydraulic engineers. But occasionally they made
mistakes—like building in the County Mayo a canal that won't hold
water!)

The cottage is as cozy and snug inside as it is tidy outside. It was
built after 1890, when the land reforms began to redistribute property
to the peasant tenants who had worked on the land for years; perhaps
it even dates to this century. Clearly the iron roof and the television
antenna are signs of modern Ireland. Next to the cottage, there is a
rough stone shed about the size of the office in which I work on this
manuscript; it is the original house on the land, hundreds of years old
perhaps, certainly pre-Famine, surviving because of the strong western Ireland conviction that one does not tear down houses lest one
offend the spirits of the ancestors who might still lurk there.

It was in this cottage that my grandfather and the other members
of his family (I don't know how many there were) were born, a
decade after the Great Famine—about 1870, I should think—during
the time of the "little famine." He left the family home to go to
America because, as the second son, he could not hope to inherit the
land.

He married my grandmother in Chicago in about 1880. He was a
teamster, in the old sense of the word: he drove a team of horses on a
horse-drawn cart. My schoolteacher grandmother, born of immigrants in London, was better educated and probably of a better social
ranking (a not unusual situation in immigrant groups, since limited
upward mobility was more readily available to women than to men
at certain stages in the immigration experience). Somewhat later, it
would appear, my grandfather's older brother came temporarily to
America but then returned to Ireland, perhaps just before 1900, and
assumed his ownership of the family farm. His granddaughter (my
second cousin, if I calculate things right) and her husband and children still live on the farm.

My grandfather never returned. On the day when he walked
down the road in Ballendrehid toward Ballyhaunis, walked or rode a
coach to the railway either in Galway or Castlebar, and sailed for
America, he must have known that his chances of returning to the
land on which he had been raised, to the friends he had known in his

youth, were slim. Yet there was no land and no employment and probably very little food for him in Ireland. For that Andrew Greeley, there was no choice but to immigrate to America.

He worked very hard in the twenty or so years of life that remained to him. Hard work in the muddy, unsanitary Chicago at the time immediately after the fire is what America meant to my grandfather. Not much, heaven knows, but more than he could have expected if he had remained in Ireland.

His brother's descendents still live on the land and are modestly prosperous by Irish standards. My grandfather's descendents have earned doctorates at the University of Chicago and write books, but are quite incapable of milking a cow or sweeping a barn. Nor are they very good at riding a bicycle, which is still the family transportation in Ireland. The life of my Irish cousins may be a healthier and happier one; they are certainly strong, vigorous, and attractive people. I wouldn't trade with them, however, and I doubt that very many people with European peasant ancestors would trade with the descendents of those who stayed behind. Unlucky grandfather, lucky me.

Immigration is a traumatic experience, even under the best circumstances. One leaves behind familiar sights, beloved places, intimate friends. If one is an immigrant to a strange land, with only the vaguest notion of what one's life will be like, with intense dread of the loneliness and isolation that is going to be one's fate, immigration is even more painful. The first huge wave of immigrants from Ireland, the Famine Irish, were also sick, hungry, mostly illiterate, and often spoke little if any English.

Those of us who have come after the immigrants, who stand on their shoulders, are eager to repress memories of the early immigrant experience, to romanticize the immigration trauma—as though Ellis Island were not after all such a bad place for the "wretched refuse of the earth." Immigration is still too close to us, too painful, too degrading an experience to be faced honestly. For every realistic description of what it means to be an immigrant, like the film *Hester Street*, there are a dozen romanticized portraits, like the meretricious one in *The Godfather* or the movingly sentimental one in *Hogan's Goat.*

There have been many different Irish immigrations to the United States. There were some Irish Catholics here at the time of the Revolutionary War, though most of the Irish regiments which fought in that war were regiments of Irish Protestants. By 1820, however, enough of the "Mere Irish" were migrating to America to stir up concern about the papist hordes that were invading our Protestant nation and to induce Irish Protestants to begin to use the name "Scotch-Irish," which had been used pejoratively of them by their American neighbors (they themselves had hitherto thought of themselves as "Irish").

At least a million Irish Catholics migrated at the time of the Great Famine, though how many of them survived the trip to America and lived in America long enough to produce offspring in the incredibly filthy and dangerous slums of New York and Boston is uncertain. Another two million migrated between 1860 and 1890, and possibly yet another half million after 1890. Thus one could estimate that somewhere between 3.5 and 5 million Irish Catholics migrated to the United States, about 10 percent of the 44 million immigrants who have come to our country since the Revolutionary War—a not unreasonable estimate considering that descendents of post-Revolutionary immigrants constitute about half of the American population and approximately 5 percent of the American population is Irish Catholic.

Because of differential mortality rates, reverse migration, and leakage from the Church (almost all of which occurred before 1850), it is difficult to estimate on the basis of immigration statistics alone what proportions of the American Irish population come from the different immigrant waves. However, relying on NORC survey data, we are able to say with reasonable certainty that about one-quarter of the Irish in America are descendents of families who migrated before 1870. Another two-fifths are descendents of those who came between 1870 and 1900. One-quarter are descendents of immigrants who came between 1900 and the foundation of the Irish Republic, and 7 percent are either descendents of immigrants who came after 1925 or are themselves immigrants from this most recent period. If you look at the matter somewhat differently, 4 percent of American Irish Catholics are foreign-born and 25 percent are native-born of immigrant parents. Seventy-one percent of the Irish Catholics in America, then, are either third or fourth generation.

While there are some interesting differences between the Famine Irish and the Irish who came after 1870, for our present purposes it is sufficient to say three-quarters of us came after the Famine immigration, two-thirds of us came before the twentieth century, and all but 7 percent of us came before the end of the Irish civil war in 1923.

One-quarter of us came, in all likelihood, on sailing ships, but most of the rest of us came on steam vessels of one variety or the other, and a small number of the more recent of us came on jet planes. One-quarter of us are from illiterate families, but the other three-quarters of us are offspring of people educated in the National Schools who could read and write and speak English fluently. Less than one-quarter of our families were here during the American Civil War and at the time of the famous New York race riots (in which the Irish surely participated but for which they are probably unjustly blamed). Three-quarters of us came after the devotional revival saved the religion of modern Ireland and are not, at least in the strict meaning of the word, refugees from religious persecution. One-quarter of us came after land redistribution had notably im-proved the lot of Irish peasants. Few of us were either affluent or financially secure, but three-quarters of our families could scarcely be characterized as impoverished refugees from famine, one step ahead of starvation or the plague. One-third of our families came when the prospect of return to the homeland in a relatively fast and safe steam-ship was not unrealistic if one was frugal enough to save the money for the passage. And the most recent of us of course are college-trained professionals who jet home every year or every other year (and perhaps some illegals or "undocumenteds" who are afraid the Immigration and Naturalization Service may ship us back to Ireland if we don't have the education that is required of immigrants today).

Hence, while the Chicago to which my four grandparents came was not a prize, it was infinitely better than New York or Boston of the previous generation as described by Oscar Handlin and Robert Ernst. My grandparents themselves (three of whom were doomed to an early death, and the other living to the time of the Al Smith campaign) were not hapless, disease-ridden Irish. There was already a substantial middle class among the Irish in New York before the Famine immigrants arrived. This middle class was inundated by the starving refugees from western Ireland but then later augmented by its industrious or more fortunate members, so that when the refugees of the "little famine" began to pour in after the American Civil War, both the neighborhood parishes and the communities were able to cope. Thus, unlike the hasty refugees of 1850, my grandparents had family and friends to meet them.

Immigration for the Irish was still not easy for those who came between 1870 and 1900, but it was simpler in 1870 than in 1850 and even less traumatic in 1900. The wretched shanties along Archer Avenue in the Bridgeport district of Chicago and the tenements described by Handlin and Ernst were not the dwelling places of every Irish immigrant until 1920. Such a notion is part of the myth that the Irish stayed impoverished in America until John Kennedy was elected President.

But immigrant life even in 1900 was not physically or psychologically easy. Discrimination was still massive. Although diphtheria and cholera epidemics were over, the death rate was perhaps twice as high in the ethnic neighborhoods. Families like my mother's, in which seven children were orphaned with the eldest still in her teens, were not infrequent. Only after 1920, and then decisively after 1940, did white immigrants in America cease to be the victims of economic discrimination and social injustice (save at the top levels of society, where the ethnics are still excluded). After 1910, however, rapid steamship trips across the Atlantic and effective public-health activities in the large cities (the Spanish influenza epidemic in 1919 led to tremendous improvements in American public-health standards) made immigration physically easier. Psychologically, it was still as difficult as ever—as it probably is even for the affluent Trinity College graduate today applying for profession or trade in San Francisco and winging his way home several times a year.

Immigration, then, was much more dangerous and difficult for those who came earliest. Those who came before 1870 were refugees in the strict sense of the word. Most of them indeed barely survived. Those who came after 1870 were not so much refugees as they were searchers for a new and better life, even if the price for such a life was traumatic uprooting.

Existence in the early slums of America was grim before the First World War but certainly no more grim than life in the old country. My three grandparents all died before their fiftieth birthday, but statistically the same fate was even more likely for them if they had remained in Ireland. In the United States they could tell themselves that there was a point and purpose in their sacrifice of the white cottages in Mayo. Their children, they firmly believed, could become successful, respected Americans; the cycle of poverty and degradation could at last be broken.

How bad was tenement life in the last century? In New York in the middle of the last century the gross density per acre was 272 people. In one neighborhood, more than 7,000 people were living in cellars. After 1863 and the building of large tenements, only 18,000 in New York City lived in cellars. In a house on Pike Street there was a ten-foot-square cellar (seven feet high, with one small window) where two families, consisting of ten persons of all ages, lived.

Rain water leaked through cracks in the walls and floors and flooded the cellars. Refuse filtered down from the upper stories and mingled with seepage from outdoor privies.* Water for bathing and washing had to be fetched from street pumps or nearby wells. Private philanthropy had erected a "peoples' washing and bathing establishment" on Mott Street in New York by the early 1850s, but most bathing was done in the waters of the Hudson or the Harlem rivers. Most of the tenements had no toilet facilities and the backyard wooden privies were not adequate to the demand.

With the lack of cesspools and sewers, some twenty-four million gallons of sewage matter accumulated in the streets and gutters of New York daily. Typhoid fever, cholera, typhus, pneumonia, and bronchitis put the population in constant danger. Nearly two-thirds of New York City's deaths in 1857 were of children under the age of five, most of them offspring of immigrants. Eighty-five percent of those admitted to Bellevue Hospital in 1855 were born in Ireland, even though the Irish constituted only 54 percent of the foreign-born inhabitants of the city. Two-thirds of those admitted to the Blackwell Island insane asylum were Irish; many of them were immigrants who had been in the country for less than a year. Gambling, drunkenness, crime, and prostitution flourished in the immigrant neighborhoods. Of two thousand prostitutes examined in 1858 at the penitentiary hospital on Blackwell Island (the city's venereal disease hospital) 538 were immigrants and 706 were Irishwomen, more than half of whom had lived in the United States for less than five years and one-fifth of whom had been residents for less than one year. Three-eighths were between the ages of fifteen and twenty, three-quarters were younger than twenty-six.**

The Irish were lowest on the totem pole. Most of the prostitutes in Cleveland were Irish. In Boston, half of the Irish were unskilled laborers (as opposed to 10 percent of the German and the black populations at the same time). In Boston in 1850, more than three thousand Irishwomen worked as domestic servants. As one news-

---

* Robert Ernst, *Immigrant Life in New York City, 1825–1863*, p. 49.
** Ibid., pp. 48–60.

paper put it: "There are several sorts of power working in the fabric of this republic, water power, steam power and Irish Power. The last works hardest of all." Charles Dickens described the Irish railroad builders in upstate New York in 1841 and scarcely could contain his disgust.

> . . . with means of hand in building decent cabins, it was wonderful to see how clumsy, rough, and wretched, its hovels were. The best were poor protections from the weather; the worst let in the wind and rain through the wide breeches in the roofs of sod and grass, and in the walls of mud; some had neither door nor windows; some had nearly fallen down, and were imperfectly propped up by stakes and poles; all were ruinous and filthy. Hideously ugly old women and very buxom young ones, pigs, dogs, men, children, babies, pots, kettles, dung hills, vile refuse, rank straw and standing water, all wallowing together in an inseparable heap, composed the furniture of every dark and dirty hut.

Small wonder that when the Civil War came so many of the men flocked to the colors. They may not have been sympathetic to the cause of freeing the slaves, but at least there was food and regular pay—and death in battle or, more likely, death from disease. The Irish immigrants may have read very carefully Father John O'Hanlon's mid-nineteenth-century *The Irish Immigrants Guide to the United States* with its careful and prudent warning about travel to the New World, adjustment to its life, and the kind of occupations an immigrant ought to seek. But there was nothing in O'Hanlon's book that could prepare them for the subhuman living conditions. Nor could O'Hanlon tell the immigrants how to cope with the nativist bigotry which, presented in the national press cartoons, depicted the Irishman as a drunken, superstitious ape. How do you, after all, deal with a bigot like Thomas Nast or with a man who would write in *Harper's Weekly:*

> Is there one [thoughtful Irishman] who is not grieved by the general result of Irish immigration to America? . . . It is not to be denied that the Irish immigration has been one of the most perplexing and menacing elements in American development. It has been the sure reliance of the demagogue and the traitor. There have been noble and generous and admirable Irish citizens in the country, but not one of the great steps of human progress which it has taken was due to the

inspiration or received the support of the Irish element of the population. Yet no other class has been so flattered. . . . These are not pleasant
things to say. But it is not by faintly echoing lies, but by telling the
truth, that the unquestionable evils of the Irish immigration are to be
corrected. And that correction is a work in which all honorable Irishmen should make common cause with all honorable Americans. So
long as the more intelligent Irish citizens in America identify themselves with the perilous and un-American political designs of the
priesthood—so long as they do not sternly frown upon the pandering
of demagogues to the ignorance and passions of their countrymen—so
long as they refuse their sympathy to the spirit of justice which has
emancipated the slave and which seeks an honorable equality of all
citizens—so long will they be untrue to the cardinal principle of the
government, and the political society which they have chosen. . . .

When intelligent Irishmen permit priests and demagogues to form
political combinations for the overthrow of the fundamental guarantee of liberty of every kind, they must not be surprised if they forfeit
the respect and confidence of all good citizens. And in exposing such a
conspiracy with all the resources of pictorial satire, it is not the Roman Church as such, it is political ambition hiding itself under the
mitre and the chasuble which is denounced. If . . . ecclesiastical Rome
has conquered Ireland, she will not be suffered, even with the aid of
her captive, to conquer America. *(October 21, 1871)*

And if that were not enough, in his *A History of the Irish Settlers in
North America,* Thomas D'arcy McGee, who was allegedly one of the
leaders of the Irish, pleaded with the American public to be kind to
the pathetic Irish.

The Irish, also, who settle in America, are creatures of their own
antecedents. The Atlantic works no miracles on them. They come to
these shores, the production of British power. Disfranchised in their
native land, the suffrage is a novelty to them; disarmed, the use of
arms is a possession not understood; ruled by a class, they abhor the
very semblance of class legislation; untrained to freedom, they make
but a poor figure, at first as free men. . . .

O, believe me, American reader, ours is a people very teachable by
those they love. Deal tenderly with their failings, they are a fallen
race. Do not pander to their party prejudices, but appeal to their
common sense and love of fair play. Do not make the weak, weaker,
and the dependent, more dependent, but endeavor to fit them for

equality, as well as liberty, so that the land may rejoice, and be secure in the multitude of its well instructed children.

The wonder is not that life expectancy was short under such conditions of exploitation and oppression; the wonder is that any of the Famine immigrants survived at all to produce children who would live to adulthood and claw their way out of the tenements as the nineteenth century came to an end. It is not unreasonable to assume that half of the Irish immigrants who came to America in fact came before 1870. If their descendents constitute only one-quarter of the population of Irish Catholics in America today, one must conclude that a large number of pre-1870 immigrants had been wiped out without a trace—and few tears shed for them at that.

Afterward things got better, a lot better. But life was still harsh for the Irish immigrants and their children throughout the remainder of the nineteenth century. Yet until the historians of the American Irish abandon their concern with politicians, writers, entertainers, and bishops and try to put together a social history of the Irish in the last half of the nineteenth and the first half of the twentieth centuries, we will have to rely on storytellers and retrospective survey data.

If James T. Farrell describes the Irish arrival in the middle class in the years before 1920, his Chicago predecessor, Finley Peter Dunne, and Dunne's spokesman, the incomparable Mr. Dooley, give us the best portrait of what life was like for the Irish immigrants and their descendents in the last quarter of the nineteenth century. Charles Fanning's two brilliant books about Dunne and Dooley * have provided us with detailed portraits of the life of the American Irish at that time. Dooley was a combination of toughness and sentiment, and four Dooley stories from *Mr. Dooley and the Chicago Irish* ** give a better feel than any social historian could possibly present of what life was like in those days.

★ ★ ★

"Poverty and Pride in the Callaghan Family"

[The St. Vincent de Paul Society is an important Catholic charitable organization. The Chicago chapter was founded in 1857 by Peter Dunne's uncle, the Reverend Dennis Dunne, of St. Patrick's Church.]

---

* *Finley Peter Dunne and Mr. Dooley, the Chicago Years,* University of Kentucky Press, 1978, and *Mr. Dooley and the Chicago Irish,* Arno Press, 1976.
** Finley Peter Dunne, *Mr. Dooley and the Chicago Irish.*

"Have you seen Callaghan to-day?" asked Mr. McKenna.

"No," said Mr. Dooley.

"It's too bad about him," said Mr. McKenna.

"It is that, it is that. Th' poor man. Th' hear-rt iv me is gray with thinkin' iv him over there alone. D'ye know, Jawn, I was th' last to see him whin he wint away an' th' first whin he come back. 'Twas early last summer he left. They'd had th' divvle's own winter an' spring iv it—Callaghan out iv wurruk an' th' good woman down with pnoomony iv th' lungs an' ne'er a dollar in th' house but what he picked up wanst in a while doin' odd jobs around. An' him as proud as a pr-rince an' patient as a nun! I mind whin th' Saint Vincent de Pauls wint out f'r to investigate his case. Well, Jawn, ye know what th' Irish is whin they have money. Head and tail up. Give me thim that haven't enough to ate iv their own to help their neighbors. I've seen th' stirabout divided whin th' eyes iv th' childher was poppin' out iv their heads. Well, the chairman iv th' comity that wint to investigate Callaghan's case was old Peter Coogan—an' ye know him—big hear-rt enough but desp'rate r'rough. Mrs. Callaghan was up whin they called an' 'twas 'me good woman this' an' 'me good woman that' an' 'th' mimbers is always r-ready f'r to help th' desarvin' poor.' Con Hogan who was in th' comity tol' me Mrs. Callaghan answered niver a wur-rud, but th' tears come to her big, gray eyes an' she held on to th' table. Coogan's father was wan iv her fa-ather's farmhands in Roscommon, d'ye mind.

"That night th' Saint Vincent de Pauls met in th' basemint iv th' church an' just as th' meetin' begun Callaghan stamped in, big an' fierce. 'Gintlemen,' says he, 'I've been given to undherstand,' he says, 'that some iv ye,' he says, 'has been around to me house,' he says, 'offerin' charity on th' tips iv ye'er muddy boots to me sick woman,' he says. 'Now,' says he, 'I'm no ora-thor,' he says, 'an' I'm f'r peace,' he says, 'but if anny iv ye is minded f'r to offer charity to me wife,' he says, 'I wisht ye'd let me know first,' he says, 'so that I can take ye'er charity,' he says, 'an' shove it down ye'er throats,' he says. 'An' that manes you, Coogan!' With that he thramped out an' no more charity was offered to Mrs. Callaghan.

"Whin summer come he got a job in Kansas an' he come to see me befure he wint away. Be nature he was a light-hear-rted man an' this night ye cud hardly hold him f'r pure joy. Be this an' be that he was goin' to make his fortune an' live like th' gintleman th' husband iv Nora Deane sh'd be—him tur-rned iv fifty an' goin' out to Topeka at wan-sivinty-five a day! I seen him off on th' thrain. I heerd he was doin' well an' th' good woman took a pew in th' church, though she'd been kneeling in the dhraft fr'm th' dure manny's th' Sundah. 'Twas th' sicond wan fr'm Doheny's near th' confissional. That's it, that's it. Th' wan McCarthy, th' plumber, rinted. I niver knowed she was in a bad way till two weeks ago Sundah whin she missed mass. Thin little Mrs. Doherty tol' me she'd found her in bed singin' th' vispers to herself.

"Thursdah night I was walkin' down th' r-road whin who should I meet but Callaghan, walkin' with his chin on his chest, an' white as a sheeted cor-rpse. I called to him but he made no answer. He walked wist a block or two an' thin come back at a tearin' gait an' wint acrost th' street. I niver guessed what ailed him till I looked an' seen that th' fr-ront windows iv th' house was wide open though th' night was could. An' as he opened th' dure I heerd th' keening. 'Tis a har-rd, har-rd wurruld."

(November 24, 1894)

★   ★   ★

"The Grady Girl Rushing the Can"

Up in Archey road the streetcar wheels squeaked along the tracks and the men coming down from the rolling-mills hit themselves on their big chests and wiped their noses on their leather gloves with a peculiar back-handed stroke at which they are most adept. The little girls coming out of the bakeshops with loaves done up in brown paper under their arms had to keep a tight clutch on their thin shawls lest those garments should be caught up by the bitter wind blowing from Brighton Park way and carried down to the gashouse. The frost was so thick on the windows of Mr. Martin Dooley's shop that you could just see the crownless harp on the McCormick's Hall Parnell meeting sheet above it, and you could not see any of the pyramid of Medford rum bottles founded contemporaneously with that celebrated meeting.

Still, signs of warmth and good cheer were not lacking about the Dooley establishment. One sign in particular, a faded one and time worn, bearing a legend touching upon Tom and Jerry, hung from the door. It met the eye of the Hon. John McKenna standing on the streetcar platform and conversing with the driver upon the benefits to civilization only possible under the mayoralty of George Brains Swift. Mr. McKenna hopped from the car and went in to find Mr. Dooley sitting comfortably behind the tall stove which was steaming from the reservoir atop. Mr. Dooley was partaking contentedly of an aromatic mixture of a golden color, slightly flecked with Vandyke brown, in which a bit of lemon peel was floating.

"Is it cold out, I dinnaw?" said Mr. Dooley, laying down his glass.

"Oh, no," said Mr. McKenna, rubbing his ear; "it isn't cold. I dropped in to get an umbrella. I'm afraid I'll get sunstruck if I go along without one."

"I didn't know," said Mr. Dooley, calmly chasing the lemon peel around with the spoon. "It isn't cold in here, Jawn, and by gar as long as it isn't, 'tis not mesilf 'd poke me nose out to learn th' timphrature. Some idjuts iv me acquaintance kapes a thermomter about to tell how cold it is, but f'r me, Jawn, I'd as soon have a mad dog in th' house. There was a man be th' name iv Denny that kep' th' block below Finucane's, an' he bought a thermomter f'r to tell how cold it was, an', by gar, th' poor, deluded man 'd be r-runnin' out fr'm morn till night to take a pike at th' thermomter, an' him in his shirt sleeves. Wan day he tuk pnoomony in th' lungs and died, Gawd rest him, in three days. I wint to his wake. They waked him in beer, but annyhow thim Dennys was always low people. Wan iv thim is a polisman now. It's dam'd little I care how cold it is so long as I have this here fire baychune me an' th' frost. Zaro or twinty daygrees below zaro an' wan lump iv coal in that there shtove, and it's all akel to Dooley. I can plant mesilf in this chair an' say to mesilf: 'Come on winter; I'm here before ye.' Thin to think iv th' poor divvles out in th' night, tortured an' sufferin' with th' cold an' nothin' to cover thim an' protect thim fr'm th' frost—Jawn, there's no divarsion more cheerin'. Bedad, half th' philo-sophy iv life is in knowin' that some wan is sufferin' whin ye're on aisy street. It is, so it is."

A rattle at the door and a short cry caused Mr. Dooley to pause and listen and finally to toddle out grumbling complaints about the Donohue goat, whose only divarsion was to batter down the tenements of dacint people. As he opened the door his grumbling ceased, and presently he came in carrying something that looked like a rather large parcel of rags, but on close inspection turned out to be a very small girl carrying a very big can.

"Glory be to Gawd," said Mr. Dooley, setting the little girl down in the chair. "Glory be to Gawd, an' did ye iver see th' likes iv that? Luk at her, Jawn, th' unfortunate chick, lyin' out there froze in this murdhrin' night with a can in her hand. Who are ye, poor thing? Let me take a luk at ye. By gar, I thought so. 'Tis Grady's kid—Grady, th' villain, th' black-hearted thafe, to send th' poor choild out to her death. Don't stand there, ye big numbskull, like a cigar store injun starin'. Go over an' fetch that can iv milk. Musha, musha, ye poor dear. Naw, naw, don't wipe ye'er nose on me apron, ye unmannerly crather. Give me a towel, Jawn, fr'm in under th' shilf where thim

Angyostooria bitthers stands. There ye are. Don't cry, dear. Does ye'er—what th' 'ell's baby talk f'r feet, Jawn?"

"Tootsy-wootsies," said Mr. McKenna proudly.

"Does ye'er tootsy-wootsies hurt ye, avick? Dhrink that an' ye'll be as warm as two in a bed."

Mr. Dooley stood with hands on his hips and saw the little Grady girl laving her purpose nose in the warm milk. Meantime he narrated the history of her father in forcible language, touching upon his failure to work and provide, his bibulous habits and his tendency toward riotous misconduct. Finally, he walked behind the bar and set out the glasses, as his custom was for closing time. He placed the cash drawer in the small iron safe in the corner and tucked a $5 bill in his vest pocket. Then he turned out the lights in the window and put on his overcoat.

"Where are you going?" asked Mr. McKenna.

"I'm goin' over to lick Grady," said Mr. Dooley.

"Then," said Mr. McKenna, "by heavens," he said, "I'll go with you."

And they marched out together, with the little Grady girl between them.

(November 25, 1893)

★　★　★

"Organized Charity and the Galway Woman"

[The winter of 1896–1897 was the worst in recent memory for the poor of Chicago. On November 30, the Bureau of Associated Charities estimated that 8000 families were destitute. As that figure grew larger, the situation was aggravated by a cold wave that struck in early December and held on until February. Accelerating demands for food and fuel soon swamped the city's relief bureaucracy, and Chicago faced a life-and-death crisis. The remaining Dooley pieces in this chapter were written during that hard winter. In the first, Dunne attacks the self-defeating regulations of the city's Relief and Aid Society with a grim vignette set in another hard winter, 1874.]

"Whin th' col' spell comes along about Chris'mas time," said Mr. Hennessy, opening the stove door and lighting a small piece of paper which he conveyed to the bowl of his pipe with much dexterity, just snaring the last flicker with his first noisy inhalation, "whin th' col' weather comes on I wish thim Grogans down in th' alley'd move out. I have no peace at all with th' ol' woman. She has me r-runnin' in night an' day with a pound of tay or a flannel shirt or a this-or-that-

or-th'-other thing, an' 'tis on'y two weeks ago, whin th' weather was warrum, she tol' me Mrs. Grogan as an ongrateful as a cow an' smelled so iv gin ye cud have th' deleeryum thremens if ye sat with her f'r an hour."

"What ye shud do," said Mr. Dooley, "is to get ye'er wife to join an organized charity. Th' throuble with her is she gives to onworthy people an' in a haphazard way that tinds to make paupers. If they'se annything will make a person ongrateful an' depindent it's to give thim something to eat whin they're hungry without knowin' whether they are desarvin' iv th' delicate attintion. A man, or a woman ayether, has to have what ye may call peculiar qualifications f'r to gain th' lump iv coal or th' pound iv steak that an organized charity gives out. He must be honest an' sober an' industhrious. He must have a frind in th' organization. He must have arned th' right to beg his bread be th' sweat iv his brow. He must be able to comport himself like a gintleman in fair society an' play a good hand at whist. He must have a marridge license over th' pianny an' a goold-edged Bible on th' marble-topped table. A pauper that wud disbelieve there was a God afther thrampin' th' sthreets in search iv food an' calmin' an onreasonable stomach with th' east wind is no object iv charity. What he needs is th' attintion iv a polisman. I've aften wondhered why a man that was fit to dhraw a ton iv slate coal an' a gob iv liver fr'm th' relief an' aid society didn't apply f'r a cabinet position or a place in a bank. He'd be sthrong f'r ayether.

"I mind wanst there was a woman lived down near Main sthreet be th' name iv Clancy, Mother Clancy th' kids called her. She come fr'm away off to th' wist, a Galway woman fr'm bechune mountain an' sea. Ye know what they ar-re whin they're black, an' she was worse an' blacker. She was tall an' thin, with a face white th' way a corpse is white, an' she had wan child, a lame la-ad that used to play be himsilf in th' sthreet, th' lawn bein' limited. I niver heerd tell iv her havin' a husband, poor thing, an' what she'd need wan f'r, but to dhrag out her misery f'r her in th' gray year sivinty-foor, I cudden't say. She talked to hersilf in Gaelic whin she walked an' 'twas Gaelic she an' th' kid used whin they wint out together. Th' kids thought she was a witch an' broke th' windows iv her house an' ivry wan was afraid iv her but th' little priest. He shook his head whin she was mintioned an' wint to see her wanst in awhile an' come away with a throubled face.

"Sivinty-foor was a hard winter f'r th' r-road. Th' mills was shut down an' ye cud've stood half th' population iv some iv th' precints on their heads an' got nothin' but five days' notices out iv thim. Th' nights came cold, an' bechune relievin' th' sick an' givin' extremunction to th' dyin' an' comfortin' th' widows an' orphans th' little priest was sore pressed fr'm week's end to week's end. They was smallpox in wan part iv th' wa-ard an' diphtheria in another an' bechune th' two there was starvation an' cold an' not enough blankets on th' bed.

"Th' Galway woman was th' las' to complain. How she iver stud it as long as she did I lave f'r others to say. Annyhow, whin she come down to Halsted sthreet to make application f'r help to th' Society f'r th' Relief iv th' Desarvin' Poor she looked tin feet tall an' all white cheek bones an' burnin' black eyes. It took her a long time to make up her mind to go in, but she done it an' stepped up to where th' reel-estate man Dougherty, cheerman iv th' comity, was standin' with his back to th' stove an' his hands undher his coat tails. They was those that said Dougherty was a big-hear-rted man an' give freely to th' poor, but I'd rather take rough-on-rats fr'm you, Hinnissy, thin sponge cake fr'm him or th' likes iv him. He looked at her, finished a discoorse on th' folly iv given' to persons with a bad moral charackter an' thin turned suddenly an' said: 'What can we do f'r ye?' She told him in her own way. 'Well, me good woman,' says he, 'ye'll undher-stand that th' comity is much besieged be th' imporchunities iv th' poor,' he says, 'an' we're obliged to limit our alms to thim that desarves thim,' he says. 'We can't do anything f'r ye on ye're own say so, but we'll sind a man to invistigate ye're case, an',' he says, 'if th' raypoort on ye'er moral charackter is satisfacthry,' he says, 'we'll at-tind to ye.'

"I dinnaw what it was, but th' matther popped out iv Dougherty's head an' nayether that day nor th' nex' nor th' nex' afther that was annything done f'r th' Galway woman. I'll say this f'r Dougherty, that whin th' thing come back to his mind again he put on his coat an' hurried over to Main sthreet. They was a wagon in th' sthreet, but Dougherty took no notice iv it. He walked up an' rapped on th' dure, an' th' little priest stepped out, th' breast iv his overcoat bulgin'. 'Why, father,' he says, 'ar-re ye here? I jus' come f'r to see—' 'Peace,' said th' little priest, closin' th' dure behind him an' takin' Dougherty be th' ar-rm. 'We were both late.' But 'twas not till they got to th' foot iv th' stairs that Dougherty noticed that th' wagon come fr'm th' county undertaker, an' that 'twas th' chalice made th' little priest's coat to bulge."
(December 5, 1896)

*   *   *

"A Bank Failure at Christmas Time"

[An adjunct of the continuing local and national depression was the failure of the Bank of Illinois on Monday, December 21, 1896. An

unfavorable report by national bank examiners had blamed "in-
judicious loans" for destroying the bank's capital, and the Clearing-
House Association of Chicago had responded by suspending it from
membership. At the end of the week, Mr. Dooley commented on the
relationship between bankers and depositors.]

"It's a quite Chris'mas," said Mr. Hennessy.

"Yes," said Mr. Dooley, "with nawthin' to break th' silence but
now an' thin a busting bank. It's a green Chris'mas f'r all th' wurruld, but a gray wan f'r thim that has their money put away in th'
sthrong boxes. Whin Sandy Kloss comes in th' shape iv a naytional
bank examiner it's time to take down ye'er stockin's fr'm th' hearth.
Ye'll need thim f'r ye'er feet."

"Well, I'm glad to see thim go," said Mr. Hennessey, the embit-
tered one. "I've been in charge iv a naytional bank examiner mesilf f'r
twinty-five years. Me assets is twinty-eight cints, two pool checks an'
a pair iv imbridered slippers that I dhrew this mornin' an' me libilities
is somewhat in excess. I'm goin' to get out a statement iv me condition. Capital stock, wan million; surplus, wan million; cash on hand,
twinty-eight cints; nee-gotyable securities, tin cints; due fr'm other
Hinniseys, thirty dollars. Dooley, there's five hundhred thousan' naytional banks iv Illinye in Chicago today, on'y most iv thim was
bor-rn with their libilities in excess iv their assets."

"Thrue f'r ye," said Mr. Dooley, "but th' conthroller iv th' currency hasn't annything to do with thim. We have polismen to look
after those lads. A nay-tional bank is diff'rent. Some day a bank
examiner dhrops in on wan iv thim an' looks over th' books. He
raypoorts th' situation to his boss in Wash'nton an' th' boss writes
down to th' prisidint iv th' bank. 'Dear sir an' brother,' he says,
'excuse me f'r intrudin' mesilf in ye'er affairs, but I'm tould ye have
been lendin' other people's money to ye'erself an' frinds, an' there's
some kickin',' he says. 'I thrust ye'll not take it too much to hear-rt if
I suggest that this is conthrary to th' laws iv th' United States. Don't
think me intrusive if I ask ye to put on a betther front f'r to quite
suspicion,' he says. 'I wudden't f'r th' wurruld hurt ye'er feelings, but
I have a jooty to perform an' that is to see that public confidence is
maintained. If ye will give th' matther a little attintion, without too
great inconvenience, an' make good some iv th' markers, ye'll be
conferrin' a gr-reat personal favor on me. With best wishes f'r a
merry Christmas an' a happy New Year, I am, yours thruly.' Well,
th' boys come together an' they look over th' markers an' decide that
they can't take thim up at wanst. Now, naytional banks always stand
by each other, f'r th' purpose iv sustainin' that confidence so essential

to—to—to confidencing th' public. That's th' point. Confidence, to inspire confidence. Th' la-ads with th' markers goes to their brothers an' frinds an' says they, 'We've got a note fr'm th' conthroller iv th' currency sayin' we've broke th' law. Thrue, we've broke oursilves too, but he takes it so much to hear-rt that we feel like doin' a good tur-rn f'r him. We've got our markers here an' we'd like to have money enough on thim to make good.' 'F'r why,' says their frinds. 'To keep up confidence,' says th' la-ads. Well, their brethren rubs their chins an' fin'lly wan iv thim up an' says: 'Th' foundation iv confidence is th' belief iv th' confidenced in th' integrity iv th' operator. This here bank has been conducted on th' wrong lines. Its methods have been un-businesslike an' it has advanced money on markers that wudden't go across my layout. I don't believe in lindin' sanction or coin to anny entherprise r-run so carelessly. Th' time has come whin th' best way to restore confidince in th' public that's been so often up agin th' game that it can r-read th' ca-ards be th' backs, is to dhrive fr'm business th' careless, th' incompetent an' th' dishonest. Besides,' he says, 'if these markers are med good, a lot that I have become bad,' he says. 'I vote "no."' So th' nex' day early th' bank examiner tacks a ca-ard on th' dure an' the la-ads begin to r-roast each other in the pa-apers, an' th' German man, not having enough money to pay his quarterly license, crawls into th' icebox, takes a light lunch of paris green an' goes into liquidation.

"There's wan Chris'mas story f'r ye, Hinnissy. It ain't what it might be f'r gayety, but it's the divvle f'r facts. Whin I see th' bank examiner playin' Sandy Kloss I want to board up th' chimbley an' put me dough in th' stove. The best a bank can git whin he's around is a r-run f'r its money."
(December 26, 1896)

★   ★   ★

There was also some gaiety and laughter, particularly in the carnivals and the socials at the parish church (just down Archer Road at Mr. Dooley's tavern and named after the patroness of spring and new life, Brigid). Fanning's collection of Dooley's early comments on life in Bridgeport presents these dimensions of immigrant life, too. It may be hard for us who live in another era to understand how they could have been even tenuously happy under such miserable conditions, yet life and love have always managed to go on, even when life was short and love deprived the advantages of a post-Freudian vocabulary. Among my mother's recollection of growing up on the near west side of Chicago at the same time Dooley was commenting on life in

Bridgeport on the south side of Chicago, there were indeed stories of poverty but far more stories of gaiety, laughter, celebration—even when you lost your mother in your grammar-school years and had to go to work at Sears, Roebuck & Co. at the age of fifteen.

★   ★   ★

A word here is appropriate about the Irish immigrants' habits of cleanliness. When we were growing up on the west side of Chicago, we had a Polish neighbor who told my mother one day that her son Albert was dating an Irish girl, but "it's all right. She's Irish, but she's clean." My mother was, as one may imagine, furious, but the truth of the matter was that the Polish woman's house was always in such impeccable order that my mother returned from it a nervous wreck. Everything was always in place in the house. You didn't dare move anything out of place, my mother added. The Polish woman scrubbed her front porch and sidewalk every day—a compulsion which most Irish homemakers have been able to avoid.

In the 1961 NORC study of college-graduate women, the respondents were asked both to rate themselves as housekeepers and to rate the satisfaction they got from keeping the house clean. The Irish ranked dead last in both categories. As my mother said, with some contempt of the Polish and Czech obsession with neat and orderly homes, "A house is meant to live in, not to admire." However, such a casual approach to housewifery—and, one presumes, to order in the work place too—was not and is not incompatible with concern to the point of obsession about personal cleanliness. If the Irish were physically dirty oftentimes during the last century in both Ireland and the United States, the reason was poverty and not personal slovenliness. The obsession of the contemporary Irish with their daily showers—one they have in common with most other Americans—has historical antecedents; citing literary sources, archaeologists tell us that any Irishman who was able to do so in the pre-Christian and early Christian era bathed every day. The archaeologists tell us, however, that in marvelous anticipation of contemporary practice, the daily-bathing Irish aristocracy were casually indifferent to the neatness of their homes—tossing ham and chicken bones and other refuse on the floor of their houses and not bothering to sweep such garbage away. Even contemporary Irish archaeologists are somewhat surprised to find in the same digs physical relics of great personal cleanliness and casual domestic indifference—one more Irish habit from the past.

I am not being critical of Irish women—and Irish men, for that matter—when I suggest that many are not as neat as they might be in their preservation of domestic order. My mother was right. A house is meant to be lived in, not admired.

★   ★   ★

So, as the nineteenth century came to an end, everything the British said about the Irish seemed to be true. They drank too much, they fought too much, they were dirty and slovenly, superstitious, and unreliable. They had indeed come to America in great numbers and had fought their way out of terrible poverty, but they were still poor, drunk, politically corrupt, and had probably reached the upper limit of their achievement. Beatrice and Sidney Webb, those delightful founders of the British Labour Party Society, after visiting in Ireland in 1892, reported that the natives were charming but "we detest them as we would the Hottentots for their very virtues . . . we must give Ireland home rule in order to get rid of this detestable race."

Earlier, a Whig journal called the *Edinburgh Review* commented on the Irish:

> They possess, no doubt, qualities of a very serviceable kind, but these qualities require the example and power of another race, more highly endowed, to bring them to perfection and to turn them to full account. . . . The Irish are deficient in that unquiet energy, that talent for accumulation, those indefinite desires which are the mainsprings of successful colonization, and they are deficient too in that faculty of self-government without which free institutions can either flourish or be permanently maintained.

And the racist English historian Edward A. Freeman wrote in 1881 to England from the United States, "This would be a grand land if only every Irishman would kill a Negro, and be hanged for it. I find this sentiment generally approved—sometimes with the qualification that they want Irish and Negroes for servants, not being able to get any other."

As the nineteenth century ground to an end, immigration tapered off for a few years because redistribution of land in Ireland greatly improved the lot of the Irish peasants. American nativists turned away from the Irish to be even more passionately concerned about the Italians and the Poles and the Greeks and Eastern European Jews who were arriving in America. The Irish, they seemed to feel, had

permanently doomed themselves to the working-class slum neighborhoods, with the exception of a few politicians and physicians. The
Irish in America had risen about as far as they were going to rise. This
curious final judgment on the fate of the American Irish still persists,
though the myth is willing to add entertainers, authors and, of
course, the Kennedys to the list of the Irish who have made it out of
the working class or the lower-middle-class communities.

Dunne left Chicago for New York and Dooley became concerned
about international issues. Nothing more needed to be said about the
American Irish. No one noticed, it seems, that the Irish were already
in the process of crossing the national average in the proportion of
their young people going to college. Something unexpected and un-
precedented was about to happen.

FIVE

The Nationalist Cause

DEDICATION TO THE CAUSE OF A FREE AND UNITED IRELAND PLAYED AN important part in the transition of the immigrants to American life. It was a symbolic goal with broad appeal around which the various factions in Irish-American life might rally; whatever their differences about method, virtually all Irish Americans agreed that Ireland should no longer be an English colony. The energies and talents of many of the leaders of the Irish-American community were consumed by nationalist devotion, as was a considerable amount of the money from ordinary members of the community. Indifference of other Americans to the cause, particularly of those whose sympathies were allegedly progressive or liberal, probably increased the Irish suspicion of ideological liberalism (though they voted more often than not for liberal candidates, on pragmatic grounds).

★　　★　　★

The history of Irish-American nationalism can be separated into four eras: 1850–1880, the time of "Young Ireland" and the Fenians; 1880–1900, the time of the Land League and clan; 1900–1921, the era of the Irish Republican Brotherhood; 1921–present, when the "Irish question" receded into the unconscious to appear again whenever the gunmen began to walk the misty lanes and the foggy streets of Ireland.*

In 1819, the first of the Irish-American nationalists, the Dublin-born writer Matthew Carey, in the midst of a life of deep involvement in the literary and political problems of his era, wrote a book called *Ireland Vindicated*. It defended both the Irish immigrants and Irish culture against the assault made by the opponents of Catholic emancipation in Ireland.

Carey was hardly a revolutionary. Those who came after him were, quite literally, rebels.** They came after the failure of the Young Ireland movement in 1848, either directly from Ireland or after escaping from exile in Australia. Literate intellectuals, they had been a failure as military and political leaders in Ireland and two of the most famous of them, Thomas D'arcy McGee and John Mitchell, produced newspapers called respectively *The Nation* and *The Citizen* in which they struggled with the dilemma of their political and social liberalism that inclined them toward an American loyalty and their nationalism that inclined them toward a concern with Irish freedom.

The Fenians were founded in the mid-nineteenth century by one James O'Mahoney, another Young Ireland exile, and established themselves as a pseudoseparate state with a president, a congress, ambassadors, and all the paraphernalia of government. They also

---

* The best book on Irish-American nationalism is still Thomas N. Browne's *Irish American Nationalism* (Lippincott, 1961). The Arno Press, in its 1976 reprint series, also has a number of useful or informative volumes: Lawrence McCaffrey (ed.), *Irish Nationalism and the American Contribution;* Robert Athearn and Thomas Francis Meagher, *An Irish Revolutionary in America;* Francis G. McManamin, *The American Years of John Boyle O'Reilley;* Michael Funchion, *Chicago's Irish Nationalist, 1881-1890;* Joseph Patrick O'Grady, *Irish Americans and Anglo-American Relations, 1880-1888;* James Paul Rodechko, *Patrick Ford and His Search for America;* Marie Veronica Tarpey, S.C., *The Role of Joseph McGarrity in the Struggle for Irish Independence;* Joseph Edward Cuddy, *Irish America and Nationalism, 1914-1920;* John Patrick Buckley, *The New York Irish and Their View of American Foreign Policy, 1914-1921.*

** The Irish "freedom fighters" from 1798 to Easter 1916 were for the most part priests, poets, intellectuals, and dreamers. The '98 rising was a bloody disaster. The various other conflicts, particularly those of the Young Ireland movement and the Fenians a couple of decades later, were more ludicrous than dangerous. Caught in the same combination of military ineptitude and popular indifference, the same fate would have almost certainly happened to the occupants of the General Post Office if the British had been more intelligent and less bloody-minded in their response to the rising. Only after 1916 did the brilliant military and political genius Michael Collins invent modern guerrilla warfare for which the British, with professional soldiers, mercenary auxiliaries, and paid informants and agents provocateurs, were no match. Collins knew that his guerrillas were, as Mao would later say, "fish swimming in the sea of the people."

became an important social and recreational component of Irish-American life. As Finley Peter Dunne's Mr. Dooley commented, Ireland would long since have become free if Sunday afternoon picnics could create freedom. The summer military encampments of the Fenians (also ruthlessly satirized by Dooley) were more ridiculous than dangerous—especially when as often was the case they turned into little more than rural drinking orgies.

However, many of the Fenians were Irish veterans of the Civil War (many of them serving under General Thomas Francis Meagher, another Young Irelander) and fancied themselves capable of waging serious warfare despite their ludicrous attempt to invade Canada in 1870. The Fenians themselves probably never had more than forty thousand members, though they had much wider popular support for their goal. They were Irish nationalists, concerned less with social justice than with freedom for Ireland; in practice, they were also frequently more concerned about social and recreational life in America and about careers in American local and national government than they were about the problem of the old country.

After the Fenians, there appeared a wave of more serious Irish nationalists who became the American counterpart of Michael Davitt's Land League and Parnell's Irish Party in the old country. The two most important nationalist leaders of this era were Patrick Ford, editor of *The Irish World* and a dedicated social reformer (absolutionist and prohibitionist as well as nationalist), and John Boyle O'Reilley, editor of *The Boston Pilot* and a moderate nationalist far more concerned with the plight of the Irish immigrants than with radical social reform in the United States or revolutionary militancy in the old country. Ford was, in other words, an American reformer and O'Reilley a leader of the immigrant community.

John Devoy, the founder of a journal called *The Irish Nation,* was an Irish revolutionary temporarily dwelling on American soil. He was deeply involved in the Clan Na Gael, the secret society which replaced the Fenians. It was much tougher, more realistic and, due to the collections of Irish Americans for a "skirmishing fund," more affluent. Monies from the "skirmishing fund" were at first used for propaganda purposes, but then some of the money went to terrorist organizations.

In Chicago, where the Clan Na Gael was powerful—in part because the Roman Catholic hierarchy was sympathetic—the Irish seemed more interested in murdering other Irish Americans than in killing English oppressors. One of the most influential in the Clan, a plausible scoundrel named Alexander Sullivan, was probably responsible for the murder of a rival named Dr. Cronin, but he certainly also played fast and loose with the Clan's funds. With the fall of Parnell in 1890, both the Clan and its more socially oriented rival, the Irish National League, went into eclipse.

The more secretive Irish Republican Brotherhood remained powerful on both sides of the Atlantic, waiting, watching, biding its time so England's weakness would become Ireland's chance. However, land reform in Ireland, the slow spread of prosperity, and the powerful role of the Irish Party in the British Parliament led to gradual political and economic improvement in Ireland. When the Home Rule Act was suspended at the beginning of the Great War, it seemed to be the answer to nationalist dreams on both sides of the Atlantic.

The IRB never believed in home rule. Britain was mired in the quagmire of Flanders. It was now Ireland's chance. On Easter Monday in 1916, the General Post Office on Sackville Street in the heart of Dublin was occupied.

American money began to pour into Ireland; it is difficult to tell how much. Surely more money than ever, because the Irish were more affluent. A man like Michael Collins didn't need much money to fight a guerrilla war, though there is some reason to believe Collins accepted his "half a loaf" in establishing the Irish Free State in 1921 because his troops were low on ammunition. Irish-American political support was mobilized.

But Woodrow Wilson ignored the pressure. Wilson had been warned by advisers that he was courting trouble and he replied haughtily, "We are utterly at a loss how to act . . . without involving the government of the United States with the government of Great Britain in a way which might create actual breech between the two." Joseph Tumulty might argue that Ireland never had a truer friend than Woodrow Wilson and Senator Thomas Walsh may have lamented that "They want to beat the League of Nations so that someday or other . . . England may get what is coming to her. And they do not want wars, even world wars, to be made impossible or only remotely possible because in some great war the British Empire may go smash." But the aging Fenian John Devoy spoke for many Irish Americans when he described Woodrow Wilson as "the meanest man who ever filled the office of President of the United States."

We have no data on the attitudes of ordinary Irish Americans toward the League of Nations or on how they voted in the 1920 presidential election. Still, historians are inclined to think—mostly, one suspects, on the basis of reading the furious statements of the Irish in newspapers—that Irish-American opposition was decisive in shattering Woodrow Wilson's dream of a League of Nations. A modest and more reasonable assessment, it seems to me, would be that Wilson could have put more pressure on the English without breaking relations; he could have demanded a more responsible solution to the Irish struggle that would not have left so many seeds of future violence embedded in Ireland. He also could have been more diplomatic in dealing with the Irish-American community, which had enough votes to get a meaningless resolution in favor of a free Ireland through the United States Senate. If Wilson had done either or both of these things, he might have increased Irish-American support for the League. But then if he had been a man capable of such tact, diplomacy, and sensitivity, he would have won over many other potential allies to the League.

★   ★   ★

The nationalist tradition has not vanished completely from Irish-American life. Just as the peace treaty of 1921 only partially freed Ireland, so it only partially eliminated Irish-American nationalism. Most American Irish are not nationalists and feel distaste and disgust for the violence in Ulster, which they do not understand. But there is a slender thread linking some Irish Americans to the fervent and occasionally bloody nationalism of the past. Moreover, the symbols of the cause—the Republic, One and Indivisible—still persist in the collective preconscious of the Irish Americans, most of whom would be hard put to distinguish Michael Collins from Silken Thomas. Precisely because it is not understood and not even examined, the nationalist tradition is an unpredictable element in Irish-American life; it is mostly unimportant, yet it is present, simmering, and potentially explosive—a threat to both the Irish and the American governments. Nor is the nationalist story easy to understand. For Irish-American nationalism lost all the fights but the last; probably won that, though the outcome is still obscure, and then set about losing again.

As I finish this book, a group of Irish-American politicians have called on Britain's Prime Minister Thatcher for a "new initiative" in Ulster, and a group called the Irish American Caucus—with the vigorous support of the Celtic congressman Mario Biaggi—is plugging away at support for the Republican cause in Ulster. Only a small amount of American money is getting through to the IRA, and it is coming from a tiny minority of the Irish population.

Yet Leon Uris, the author of *Trinity* and a republican sympathizer (though surely opposed to violence), could attract fifteen hundred Chicago Irish men and women to a meeting which normally would only have a couple of hundred in attendance. The nationalist cause, it may seem to those it makes nervous, is a time bomb ticking away. I think they need not be so nervous. The Irish Americans of the third and fourth generation (most of us) are far too respectable to get mixed up with the Ulster gunmen.

⋆ ⋆ ⋆

Toward the end of the marathon negotiations that resulted in a peace accord between Israel and Egypt, Israeli Prime Minister Menachem Begin, speaking to a group of Jewish leaders in the Waldorf Astoria Hotel in New York, and to the country on national television, commended American Jews for the enormous influence they had had on their government during the long course of peace negotiations. Believe me, he said in effect, without your influence things would have gone very differently.

Despite protests, Americans take it for granted that collectivities within the nation may campaign vigorously for a foreign cause, particularly a cause of a nation with which they identify. One may be prepared to concede, as I am, absolute legitimacy of American Jewish support for Israel and still wonder why the American Irish were not successful in urging their government to support freedom for the Republic of Ireland. The two situations, of course, are not strictly comparable, but mostly because the Republic of Ireland was born, more or less, in 1916 and Israel in 1948, three decades later. The Irish community in the United States was certainly as militantly organized to support freedom for Ireland as Jewish Americans are today. The Irish were becoming members of a politically powerful middle class and controlled many of the large city governments around the country.

It may also be true that the Irish did not have the influence in the world of the mass media that Jews do today, but there were many important Irish reporters and editors. Irish political power at the ballot box probably exceeded the political power of the Jewish community after the Second World War. The holocaust gave special poignancy and power to the demand for a free Israel; so should the Famine have given special poignancy and power to the demand for a free Ireland. Why did the Irish fail to persuade their government and the cultural leaders of the nation that Ireland has a right to be free, while the Jews succeeded in persuading the government and much of the nation's cultural elite that Israel has the right to exist as a free nation?

Woodrow Wilson deliberately and callously ignored the demand of Irish Americans to support freedom for the Republic of Ireland, thus confirming the conviction of many American Catholics that Wilson was an arrogant and self-righteous bigot. Wilson's opposition to the Irish cause contributed substantially to the defeat of the League of Nations and the Democratic rally of the 1920 presidential election. Yet such a demonstration of political power had no impact on the Democratic Party. During the Second World War, Franklin Roosevelt conspired with his ambassador in Dublin to claim that Prime Minister De Valera and the Irish government were pro-German (when, in fact, they tilted in the opposite direction), as part of an explicit and deliberate strategy to turn the Irish Americans away from support for Ireland and so that they would not torpedo Roosevelt's version of the League of Nations. They could have saved themselves the effort because once Ireland emerged as a mostly free nation, the American Irish lost interest in such residual questions as the six-county Protestant enclave in the north. Roosevelt, like Wilson, was concerned about justice and freedom all over the world but quite unconcerned about it in Ireland. He was afraid of the political power of the Irish Americans and characteristically resorted to treachery rather than responsiveness in dealing with that power.

It is unclear how strong was the commitment of the ordinary Irish American to the cause of freedom for his homeland. Many Irish-American politicians, for example, supported Woodrow Wilson and his League of Nations with little fear of punishment from their voters. Parallel behavior would be unthinkable for any Jewish-American politician. The emerging literature on Irish-American nationalism focuses on the nationalists, their organizations and internal fighting, and their financial contribution to the revolutionary cause in the homeland. It does not reveal how broad or deep was the support in the Irish-American community for the nationalist cause.

To most American Jews, Israel is at the top of their agenda of political priorities. It is doubtful that the same could be said about the Irish Americans in the first decade of this century. After the Anglo-Irish treaty of 1921 they were neither well informed nor passionately committed to the cause of the revolutionaries. One suspects that most Irish Americans were indeed sympathetic to the revolutionary cause and agreed with the leadership of the nationalist movement that when Ireland took its rightful place in the family of nations then the American Irish might begin to win some respect from the English Protestant host culture (their expectations, as it turned out, were wrong but that's another matter). Nonetheless, they did not identify their own welfare nearly so strongly with the welfare of the Republic as American Jews identified with the cause of Israel.

England was, of course, an ally of the United States, one with whom we had just fought a major and successful war and one from whom we had drawn much of our language, culture, and legal tradition. England was not a temporary ally of convenience like Saudi Arabia. Wilson not only needed David Lloyd George's support in drafting a Versailles treaty, but also had, as did most Americans, a powerful political and cultural sympathy for England and a consequent distaste and disdain for the uncivilized revolutionaries across the Irish Sea. The Irish nationalists in the United States were therefore not only contending for their own cause but contending against a powerful and respected ally.

Yet another factor was at work: the American Irish were never able to persuade their government or their nation's cultural elite of the moral rightness of their cause. The American nation could be moved by powerful emotional sympathy—for the Hungarians against the Austrians, the Armenians against the Turks, the Chinese against the Japanese, and for the Indians against the British, but not for the Irish against the English. Somehow or other, the Irish have never been able to qualify as a fashionable evicted people.

Concern for human rights in Rhodesia, Chile, and Franco's Spain has in recent times all but obsessed the nation's intellectual and cultural elite. The issue of human rights in Ireland, however, even today, scarcely gains any notice at all. Violence, which in Rhodesia and South Africa becomes admirable because it is "revolutionary," is quickly categorized as "senseless" when it takes place in Ulster. The residues of colonialism are objectionable in Asia, Africa, and Latin America. American efforts at colonialism in Iran and Vietnam are thought to be outrageous, but the residues of British colonialism and the "plantations" of Ulster are taken to be legitimate and even necessary. The English argument that they must remain in Ireland in order to avoid a "bloodbath" is repeated sanctimoniously by the same people who ridiculed such a defense for the American precedence in Vietnam. Ultimately then, one speculates, the reason for national support for Israel and the lack of national support for Ireland is that freedom for Israel was viewed as a morally legitimate cause and freedom for Ireland has never been, and indeed is not now, a morally legitimate cause in the eyes of most Americans.

There are paradoxes, however, in the Irish-American nationalist movement. Even though it failed to convince the American government and people of the righteousness of its cause, it still was probably of decisive importance in the creation of the Irish Republic; in part because (second paradox) Irish-American nationalism was more militant than Irish nationalism. Even today, there is far more vocal and vigorous support of the Irish Republican Army in the Irish American bars in Queens and Manhattan than there would be in comparable pubs in Dublin or Cork or Galway. So, too, in the past there was probably more sympathy and certainly more money in the Irish-American community to support the organization that moved into the General Post Office on Easter Monday in 1916. It took characteristically inept British repression of the Easter Rising to mobilize support for its cause in Ireland. In Boston and New York there was already plenty of support.

Hence, a third paradox. While the nationalist cause may not have been high on the agenda of many Irish-Americans, it was probably more important to them than it was to their Irish counterparts, who had prospered both politically and economically in the quarter of a century before the Great War, and who expected, perhaps with misplaced confidence, that home rule would come after the war was over.

The key to these paradoxes perhaps can be found if one looks at the Irish-American nationalist phenomenon today. There are certain nationalist sympathizers in Chicago, who come almost entirely from two very distinct groups: recent revolutionary émigrés and third- or fourth-generation Irish Americans looking for a cultural identity. Neither group is likely to exist in appreciable numbers in Ireland. Revolutionary émigrés have, by definition, emigrated; often they have lost contact with both the political and revolutionary situation in the homeland.

If such Irish-American writers as Jimmy Breslin and Gail Sheehy and Pete Hamill are more concerned about the cause of the IRA than are their counterparts in Dublin, the reason most likely again is that they need a cause to parallel their Jewish colleagues' support for Israel. Indeed Pete Hamill once wrote quite explicitly that "the new" Irish of New York were superior to the old Irish because they had begun "to think like Jews" (as classic a manifestation of self-hatred, incidentally, as one could possibly find). It is easy to support gunmen, some of my friends in Ireland have remarked, when you are three thousand miles away from the gunfire. They don't seem to appreciate that when you are three thousand miles away it may be more necessary to support a revolution than when you are on the spot, especially if you are someone who has been driven from the country by a previous episode in the revolutionary tradition or if you are in desperate search for something that will define you or give you worth over another, allegedly superior, cultural tradition in your environment.

The present Irish government and intelligentsia are caught in a dilemma. They revere the symbols of 1916 but denounce those who use the symbols in Ulster today and those Americans who do as their predecessors did in 1916—contribute financially to the cause that utilizes the same symbols. Connor Cruse O'Brien, Minister of Post and Telegraph in the coalition government that preceded the present Fianna Fail (De Valera's party) in Ireland, was at least consistent. O'Brien was ready to reject the men who used the symbols in 1916 with the same impartial enthusiasm with which he rejects those who use them today.

The paradoxes after a while become ironies: the coalition government often seemed more interested in protecting the sensitivities of the Protestants from the north and cutting off American aid to the IRA than it was in protesting the continued discrimination and oppression in the bastardized six-county province of Ulster. Indeed, when I wrote a column tracing the historical antecedent of the Ulster situation, describing objective conditions of Catholics in that province (while at the same time opposing violence in Ulster), I received a letter from an official of the Irish government blaming me for the violence in the north and a pompous and patronizing reprimand from Professor Brian Tierney of Cornell University. Tierney asserted that I was every bit as much a murderer as if I had shot down someone in the streets of Ulster.

The tortured logic behind these protests seems to be that if you tell the truth about Ulster, Irish Americans will support the IRA and that, in turn, will lead to murder. The IRA, of course, has not needed American contributions in the past. In the absence of such contributions it could either rob banks, as it used to do, or collect more money from Colonel Qaddafi, the Lybian strong man. There is no reason to think that anything the government of the Republic of Ireland could do would really reassure that Protestant colonial minority in the north. Finally, there is no reason to believe that an objective statement of the facts of the Ulster situation—and no critic denied the accuracy of my factual descriptions—really is going to increase the tiny minority of Irish Americans who sent money to Ulster.

I am, be it noted, neither a nationalist nor a republican (of either the Irish or the American variety), but I am inclined to think that Connor O'Brien may have been intellectually right even if he was politically wrong. Home rule would have occurred eventually anyhow and it would have been home rule for the whole island.

The English government could have imposed unity on the whole of Ireland in 1921 if it had been brave enough and intelligent enough to do so. Harold Wilson, a left-wing socialist, could have enforced the power-sharing compromise in the north of Ireland in 1973 if he had had the courage to do so. However one may lament the extremes of Irish nationalism, Irish revolution, and the mistakes the Irish gunmen may have made, all have been in response to even worse English mistakes.

If the revolution against colonialism is right in the third world, then it is right in Ireland, too. If Camillo Torez, the priest who died in guerrilla warfare in Latin America, is a hero—and many Catholic liberals would make him so—then so are the IRA gunmen who are shot in Ulster. If violence is excusable in Rhodesia and South Africa, then it is excusable in Ulster. If the new nations in Africa have a right to territorial integrity, so does the new nation of Ireland. If colonialism is wrong in India, then it is wrong in Ulster. If ethnic minority groups have to learn to live with national governments in the third world, then why is it inconsistent to demand that the Protestant minority group in Ireland learn to live with a national government? I do not approve of revolutionary violence (at least in most cases), but neither do I approve of inconsistency or the double standard or the ridiculous notion that Irish Americans can be blamed for the failures of the British and Irish governments to arrive at peace and justice in Ulster. Peace will occur in Ireland only when the economic and political oppression of the Catholics in the north ends and when some deference is paid, however minor and however symbolic, to the fact that Ireland is one island and one nation, not two.

In one important respect, both the Irish and the American Irish have been trapped in an historic ambiguity (neither paradox nor irony) over the cause of Irish freedom. On the one hand, they do not like the violence and the killing, and on the other hand, they are sympathetic with the nationalist or republican cause. The dilemma of the Irish government today is that on the one hand the majority of its people (perhaps 95 percent) rejects the violence of the IRA, but on the other hand, a majority (perhaps 65 percent) believes that the British ought to leave Ulster and a unified Irish nation ought to exist.

Much less well informed, the American Irish probably would divide along the same lines and are utterly baffled by what they take to be the appeasement stance of the Dublin government. William Cosgrave, the head of the coalition government, came to Chicago once and at a large civic dinner denounced contributions to the cause of the IRA. In a response, Chicago's Mayor Richard Daley prayed for peace and justice. "What's a madda wid dem?" hizzoner later said to me. "How can dey be silent about de injustice in da north?" Daley was not a nationalist. He cut off the flow of funds to Irish Northern Aid as soon as one of his agents reported that Northern Aid might be for the IRA. But he could not comprehend why government officials of the Republic of Ireland had remained silent about the historic and contemporary injustices in the north. Neither can most Irish Americans.

The Irish, both in Ireland and in the United States, despite the stereotypes, are a peaceful, nonviolent people. (Anatole Broyard, a book reviewer for The New York Times, once wrote about the bloody, violent history of Ireland. It was, of course, the bloody and violent history of a nation that was being invaded, since the Irish have not engaged in aggressive war since the time of Neill of the nine hostages and it was mostly Irish blood being shed—facts which did not seem to trouble Mr. Broyard very much.) The overwhelming majority of the Irish on both sides of the ocean has always wanted a peaceful evolutionary solution to the problem of the Irish aspiration for freedom. Both sides would undoubtedly have settled at one point early in the century for a dual monarchy modeled on the Austro-Hungarian regime. But the English could never really accept an evolutionary solution, and neither then nor now could they or their American cousins truly admit that the English presence in Ireland is a monumental historical injustice and that the Irish aspiration for national freedom is as legitimate as that of any other people in the world—and as moral.

The result has been revolutionary violence since 1798 and an ambivalent Irish–American nationalist movement since 1850. Only when England and its American admirers and allies are willing to assume responsibility for its historical crimes and its current subsidy, military and economic, of injustice can one expect the fires of Irish-American nationalism to be finally banked. There will always be revolutionaries; there will always be émigré revolutionaries fleeing to America; there will always be young Americans seeking a cultural identity by allying themselves with a romantic cause in the land of their origins.

There exists no empirical evidence about the attitudes of the American Irish about Ulster. No one on any side of the argument has been willing to fund such research, probably because everyone is afraid of what it might reveal. I suspect one of the findings, however, would be that most American Irish have learned what little they know of Irish history from reading *Trinity* and *The Year of the French*. A passionate desire for respectability precluded the Irish-American family from keeping alive any sense of its Irish past; so did the Irish-American Church and the schools, as far as that goes. One suspects that most Irish Americans turned away from the nationalist spirit after 1921 with an enormous sigh of relief. They wanted Ireland to be free, yet the perennial "Irish question" in American politics was an enormous embarrassment to them in their search for discreet American respectability—a reaction whose parallel would be inconceivable to American Jews.

★   ★   ★

The history of Irish-American nationalism is depressing. Most Irish Americans are spared because they have little interest in the subject. Some of the men, like O'Reilley, were admirable, others such as Carey and McGee were surely gifted. While others, like Joseph McGarrity, were dedicated patriots, men like John Devoy were little better than schemers and conspirators; some, like Alexander Sullivan, were downright scoundrels. Often their internal affairs and their personal political ambitions became far more important than the cause of Irish freedom. The money with which they financed terrorist activities, such as the Phoenix Park murders, did little for the cause of Irish freedom (until years after 1916), and the military machinations were for the most part ludicrous. The activists were surely a minority (the Clan probably had no more than forty thousand active members) and often they exploited the sympathies of the poor Irish working men as a pretext for raising funds that went to the maintenance of the organization, to the personal fortunes or the political ambitions of the nationalist leadership; bright dreams, revolutionary

visions, brilliant rhetoric but also chicanery, conspiracy, and corruption. Perhaps this is so with all nationalist movements.

Many of the American Irish were bitterly opposed to the nationalists. Most churchmen, many elected Irish political officials, and a
substantial proportion of the Irish upper-middle and upper class saw
no reason why Irish-American money ought to go to the support of
visionary terrorists. Just as the nationalist leaders argued that a free
nation would bring respectability to the Irish in America, so the
antinationalists argued that Americans would never respect the Irish
as long as there were the revolutionary terrorist organizations in the
Irish-American community.

Both arguments were probably wrong: neither the emergence of a
free Ireland nor the disappearance of the terrorist organizations
would make the Irish any more respectable in the eyes of the American elite. Still, those who were more concerned about America than
Ireland wished the national issue would go away. So, from that
fateful Monday in April 1916 until the defeat of the League of Nations, even the most respectability-obsessed Irish Americans had to
grudgingly admit that it was time for Ireland to be free. Nevertheless,
the Irish nationalists were never able to make the cause of respectability work in their behalf since they could never arouse total commitment from the Irish community.

The nationalists became irrelevant after the "Free State" treaty of
1921. Most American Irish could no more understand the bloody
civil war (in which Collins died) between pro-Free State and the
anti-Free State forces than they can now understand the complexities
of the conflict in Ulster. It is as though the Irish communities in the
U.S. sighed with relief when the Free State was born. The nationalist
issue was over and now they could settle down to the serious task of
becoming respectable Americans—which, after all, was the reason
why most of them had come to America in the first place.

Virtually all of the immigrant groups had been split into nationalist and Americanist camps. In the first decades of this century, for
example, the Poles in the city of Chicago were even more sharply
split than the Irish; they established separate parishes only a couple of
blocks away, one for the nationalists and the other for the America-
nists. Such a division is perhaps inevitable when most refugees are
economic fugitives and only a few are political and revolutionary
fugitives from a nation that is ruled by a foreign power. Victor Green
has demonstrated that Eastern European nationalism was able to

exercise widespread influence on Czech and Polish Americans only when the causes of a free Poland and a free Czechoslovakia became important American goals in the Second World War. Then it was possible to be a nationalist and an Americanist at the same time. The Irish were not that lucky. However, once the homeland is free, the appeal of the nationalist cause wanes (even in the case of Poland and Czechoslovakia, where there are both new political oppression and new waves of revolutionary émigrés) and most of the immigrants and their offspring settle down to the essential task of becoming successful Americans.

However, as long as there is oppression and injustice then a new generation, some of whose members seek identity in a nationalist cause, may start the fires of nationalism burning again.

What final judgment, then, on Irish-American nationalism? It is arguable that Ireland might not be a free nation without the support of the militant nationalist minority and the sympathetic majority in the United States. For all its narrowness, for all self-serving opportunities, for all of the foul-mouthed braggarts, it is still true that Irish-American nationalism at a critical time played an important, possibly decisive role in the drama which de facto led to the emergence of a free Ireland. Irish-American nationalism failed all along the path of its history and expired for all practical purposes at the moment of victory. Despite all its failures, the cause for which it stood did manage to win a partial victory. By the standards of the last half millennium of Irish history, even partial victories have been few and far between.

What impact did the nationalist movement have on Irish-American life? Despite the substantial literature on the subject, most books about the American Irish (John B. Duff's *The Irish in the United States,* William Shannon's *The American Irish,* and Marjorie R. Fallows's *The Irish Americans)* pay no attention to the nationalist movement. In his *The Irish Diaspora in America,* Lawrence McCaffrey devotes several chapters to Irish nationalism but does not assay any evaluation of the impact of the nationalist movement on the Irish in America. Could it be that the movement was mostly irrelevant? Is it an interesting historical curiosity but a distraction in any effort to understand the American Irish?

I think such a conclusion would go too far. The nationalists were doubtless often as ridiculous as Finley Peter Dunne and his Mr. Dooley claimed they were, but nationalism, broadly defined as pride in one's heritage, had to have been very important for many immigrants and their offspring. The nationalist cause was at times a distraction—and the reactions of many of the clergy and most of the well-to-do laity make it clear that they did indeed consider it a distraction. It was also at other times a source of hope and pride and reassurance. One might not be a nationalist oneself, but one could take consolation that there were those who on days besides the seventeenth of March were hoping that "Old Ireland might be free." The existence of a militant nationalist cause as an available symbol for self-validation might well have facilitated the upward mobility of many Irish Americans at a time when they were still despised by the host society and still plagued, however unconsciously, by their own self-hatred. After the disappearance of the revolutionary movement, about which most of them were ambivalent, most Irish Americans turned for cultural validation to St. Patrick's Day and "Irish Eyes Are Smiling," heroic feats with "the creature," stories about leprechauns, and the autumn Saturday afternoon triumphs of the fighting Irish of Notre Dame.

Whatever the limitations of the nationalist movement, it certainly did not constitute much of an obstacle to Irish-American success. The rhetoric at the Fenian picnics may have seemed ridiculous to Finley Peter Dunne and dangerous to Mr. Dooley, but sometimes I think that Fenians' picnic rhetoric is much to be preferred to the sound of well-to-do Irish singing "My Wild Irish Rose" (even worse, Kevin Barry or Roddy McCauley) in a Chicago bar or a Grand Beach recreation room on a Saturday afternoon as the Irish of Notre Dame—many of them dark-skinned—wipe up the mud, once again, with some hapless foe.

Maybe not, though. The Irish and the pseudo-Irish of Notre Dame at least do not assassinate people.

SIX

Achievement

I PROPOSE AS A SYMBOL OF THE CURRENT STATE OF IRISH CATHOLIC achievement in the United States Senator Daniel P. Moynihan of New York—an action which when combined with my discussion of Richard Daley in a subsequent chapter is almost guaranteed to bring down upon my head the wrath of a certain type of liberal intellectual.

I cite the senator for a couple of reasons (in addition to my delight in shouting and snarling in defiance at that certain kind of liberal intellectual). First of all, the senator is, I think, the first Irish Catholic with a Ph.D. to arrive on the floor of the United States Senate; and secondly, while a certified card-carrying academic, the senator, like many another Irishman with a Ph.D., doesn't play the academic game the way it is "supposed" to be played—which is one more reason for that certain kind of liberal intellectual to turn purple at the mention of his name. In early books about the American Irish, the symbol of Irish success was the athlete or the entertainer (James Cagney or Bing Crosby) or the affluent entrepreneur (Joseph Kennedy) or the successful bank-president financier or corporation president; more recently it is the newspaper editor (Michael O'Neill of the *New York Daily News,* for example). In fact, however, such personages are no longer a good symbol of where Irish Catholics are in the United States. As I will attempt to document in this chapter, the present condition of the Irish Catholic population is such that the most interesting phenomenon is not the rise to affluence but rather the emergence of a substantial Ph.D./intellectual class whose members use ideas as a means for rising to (moderate) wealth and (considerable) power.

Any careful reading of the empirical evidence makes it clear that in the generation under forty there is a swarm of Irish Catholic intellectuals. However, one must still deal with the analysis and the impressions of those who are skeptical that the Irish have arrived at affluence, much less intellectualism—including, in his *Beyond the Melting Pot,* the aforementioned senior United States senator from the Empire State. Thus, from one viewpoint, Senator Moynihan represents the movement of the Irish population beyond achievement and affluence to intellectuality, and from another point of view, he also represents the skepticism about Irish affluence. It serves him right, says I.

The senator cannot be called part of the new generation of Irish Ph.D.'s because he is a decade older. He, like many of us who grew up during the Depression, knew both impoverishment and poverty at various times despite his middle-class background (his father was a journalist). Most of those in the new breed of Irish Ph.D.'s are the product of post-World War II affluence, and while they may have had to scrimp to get along on research assistants' salaries for a couple of years, they do not know and cannot imagine the demoralization and poverty of the Great Depression.

Furthermore, the new breed of Irish intellectuals is anything but alienated from the broad Irish Catholic community, while the senator, who is surely benevolent toward the community, can scarcely be reckoned an active participant in it. Despite these differences, however, the somewhat younger Irish Ph.D. types have one thing in common with their flamboyant predecessor: the same kind of liberal intellectuals who hate Pat hate the rest of us too. They hate us when push comes to shove and not for the stands we may take on integration or on tuition tax credit or on foreign policy; they hate us because we are Irish and because we are Catholic.* They are very likely never to stop hating us as long as we are either of those things.

---

* This book is not the place to discuss in detail the persistence of anti-Catholicism in America, and in particular its persistence among liberal intellectuals. Lou Harris, the only pollster who seriously investigates the prejudice, has found that about one-quarter of the

In the years after the Second World War, about one-fourth of the higher academy (top state universities and private universities) suddenly became dramatically and obviously Jewish. In the years after 1960, another fourth of the academy became more gradually, more quietly, and more surreptitiously Catholic. So quietly, in fact, that neither the Church nor the academy had noted the change—a phenomenon which seems to delight many of the new Catholic intelligentsia, apparently because of their conviction that if large corporate institutions don't recognize your existence they won't be able to do anything to you. While the Irish constitute only about one-fourth of the Catholics in the United States, they constitute approximately half of the new Catholic Ph.D. intelligentsia; they are overrepresented, it would seem, in such disciplines as political science and English and history; proportionately represented in such disciplines as philosophy, economics, and the physical and mathematical sciences; and underrepresented in sociology and psychology.* Graduate-school-trained Irish Catholics are also swarming into governmental administrative positions at the national, state, and local levels, having discovered a new access to political power besides coming up from the precinct—though many of the graduate-school-trained administrators also come up from and still have roots in the precincts.

Most of the new Irish intelligentsia are more discreet than the senior senator from New York. Some play the academic game seriously and out of conviction. They believe it is proper to defer to senior professors (who, with the decline of tenured slots, become some of the most arrogant slave masters the world has ever known), sticking only to the most narrowly specialized subject matter and refusing to do or say anything that is not scholarly because of the

---

American people hold positions which can fairly be described as anti-Catholic. More than one-third of those who live in the Northeast and those who described themselves as liberal also subscribe to anti-Catholic positions (the Jewish rate, however, is somewhat lower than the national average). Senator Moynihan is quite correct in his oft-repeated charge that anti-Catholic nativism has even greater durability than racism and anti-Semitism in American life. Nor does one have to be around a certain kind of academic liberal—not necessarily typical—for very long to know that these folks hate our guts and do so in the serene confidence that disliking the Irish, far from being liberal, is an act of positive virtue.

* Sociology is, I think, the most anti-Catholic of all the academic professions. The American Sociological Association has in recent years commissioned a number of guilt-producing studies about the underrepresentation of women and blacks and Hispanics in the profession. One report even lamented that the overlooked "minorities" represented 15 percent of the American population. No one in the profession, however, has bothered to note that Catholics, who are drastically underrepresented in sociology, represent 25 percent of the population.

conviction of some senior professors that if you ever do anything that can be read by ordinary people you cease to be a scholar.

Other Irish Catholic academic types deal with the oppressiveness of the tenure system the way their ancestors dealt with the Penal Laws—they conform externally and laugh up their sleeves at the foolishness of the scholarly game. Yet others go the Moynihan route—doing their research, publishing their scholarship, and being who and what they damn please with utter disregard of the solemn and serious canons of the academy. At the better state universities, they survive and flourish. At private universities, like the University of Chicago, not very many of them are hired, so the question of survival becomes irrelevant.

The Irish Catholics will not, it might be said, reshape the academy or its Sufragan Sees, the arts and literature and the national elite media. But just as they flooded into the cities a century and a quarter ago, the Irish are now flooding into the academy and they have come to stay. Furthermore, just as those Americans who thought the Irish would shortly abandon their superstitious faith when they became Americanized were wrong, so too are those "liberal intellectuals" who believe that after a short period of socialization the Irish Catholic with a Ph.D. is going to leave his religion and his value system behind. The Irish have come to the Ph.D. world, they have come to stay, and they are going to stay as Catholics.

This is as dramatic a quiet revolution and as unnoticed as an earlier revolution at the end of the century, when the Irish began to move out of their impoverished slums in American cities and in very substantial numbers push their way into the lower middle class.

In his introduction to the Modern Library edition of *Studs Lonigan,* James T. Farrell insists that that classic of Irish-American literature was not, contrary to some popular impressions, written either about offspring of the slums or about juvenile delinquents. The Lonigan family was not poor. Studs may have engaged in occasional delinquent behavior, but he was not an habitual criminal; and the houses he lived in on Indiana Avenue and later on Wabash Avenue were anything but slum tenements. According to Farrell, he was telling a story about "spiritual poverty" in the midst of increasing economic affluence. The descendents of the immigrants, he tells us, learned to be successful in America at the price of spiritual deprivation, a spiritual deprivation that was so great that in the case of Studs it doomed him to failure.

For all its brilliance, there is an inconsistency in *Studs Lonigan.* Did

the protagonist fail because of spiritual poverty? Or was it because of
personality characteristics—particularly those which drove him to destroy his relationships with women—rooted in his relationship with
his own mother? Or was Studs Lonigan finally destroyed by a combination of bad health and the disaster of the Great Depression?

One has to say that a lot of Irish as impoverished as Studs, and as
crippled in their relationships with the opposite sex, managed to
survive the Great Depression physically and to become, by the measures of success in America, extremely successful.

Perhaps, after all, the tragic flaw in Studs Lonigan was weak lungs.

The world of the Lonigan and Danny O'Neill trilogies, the world
in which James T. Farrell himself grew up, is enormously different
from the Chicago of Mr. Dooley and Finley Peter Dunne. Dunne left
Chicago in 1900, the year Studs Lonigan (and James T. Farrell) was
born. The Bridgeport of Mr. Dooley was a community of poverty.
The Indiana Avenue block where Studs Lonigan and Lucy Scanlon
lived was a community of emerging middle-class respectability. The
inhabitants of Bridgeport were policemen, firemen, steel workers,
street-car conductors, stockyard laborers; Lonigan's father was a
painting contractor with employees of his own, and Danny O'Neill's
father was senior supervisor at an express company. Fear of unem-
ployment, disease, and bitter cold winters permeated Bridgeport—
along with Mr. Dooley's fear that as they began to make money the
Irish would lose their distinctive values and culture. This is the dilemma that haunted the intellectuals of every immigrant group: did
one have to give up one's own culture to escape from poverty?

James T. Farrell, writing two decades after Dunne, shared his
ambivalence. In order to escape from poverty, they were becoming
Celtic Babbitts, with spiritual poverty the price of material affluence.

In retrospect, one may wish to argue that only members of an
intellectual elite—a newspaper editor like Dunne or a novelist like
Farrell, both of whom had fled to New York—could afford to take
the issue seriously. Patrick Lonigan's parents had left poverty in Ireland. The son saw a chance to escape from poverty in the United
States, to leave the slum cottages of Bridgeport—as any sensible human being would.

For our purposes, however, the important fact to be learned from
Farrell and Dunne is that the transformation of the Chicago Irish,
which Dunne saw beginning in the last decade of the nineteenth
century, was well on its way that fateful June afternoon in 1915 when

Studs Lonigan graduated from St. Anselm's grammar school. If one wishes to chronicle the success story of the American Irish, one must focus on the years between 1890 and 1930 and in particular on the years between 1900 and 1920. It was precisely in those two decades at the beginning of this century that the Irish "turned the corner" and, economically at least, became part of the mainstream of American life.

In the National Opinion Research Center's (NORC) 1977 and 1978 General Social Survey, 26 percent of families in America reported an annual income in excess of $20,000; of those who describe themselves as British Protestants, 30 percent reported more than $20,000 in income; and 47 percent of the Irish-Catholic families reported more than $20,000 in income, a little higher than the 46 percent of Jewish families and 43 percent of Italian families. Irish Catholic occupational prestige, on a scale of 100, was 42.0, as compared to 39.8 for all American white families, 38.6 for Italian families, and 42.1 for British Protestant families. The mean number of years of schooling of Irish Catholics is 12.6 as compared to the national average of 11.8, 12.7 for British Protestants, and 11.4 for Italian Catholics, and 13.7 for Jews. Of the Irish Catholics, 32 percent were professionals or managers, as compared to a national average of 25 percent, an Italian figure of 22 percent, a British Protestant figure of 33 percent, and a Jewish figure of 40 percent.

Thus, in terms of education, occupation and income, Irish Catholics are notably above the national average for other whites. In education and occupation they are also now even with the British Protestant group and substantially ahead of that group in income. Finally, while they lag somewhat behind Jews in occupational prestige and education, their average income in the years from 1975 to 1978 is slightly ahead of both the British Protestants and the Jews.*

Thus, in metropolitan regions outside the South, Irish Catholics are four-tenths above the national white average in education; 2.4 above the national average in prestige; and $2,170 above the national white average mean income.

For more than half a decade these persistent findings generated at the National Opinion Research Center about the economic, educa-

---

* Every time NORC releases figures on income by religion it receives a number of letters from American Jews charging it with stirring up anti-Semitism by reporting that Jews are the most affluent group in America. In response, one can only say that the economic success of American Jews is no great secret.

tional, and occupational success of American Irish Catholics have been a matter of public record. They do not seem to have made much of an impact on the myth of Irish failure. Thus, Thomas Sowell, in a recent book on black economic problems, encourages blacks to imitate Italian Americans, who have been successful in this country, and not imitate Irish Catholic Americans, who have been unsuccessful. The sole basis for his conclusions about the Irish Catholics is census data (from the current Population Survey) which lump rural and Southern Irish Protestants with Northern and urban Irish Catholics.

The intellectual challenge then is not to explain the failure of the Irish Catholics but to explain why their success, repeatedly documented in at least three different independent large-sized national samples, is still denied by Irish and non-Irish alike.

In the World War I era, the odds were a little better than one to five that a typical American would attend college, but the Irish Catholic ratio was one to four. Thus, precisely at the time that Studs Lonigan was graduating from St. Anselm's, the Irish had already crossed the national average for non-Hispanic white Americans in college attendance (among those of college age at that time). The Irish have stayed above the national line ever since, and during the Vietnam generation the rate of college attendance among Irish Catholics was still higher than the national curve.

Similarly, the odds were little better than one to three of Americans falling into a managerial or professional occupation in the last half century. Even for the Irish growing up at the time of Studs Lonigan, the chances of being a manager or professional were already higher than the national average and they have remained so ever since, at about the rate of one to two. Finally, for young people growing up in the World War I era, the chances were approximately even for ending up in a white-collar occupation. For Irish Catholics, however, the chances were better than two to one and they have remained at approximately that rate ever since.

Thus, when Studs Lonigan was deciding not to finish high school, a higher proportion of Irish Catholics of his generation was choosing to attend college than the national average for those from typical white American families. Similarly, while Studs's occupations were almost all blue-collar, Irish Catholics were already proportionately in the white-collar category, indeed even disproportionately in the professional and managerial categories.

The Irish "success" in America, then, happened when Woodrow

Wilson was President, indeed at the very time that the National
Commission on Immigration was arguing that the Catholic European immigrant groups were not capable of occupational success. (It
would take a couple more decades before the Italian and Polish ethnics proved that the nativist immigration commission was wrong in
their case, too.) Irish Catholics, to put it simply, have been the most
successful of gentile ethnic groups for better than sixty years and yet
American scholarship, Irish and non-Irish alike, seems not to have
been able to perceive this phenomenon. There are a few very rich
Irishmen, like the Kennedys, and then all the rest are lower-middle-
class Irishmen like Archie Bunker (who, of course, is Irish—no matter
what anyone says). That there was an Irish world full of Patrick
Lonigans three-quarters of a century ago seems to have escaped both
novelists and scholars alike.

Two arguments are frequently cited by those scholars who are
prepared to take the NORC data seriously. One is that Irish income
is higher because the typical Irish family has multiple wage earners. In
fact, working spouses and working children are no more likely in the
Irish Catholic family than in any other family. It is also asserted that
while the Irish may well be white-collar workers and even professionals, they have not made it into the most prestigious professions.
Such an argument ignores the fact that the NORC occupational-
prestige score cited previously is indeed designed to measure precisely
the prestige of an occupation. It also ignores the fact that if a group is
the best educated and the most affluent of the gentile groups in
America and is excluded from prestigious positions—the presidency of
large foundations, the directorship of major governmental agencies
dealing with research, professorates at distinguished private universities—discrimination in those occupational categories might be a
much more plausible argument than drinking or parochial schooling
or religious superstition.

It is argued that whatever their other successes in the United States
may be, Irish Catholics in the United States have not been successful
in the intellectual and cultural world. An endless supply of Irish
Catholic storytellers defeats the cultural argument out of hand.
Catholics are now more likely than white Protestants to attend graduate school and choose academic careers, and they are now as likely
to be on the faculties of high-quality universities as are other Americans. Furthermore, Irish Catholics are disproportionately involved in
this academic flourishing among American Catholics. They are not

yet to be found in appreciable numbers on the faculties of Harvard or the University of Chicago. But a quarter of a century ago Jews were certainly not at Harvard, and if Harvard and the University of Chicago haven't had many Irish Catholic faculty members, the same cannot be said of the great state universities like Wisconsin, Michigan, Illinois, California (and, I might add, Arizona). Despite their religion, the size of their families, their parochial schooling, and their drinking, Irish Catholics have arrived in America; indeed, they arrived a long time ago—my father and mother were meeting at Twin Lakes when Studs Lonigan was having his tragic, unsuccessful final chance with Lucy Scanlon, and Al Smith was running for governor of New York—1920 rather than 1960 was the turning point for Irish Catholics.*

Data reported in this chapter, combined with the literary evidence of writers like James T. Farrell, call for a rethinking of the American historical myth of the story of Irish Catholics in American life. The myth stressing the suffering of the immigrants in the slums of New York and Boston; the success of entertainers and athletes and politicians; and the emergence of a few wealthy families like the Kennedys simply neglect the complexity and the diversity of the American-Irish experience and of the early success of the Irish in America. There is some willingness to grudgingly admit that the Irish have finally "made it" in America, but the concession is made with the qualification that it took them "longer." One must respond, "Longer than whom?" The major Irish immigration, we have demonstrated, was between 1870 and 1900. By 1910, the Irish were already going to college and choosing managerial and professional careers at a higher rate than that of typical white Americans. The Irish success may not have been quite as spectacular as that of Jews (who, it seems, are normally the implicit comparison group), but it took the Irish no longer than it took the Jews to push their way solidly into the affluent middle and upper middle class, and they did it in less time than did many other immigrant groups (though the other immi-

---

* Fourteen percent of Americans have attended graduate school and 20 percent of Irish Catholics. In my *Religion and Career*, as long ago as 1961, I refuted the allegation of self-critics within the Catholic and Irish Catholic communities that this graduate-school attendance was disproportionate to law, medical, and business schools as opposed to the presumably superior arts and sciences graduate schools. Whatever was to be said of graduate training sought by Irish Catholics before 1961, since then they have been overrepresented, not underrepresented, among those choosing academic careers.

grant groups were hampered by the nativism of the twenties and the Depression of the twenties and thirties). It is also said, as an additional qualification, that the Irish made it through politics, as though affluence achieved through political careers is less worthy or less impressive than affluence achieved through the construction trade or the manufacture of clothing. In fact, although Irish Catholics are twice as likely as the national average to work in government jobs, most Irish Catholics are not in politics or related fields. A claim made by an alienated Chicago Irishman, William Lahey, in an August 1978 issue of *The Irish Times,* that Irish Catholics achieve success in Chicago solely through politics, and that by murdering blacks and Hispanics, is contrary to all the available data and also to common sense—though it proves that there are no outer limits to Irish self-hatred in Chicago or in Dublin.

Actually, the myth is wrong at both ends. Not only did Irish Catholic success come early in America, but not all of the immigrants were starving, illiterate, impoverished refugees. There was an emerging Irish professional middle class in New York City before 1850.* This middle class grew and expanded during the Famine years. Some of the children of the Famine immigrants managed to survive and get into that middle class. Many of the post-Famine immigrants (especially those who came after 1870) were well educated for their time and were poor but hardly impoverished.

The existing survey data do not permit us to reconstruct demographic, educational, and occupational changes in the Irish Catholic population from 1870 to 1900. However, it would appear that in the years between 1865 and 1895, there was a steady growth in the Irish middle class, a growth that kept pace, perhaps just barely, with the enormous number of immigrants. Then from 1895 to 1905—the end of the era of Dooley and the beginning of the era of Studs Lonigan—there was a dramatic quantum leap in which the social status of the Irish Catholics was transformed. That is when the Lonigans moved from Bridgeport to Indiana Avenue. It is curious that this extraordinary phenomenon occurred without anybody, other than perhaps James T. Farrell, apparently noticing it. It was at that very time that some Irish leaders were saying defensively that the Irish could integrate themselves into American life as well as the Germans had. In fact, at that very period the Irish had already begun to surpass the

---

* See the works of Jay Dolan and the Birdsell diaries edited by Nelson O'Callihan.

Germans in achievement in America. A half century later they still aren't getting credit for it.

The work of Stephen Thernstrom on the Irish of Boston is often cited as evidence of the lack of Irish Catholic success in America. Professor Thernstrom is a friend and colleague and never, as far as I know, has he seen any conflict between his research and mine. One need say though that Boston is not America, however much it may appear so from within the boundaries of Harvard Yard. If two scholars using separate data sets come up with different answers, the appropriate conclusion is not that one refutes the other, but that there is a difference in the two populations being studied, one being Boston and the other being the whole of America. However, the difference between Thernstrom's findings and my own presents the possibility that the myth of the Irish in America may have been created within Harvard Yard by those who did not perceive that there are Irish outside Boston, and indeed even outside Cambridge.*

One of Thernstrom's students, Jo Ellen Vinyard, in a doctoral dissertation done at the University of Michigan, *The Irish in the Urban Frontier in Nineteenth Century Detroit,* provides a clue to the apparently conflicting findings of Thernstrom and NORC's research team. Beginning in 1880, the United States Census Bureau enumerated by ethnicity those persons in a wide range of occupations in fifty principal cities. Vinyard selected a sample of eighteen of these cities on the Eastern seacoast and nine, like Detroit, in the "westward moving urban frontier" (San Francisco was the tenth city).

At that time, in each city, the Irish were clearly overrepresented in the unskilled categories in comparison with both the rest of the population and the Germans. Furthermore, the inland cities were just beginning their enormous industrial expansion. In Professor Thernstrom's work, the second-generation Irish (those born in Boston) were not only lower than native Americans in status but also lower than the Germans. In Vinyard's study, the proportion of Detroit's

---

* In presenting a paper at the Merriman Summer Institute in Ennis in County Clare in the summer of 1976, I found Irish scholars who were in attendance at that worthy session terribly troubled about the South Boston school case. They couldn't understand why I was not embarrassed and ashamed about what was going on in South Boston. Oddly enough, they found my response completely unsatisfying: to begin with, South Boston has something to complain about. Furthermore, South Boston isn't typical. Finally, the judge and the NAACP's lawyer in the case were also Irish Catholics. For reasons that escape me, the Irish intellectuals *want* to believe that Boston, and indeed South Boston, is typical of the Irish in America.

Irish youth in the laboring class was only 16 percent compared to 42 percent of their German contemporaries. In short, the Irish were doing much better in an expanding industrial metropolis like Detroit than they were doing in a mature city like Boston.

Vinyard offers a number of explanations for this change. First of all, it may be that those who migrated to the Midwest were more industrious and had available to them resources that enabled them to go beyond the East Coast ports. Secondly, Detroit and the Western cities were entering a period of rapid industrial growth in which the immigrants might be expected to profit, especially since they arrived there at virtually the same time as anyone else. Thirdly, there were more foreign-born than native-born in cities like Detroit and Chicago and hence more opportunity for them to move into positions of influence in the cities, since the native-born did not yet have control of the cities' political structures. Fourthly, in newly emerging industrial cities there was likely to be more egalitarianism and less nativist prejudice. Their social structures and their cultures were more flexible than those of East Coast cities.

There were then more opportunities in the Midwestern cities than the East Coast cities for the Irish, and perhaps also more Irishmen who were more likely to seize the opportunities. Combining Irish Catholic respondents from several different studies and then dividing them into four regions—New England, Middle Atlantic, Midwest (east north-central and west north-central), and other—my colleagues and I have discovered that 40 percent of the New England Irish have attended college; 36 percent of the Middle Atlantic Irish; 45 percent of the Midwestern Irish; and 33 percent of the Southern and Western Irish. The Irish in the Midwest have somewhat more education than their counterparts in the rest of the country at the present time.

In the era of the Great Depression, 22 percent of the Eastern Irish Catholics of college attendance age (born between 1910 and 1920) went to college as compared to 43 percent of those in the West (Midwestern and "other" combined). This educational advantage of the Western over the Eastern Irish persists even to the Vietnam generation, in which 44 percent of the Eastern and 58 percent of the Western Irish attended college.

The numbers of respondents are few, and the proportions fluctuate, but the trend and the tendency are unmistakable. College attendance has been more frequent among the Irish living in the West and the Midwest than in the East for the last half century. Dr. Vinyard's discovery about the tendency in 1880 does not seem to have gone away even in the present.

The National Opinion Research Center's alcohol study covered four cities—Boston, New York, Chicago, and Minneapolis. All the respondents were parents of adolescent children. The Irish in Chicago and Minneapolis were more likely to be white-collar workers and professionals than those in Boston: 39 percent of the Chicago Irish and 38 percent of the Minneapolis Irish were professionals or managers while only 26 percent of the Boston Irish were. Similarly, 54 percent of the Boston Irish were white-collar workers as compared to 71 percent of the Irish in the two Midwestern cities. There was no difference between the Bostonians and the Chicagoans in college attendance, but 27 percent of the Bostonians, 32 percent of the New Yorkers, 33 percent of the dwellers in the Twin Cities, and 50 percent of the Chicago Irish earned more than $25,000 a year. The Chicagoans, in other words, were twice as likely as the Boston Irish to make more than $25,000 a year; and indeed, when the New Yorkers and the Bostonians are combined and compared to the Chicagoans and the Minneapolitans combined, there is a clear statistical difference between the Easterners and the Midwesterners.

The Chicago Irish also get a better return on their college investment. Among those who attended college, 22 percent of the Bostonians and 33 percent of the Minneapolitans earned $30,000 a year or more, and 49 percent of the Chicagoans earned more than $40,000 a year. Chicagoans, then, are more than twice as likely than their Boston counterparts who have attended college to be earning above $30,000 a year.

Finally, the Bostonians and the New Yorkers are lower on measures of both personal efficacy and achievement orientation than are the Chicagoans, though it is impossible to say whether this difference (surely not substantial, but suggestive nonetheless) is a result of antecedent personality factors or merely a reaction to an environment in which there is indeed a reason to feel efficacious and to expect to achieve.

The data we have discussed in the last several paragraphs come from four separate studies based on independent sampling and data collection for each study. Therefore, one can say with considerable confidence that the basic finding of greater Irish success in the Midwest than in the East, and particularly in New England, is valid. It is much more difficult to explain the finding. As Vinyard herself observed, the explanation could be either selected migration or social structure or a combination of both. Those who migrated to Chicago may have been more ambitious; they may also have come to a city where there was more room for ambition. Patrick Lonigan may not have begun his painting contractor business in Boston because in that city there were already enough such contractors and there was a prejudice against hiring Irish painters. It may also have been that in Chicago, which was expanding more rapidly than was Boston, there was more painting to be done.

It seems indisputable that Boston, however admirable a city it may be, is not the United States; and the Boston Irish, however admirable a people they may be, are not typical of the American Irish. Although the nation's cultural and intellectual perspective may be shaped in Harvard Yard and on the side streets of Cambridge, that perspective is inadequate to an understanding of the experience of the Irish in America. The Harvard perspective may not have created the myth of the unsuccessful American Irish, but it certainly reinforces and perpetuates that myth.

If Studs Lonigan's lungs had not betrayed him, if he had survived the terrible trauma of the Great Depression, he doubtless would have made an enormous amount of money, moved to the Beverly district on the southwest side of Chicago, joined the country club (in the 1930s, an exclusive Protestant preserve), been a pillar of the Church, and probably have voted for Richard Nixon in 1960 (and probably would never have been able to forget Lucy Scanlon either—who would also probably have moved to Beverly). But the post-World War II affluence of America was not the cause of the success of the American Irish. On the contrary, they had already struggled into the middle class before the Great Depression, had suffered through that Depression like other members of the middle class, and were thus strategically placed—if they were young enough and healthy enough —to take advantage of the post-1945 affluence.

When I graduated from high school in 1946, only a few of my male classmates and, as I remember, only one of the women with whom I went to grammar school planned to go to college. Eight years later, when I was ordained and sent to an Irish neighborhood of about the same cultural and social level as the one in which I had been raised, it was taken for granted that everyone would go to college. But this astonishing transformation merely meant that the

Irish were staying somewhat ahead of what was going on throughout the rest of America. If the suburban professional Irish are ahead of the pack in the mid-1970s, the principal reason is that their parents were already ahead of the pack in the 1920s and 1930s.

There was a considerable price exacted by the energetic commitment to success and respectability of the Irish Catholics in the United States in the generation of my parents and of Patrick Lonigan. Irish Catholics may well have had to endure a spiritual poverty in order to achieve material affluence, as Farrell argued. Irish Catholics today may still be somewhat narrow and flawed humans because the intellectual and cultural heritage of the past was stifled in their drive for success. They may sit on our country-club verandas and sip martinis in the autumn sunlight while watching a Notre Dame football game on TV when they should be reading serious books and *The New York Times*.

Still, they have made it and made it big—and no one (to switch the cliché) is going to take it away from them.

SEVEN

Family and Personality

FROM JAMES T. FARRELL TO MARY GORDON, THE RIGIDITIES OF IRISH Catholic family life have been celebrated in fiction; from Mary Mc-Carthy to Phil Donahue, sometime Irish Catholics have blamed their personal and emotional problems on their Irish Catholic family background and heritage. Reporter Pete Hamill even wrote an article, when he gave up drinking, in which he blamed his Irish Catholic background for the fact that he drank too much. The images of the cold, stern, demanding mother (Studs Lonigan's mother pushed him toward the priesthood) and the weak, heavy-drinking, sexually incompetent father have become part of the mythology of American life.

Within the Irish Catholic community there is a parallel mythology—the story of the brilliant, witty, and well-meaning but wild, erratic, and heavy-drinking Irishman "straightened out" and made to "act right" by his sensible, tough-minded, long-suffering wife (and daughters).

There are assets and liabilities in the ways that various subcultures may organize their family relationships. In some Irish families, the woman, a combination of toughness and tenderness, provides a superb androgynous model for her daughters and sons and achieves a happy equality in her relationship with her husband. Such a pattern makes for intense warmth and intimacy, even if the man is more cautious than most about wandering too far from his family responsibilities. In many if not most Irish political families, it is the woman who has the superior political instincts and skills (and the more "typical" the Irish family structure, the more likely that its offspring will become politically involved—perhaps because he or she has become so skillful at reading the very subtle and indistinct cues by which communication is arranged in many Irish families). The typical Italian family, far more affectionate than the typical Irish family, produces politically uninvolved young people probably because the emotional demands and the emotional rewards of family life are more than enough of a challenge for a young person.

At its best, then, the Irish organization of family life functions well. At its worst, it can be a disaster like the mythology claims. In between the best and the worst and on the average, it has certain unique problems that no responsible portrait of the Irish Catholic family can ignore. The problems might not be as serious as the mythology portrays; nonetheless, the problems are serious enough.

Perhaps the most difficult of the complexities of Irish family life is that so many of us find it so hard to express the love and affection we feel, a trait which is hardly compatible with the old Celtic heritage in which men and women alike blathered all the day long and well into the night about how enamored they were of the current object of their affection. Such grandiose romanticism seems to have been pretty well crushed out by the famines and the Penal Laws.

There is the story about the old man who was dying; at his bedside stood his wife of fifty years. "Shamus," she said, "never once in all the fifty years that we have been married have you ever said you love me."

"Ooch, woman," replied Shamus, "surely there was no need of that. You knew it all along, didn't ya?"

There is a considerable difference between that mythological dialogue (with some pertinence to contemporary Irish American life) and the seemingly endless dialogues between Diarmuid and Grainne in which those two ill-fated lovers went on at very great lengths about the depth of their feelings for one another. Since the Great Famine, it would seem, both Irish and Irish-American women and men have had a much harder time in being affectionate than they used to. (If one is to believe at least one survey, Irish Catholics do seem to have sexual intercourse at a rate slightly higher than the national average. The survey does not reveal, however, what, if anything, they say to one another before, during, and after the experience.)

Because the mother plays a stronger role in the Irish Catholic family structure than she does in most other ethnic communities, the mythology of the dominant and domineering Irish mother is based on fact. But the reverse side of the picture is ignored by the mythology: precisely because the culture produces strong women, Irish Catholics are the most likely of any gentile ethnic group to endorse the pro-feminist position.

In anthropology and in literature, the dominant role of the Irish mother has been the subject of wonderment, amusement, and complaint. The statistical evidence does indeed support such an image. In both the grandparental and parental family, the Irish Catholic mother is more likely to make decisions and to decide on punishment by herself and more likely to be described by her children as "easier to talk to." Few would deny today that the Irish family ideal and practice of the strong woman is an appropriate model. Yet, in a way, might it not also be said that the Irish family structure stands as a warning to feminism of what can go wrong if strong women are not also tender and affectionate?

According to the mythology, the Irish Catholic family is a cold, authoritarian, and repressive family characterized by late marriage, domineering women, and sexually inadequate, unfulfilled men. It is also asserted by the mythology that the Catholicism of the Irish, in addition to producing sexual repressiveness, also creates models for women which bind them to the roles of housewife and mother. Both Irishness and Catholicism, in other words, produce men and women who are frustrated, unfulfilled, and unhappy.

Enough has been said in previous chapters to prepare us for strong and indeed sexually aggressive women. If the contemporary Irish are also sexually repressed, the fault can scarcely be with the ancient Celtic heritage which, as we have seen, was anything but prudish and repressed. The attitudes toward sex and family that developed as a means of economic survival in post-Famine Ireland may well have had an influence on contemporary Irish-American relationships; but it cannot be said often enough that the culture of western Ireland in the second half of the nineteenth century was not so much Irish or Catholic as it was a culture of survival. No one claims that slavery in the American South produced behavior patterns that are distinctively West African. The parallel drama in western Ireland produced behavior patterns that were necessary for economic survival, but they had little to do with ancient Irish cultural heritage.

Bachelorhood and spinsterhood have pretty much been eliminated as frequent cultural patterns among the American Irish. Only 14 percent of the men and 12 percent of the women are not yet married, and more Irish Catholic men and women are currently married than the national average. Irish Catholics do marry at a somewhat older age than other Americans. Today, the typical Irish Catholic man marries at 24.5 years and the typical woman at 22 years, both a little more than a year older than other Americans. But they do not delay their marriage until the early thirties (the age at which my parents and aunts and uncles were married in the early part of the century in the United States). Such a practice is as much a relic of the past among contemporary Irish Catholic Americans as it is in contemporary Ireland, where the age of marriage is the *lowest* in all the Common Market countries.

Even though the Irish have almost completely rejected their church's teaching on birth control, they still have the largest families of any white ethnic group. (The Irish family has an average of 2.28 children; the average among blacks is 2.49 children.) This is not the result of past childbearing before the birth control decision was made. The Irish also have the second highest estimate of the *ideal* number of children—3.37 compared to black Americans' 3.76 and a national average of 3.01.

Many people familiar with both cultures have remarked that, regardless of ethical imperatives, the Irish and blacks simply like babies. To the Irish this affection for babies has not diminished even among those under thirty. Younger Americans have a smaller estimate of the ideal family size—2.7 children—but Irish Catholics under thirty continue to be three-tenths of a child above the average; and 28 percent of all married Irish Catholics expect to have more children as compared to 20 percent for all married Americans (and 13 percent for all married British Protestants). Not only are there a few Irishmen still around, there are likely to be even more of them in the years ahead.

Nor is this desire for larger families a result of Irish Catholic machismo (an idea whose hilarity can only be appreciated by an Irish man). Men of all ethnic groups are somewhat more likely to expect more children than their wives, but the margin is reversed for Irish

Catholic men; it is the Irish women who have the highest expectation of family size—3.5 as compared to 3.0 for other Americans regardless of sex, and to 3.3 for Irish Catholic men.

There is also considerable talk in the Irish Catholic family. They are the most likely of the four ethnic groups we have studied to report frequent conversation with their spouses (15.1 hours a week) and with their children (17.9 hours a week), three hours more in each case than Italian Catholics and four hours more than Jews. However, the conversations deftly avoid quarreling. More than half of the American adolescents reported that their parents quarreled often or sometimes, but only two-fifths of the children of Irish Catholic parents reported similarly. Thus, both conflict and affection are carefully controlled in the Irish Catholic family.

The dominant role of the Irish mother seems to be more noticed by the daughters of such families than the sons, though it is Irish Catholic male adolescents who are more likely than anyone else to report that it is the mother who "grounds" them when they are in trouble. Irish Catholic women are the most likely to remember that their mothers made the decisions in the family and inflicted punishment when they were growing up.

There are differences of 20 points between Irish women and Irish men in their recollections of maternal power. Among contemporary Irish Catholic teenagers, men and women alike, the mother is the dominant figure both in inflicting punishment and in being available for conversation. I'm not suggesting—and the evidence does not support such suggestion—that men are invisible in Irish Catholic family life or that a large number of decisions are not made by both mother and father acting together. However, in the Irish Catholic family, more than in any other family studied, the woman is more likely to play a solitary influential role, just as the cultural heritage, the folklore, and the literary tradition would have predicted.

All adults are more likely to say they were very close to their mothers than that they were very close to their fathers. But Italians in both generations are more likely to report very close relationships with their parents than the Irish. In the adolescent generation, so too are Jewish and English Americans. "Very close" is of course a subjective measure. It may be that the Irish have different standards than other ethnic groups as to what constitutes "very close." However, somewhat lower estimates of affection in Irish family life certainly concur with the ideas expressed in so much Irish literature—that we do not love our parents, our children, or our spouses, but, as in Brian Friel's *Philadelphia, Here I Come,* we find that the words of affection, like the words of antagonism and animosity, get stuck in our throats. Affection and anger, one suspects, are no less powerful in Irish family life than in other families; they are, however, more difficult to express, a paradoxical condition in a group so given to talk and to flamboyant and poetic use of language.

Most research on family structure indicates that "power" and "support" are two useful concepts for rating the different ways in which families organize themselves. "Power" stands for the concentration of authority in the family, indicates whether authority is concentrated in the parents and, if it is concentrated in the parents, whether it is concentrated in one parent in preference to both parents. "Support" indicates the amount of affection that is exchanged among family members. If one carefully examines the research literature on four American ethnic groups, one is led to expect that Italian families will score low on power and high on support (being democratic and affectionate in their organization), Jewish families high on power and high on support (being both authoritarian and affectionate), Swedish and English-American families low on both support and power (being low on authoritarianism but also low on affection), and Irish families high on power and low on support. The research my colleagues and I have done in a number of different projects confirms beyond much question this difference in family structures. Authority is more centralized in the Irish family, even among the well educated, as often as not in the hands of the mother, and explicit affection is not communicated as much as it is in the other ethnic groups' families. This is not to say that the Irish family is utterly and totally authoritarian; it is, of course, part of the American system of democratic family structures. However, it is less democratic than the Jewish or English or Scandinavian families if unquestionably more democratic than most families were a generation or two ago. Furthermore, there is lots of explicit affection in Irish families; however, less than in Italian and Jewish families.

More authoritarian and less affectionate than other families the Irish Catholics may be, but one can find little evidence of "sexual repressiveness." There are virtually no differences between Irish Catholics and other Americans in attitudes toward premarital or extramarital sex, and the Irish Catholics are 13 percentage points *less* likely to condemn homosexuality as being always wrong than are

other Americans. The Irish Catholic score on a scale of sexual permissiveness is above average, and while lower than the Italian, Jewish,
and black scores on the scale, it is still substantially higher than the
British Protestant and Irish Protestant scores. Just as there are no
jokes about alcoholic British Protestant men, there is no literature
about sexually frustrated and repressed British Protestant women. If
attitudes are indicative of behavior, the Irish are in fact less sexually
repressed than the British Protestants.

(Irish Catholics, as might be expected, are less likely to approve of
abortion than are other Americans. Nevertheless, 67 percent of them
approve of legalized abortion when there is a chance of a serious birth
defect, and two-fifths of them would approve of abortion in a case
where a single woman does not want to bear a child—only 8 points
less than the approval for such an abortion by other Americans.)

The other side of the dominating and dominant Irish Catholic
mother is the Irish attitude toward feminism. They are more likely
than other Americans to approve of a woman pursuing a career; to
reject the notion that women belong in the home; to say they would
vote for a woman for president; to reject the notion that men are
better suited emotionally for politics than women. On the NORC
feminism scale, Irish Catholics are second only to Jews in their support for feminist positions. Furthermore, just as on the sexual permissiveness scale, so on the feminist scale the high score of Irish Catholics
is not a function of their superior educational attainments. Irish
Catholic support for greater involvement of women in contemporary
life is, incidentally, to be found on both sides of the Atlantic. A much
more elaborate set of questions administered by the British Gallup
organization to all the Common Market nations found that the Irish
(followed by the Danes) consistently have the most "progressive"
views on the appropriate role for women. Neither in Ireland nor the
United States, however, should Irish support for feminism surprise
anyone who knows the ancient Celtic laws and traditions that accorded women great freedom and power.

Interestingly enough, there is little difference between Irish men
and women in their support for feminism. Jewish women and black
women are far more likely to be feminists than Jewish or black men,
while British Protestant men are more likely to support feminist
positions than are British women, but the feminist scores for Irish
Catholic men and women are virtually the same. There is then some
confirmation of the survival of an ancient heritage in which both

sexes take for granted the right of women to be involved beyond the family. Irish Catholics are, incidentally, more likely than any other Catholic group to support the ordination of women priests. Indeed the majority of support for the ordination of women can be found only in one demographic category within American Catholicism—Irish Catholic men over forty-five. A possible explanation of this phenomenon is that once you're an Irish male in your late forties you are likely to have experienced at least three sacred women in your life—your mother, your wife, and your daughter. You might just as well ordain them then; it's not going to add anything more to their sacred power.

Does the Irish family structure have any impact on the adult life of children who are reared in such families—other than that they seem to imitate, as a group, the same family pattern they experienced while growing up? While one can find little evidence on our personality scale of differences among adolescents, Irish Catholic adults are lower than both Jews and English Protestants in measures of achievement orientation and personal effort (and there is some indication that adolescent Irish are also lower than Jewish adolescents on these measures). I have always been struck in my work with graduate students at how much more breezily self-confident are the Jewish students than are the Irish Catholic students. The Irish may eventually catch up but it takes them substantially longer to be articulate and self-confident in the environment of a high-powered academic research center. They are indeed likely to sit off in a corner, morosely silent and almost invisible for the first several quarters, to be noticed by senior staff members only when they turn in their first brilliantly written paper, which they have almost certainly written entirely by themselves.

Irish men, however, are not very different from other men in achievement motivation. It is the Irish women, particularly in comparison with Jewish women, who seem to have low achievement and efficacy orientation. Paradoxically, given the feminist orientations of the Irish and the important role the woman plays in Irish family life, the "Jewish American Princess" is both more ambitious and more self-confident than her Celtic American counterpart.

On other morale measures, however, Irish Catholic Americans score higher. Their feelings of life satisfaction are higher and their feelings of alienation lower than those of most Americans, and they are also more likely to report that their personal lives and their marriages are very happy; that their health is excellent; that their financial condition is above average; and that their financial condition has improved during the last five years. They obviously haven't been greatly hampered in their quest for success and happiness by their family life and by the personality characteristics that have emerged from that family life.

Like everything else Irish, family life is filled with paradoxes. The Irish are expressive but hard put to cope with affection or conflict; they accord great power to wives and mothers, but these same women score rather low on achievement and efficacy; they enjoy children, intend to have more children than any other white group in America, but their commitment to the rights of women beyond the family is stronger than that of any other gentile group in America; their childhood experiences would seem to impede both success and happiness, and yet their success and satisfaction scores are above the average—with the satisfaction existing even independently of the success, since the low Irish scores on anomie and high scores on satisfaction persist even when education is taken into account. The paradoxes and contradictions then have not been resolved, but neither have they been permitted to get in the way.

EIGHT

Religion

The most influential official representative of the Irish Cath-olic religion in the United States does not even have an Irish name, though his association with things Irish is indisputable. Nor is he a prelate in the ordinary sense of the word, not a cardinal and not a bishop, not even a monsignor. Fulton Sheen is dead. Francis J. Spell-man is dead. Richard Cushing is dead. The Irish-American cardinals at the time of this writing—Los Angeles's Manning, Chicago's Cody, St. Louis's Carberry—have little impact on the Church outside of their own dioceses and lack both the charisma and the force of char-acter to represent Catholic religion, most Catholic laity, or people outside the Church. Indeed, the first three presidents of the American hierarchy in the reorganization after the Second Vatican Council were Welsh (Deadan), Polish (Krol), and Italian (Bernardin). The fourth president, San Francisco's John Raphael Quinn, was the first Irish American to be elected, though Quinn himself repeatedly dis-counts the importance of the ethnic factor in his background.

The most influential Irish Catholic priest in America, both inside and outside the Church, is Notre Dame's President Theodore M. Hesburgh, for thirty years the man behind the Fighting Irish. In every presidential administration for two of those three decades,

Hesburgh has represented the Church in Washington and in United
Nations meetings, at the Rockefeller Foundation, in Anarctica, in
organizing and promoting the Green Revolution, on the United
States Civil Rights Commission, at world conferences, in the councils
of the mighty, and in poor parishes in Mexico, as well as in the
confessional box at Notre Dame. The skill, tact, passion, and grace of
"Father Ted" *is* the Catholic Church for an extraordinary number of
Americans of whatever age or sex or race or status. From his Irish
mother he inherited—he claims—flexible, pragmatic, and political
skills and the ability to turn a phrase. And while for the last five years
that I have known him he has seemed exhausted, he is still the most
influential priest in America and reflects better than anyone else the
world beyond the Church, the genius of Irish American Catholicism.

Socially liberal, administratively pragmatic, passionate in his enthusiasm and commitment, tough when he needs to be, and gentle
most of the rest of the time, Hesburgh is, at the core of his personality, still a parish priest who also happens accidentally to be a university president and, even more accidentally, happens to walk in the
halls of the powerful and the mighty. There have been many Irish
churchmen in the United States that a lot of us would not like to
think of as representing Irish Catholicism. Few people looking at the
Hesburgh record would want to quibble at the claim that his life and
his ministry as a priest represent Irish American Catholicism at its
best, especially as he plays his parish priest role, even if its particular
manifestation is the role of parish priest to the world.

That Hesburgh is not an archbishop or a cardinal (and that his
current sidekick at Notre Dame, Monsignor John Egan of Chicago, is
not an archbishop) is a reflection less on Notre Dame and on
Hesburgh (and Egan) than a reflection on the backruptcy of American Catholic leadership. After the Second Vatican Council, the curia
sent two apostolic delegates to the United States who were determined to punish the American Church for its progressive contributions to the council. In the years between 1963 and 1973, virtually all
the men raised to major archdioceses in the country were incompetent nonentities. That Hesburgh did not become an archbishop and a
cardinal, as did one of his predecessors at Notre Dame, was not an
accident but a matter of deliberate curial policy. Rome did not want
to have to deal with a passionate, charismatic, influential pragmatist.
Hesburgh, a man utterly without ambition for the purple or the
crimson, did his own ecclesiastical career no service when he bluntly

told Pope Paul VI that the famous 1968 birth control encyclical was a mistake. Hesburgh and Paul had previously been very close friends, but Paul VI came to use the birth control encyclical as a test of loyalty and Hesburgh failed the test.*

The Fighting Irish kept right on winning, however.

The genius of Irish American Catholicism is incarnated in the pragmatic parish priest. The immigrant pastor protecting the faith of his poor and oppressed flock; the middle-class pastor turning democratic and collegiate as his people change; the suburban pastor presiding lightly with a bizarre coalition of the postconciliar parish—these men have given American Catholicism its shape and have had a considerable impact on the rest of the Catholic Church in the United States. At their worst they have been tyrants, braggarts, alcoholics, dummies, faddists, and political wheeler-dealers; at their best they have been some of the most astute social and religious leaders the world has ever known. They have been Catholic in their world view and Irish in their political sensitivity and skills; not intellectuals perhaps, but willing and ready to innovate, experiment, try out a new idea (sometimes a new idea every six months or a year). "Father Ted" has played at the center stage of American life in the role of the parish priest.

★   ★   ★

Catholicism in Ireland is the product of a cultural background different from those in Europe and was transported to the New World at a very special time in its history. Irish Catholicism has survived and flourished in the United States. But the particular variant of Catholicism which has come to be defined as Irish Catholicism in America is by no means typical of the Catholic heritage developed in Ireland for the last fifteen hundred years.

Conversion of the Irish to Christianity was easy, though gradual. Paganism was not so much replaced as absorbed. St. Brigid kept her shrine and her sacred fire in Kildare and her mission as patroness of

---

* Hesburgh stories abound. My favorite has to do with a Fourth of July dinner at my house in Grand Beach, Michigan (whither Ted comes each year). On this particular Fourth of July, among my guests was a former seminary classmate who is a Navy chaplain. Upon introduction, Hesburgh shook his hand vigorously and said, "What kind of ship are you on, Father? A carrier? *Essex*-class? I think I have been on almost all of them." Then he went through the names of the *Essex*-class carriers, as my classmate would later inform me, *in the order in which they had been launched.*

poetry, spring, and new life. Lug became Jesus; the sun symbol of the Brigid cross was defined as standing for Christ and the Light of the World. The so-called Celtic crosses—pagan intercourse symbols—were interpreted as standing for Jesus and Mary. The druids became monks, and the druid groves monasteries. Perhaps nowhere in the world was the process of "baptizing" everything pagan so complete, so enthusiastic, or so systematic as in Ireland.

The missionaries had rich raw materials with which to work. The pagan Celtic religion had charming and gracious deities, and it celebrated life joyfully and was firmly committed to a belief in life after death (indeed, to reincarnation). The blending of Christianity with the various layers of paganism created a new religion thoroughly Catholic in its convictions and zeal but dependent on its pagan past for much of its symbolism. English and continental Catholicism would always be offended by this mixture; there was something not quite "right" about Irish Catholicism from its very beginning.

One of the most striking aspects of American Irish Catholicism is its papalism. Nowhere in the Catholic world, with the possible exception of some of the offices of the Roman curia, has the cult of papal personality been so strong as it is in the United States. While the disastrous reign of Paul VI has freed many Catholics from this cult—and made not a few of them contemptuous of the papacy—it is certainly true that in the hierarchy and many of the older clergy, loyalty to the papacy is at the very core of the Catholic world view. One need only experience the servility with which most American bishops deal with the apostolic delegate to understand the strength of this papalism. On the other hand, the Irish remember that a pope turned them over to the tender mercies of the English. They know also that the papacy was frequently willing to give the English government considerable control over Irish ecclesiastical affairs. They are aware of the papal condemnations of many Irish freedom organizations (including the Fenians). They may even recall that a relatively independent Irish ecclesiastical tradition grew up and flourished in the early Middle Ages, when Rome was a city torn by the factional quarrels of noble families with the pope as a pawn of noble women.

The Irish bishops seem a good deal more jealous of their own prerogatives and the independence of their tradition than do their American counterparts. It is not that the Irish hierarchy, clergy, and laity are in any sense antipapal or that the pope couldn't count on their support. I think, rather, that the Irish Church is less concerned about Rome and feels quite capable of going its own way. Irish-American Catholicism seems to feel deeply inferior vis à vis Rome; Irish Catholicism seems to feel just a trifle superior.

Perhaps with cause, since Irish Catholicism is very ancient. In one of the periodic conflicts that raged between Ireland and Rome over the daying of Easter, St. Columbanus could proudly claim that his calendar was more ancient in origin than the Roman calendar. The stance the Irish took in these controversies with Rome was that they were the conservatives defending the tradition against Roman innovation. Typical of this perhaps is St. Patrick. The best of modern scholarly efforts conclude that St. Patrick was an historical figure and that his *Confession and Letter* are authentic. All other materials about him are probably later legends composed to support the claims of superiority of his see of Armagh.

There were territorial dioceses and territorial bishops in Ireland from the time of St. Patrick, but the predominant ecclesiastical organization was around the monastery and the *paruchia*, the confederation of monasteries extending far beyond the boundaries of the individual kingdoms. Either the bishop became a minor functionary of the abbey, responsible for ordaining priests, or he became a member of the staff of the king. Unless he also happened to be the abbot of the monastery, he had little power.

Eventually many of the territorial bishops did become abbots, and the monastery system became for all practical purposes the Church structure of Ireland—much to the horror of strict Roman canonists. There were a number of reasons for this development: the lack of cities and towns which could be diocesan centers, the personal rather than territorial Irish approach to fealty, and the custom of holding land as a family group rather than as individuals. The system worked rather well in Ireland, but it was a constant source of shock to English and continental observers. One of the reasons for Pope Adrian IV "giving" Ireland to his English relatives was that he hoped for a reform of the Irish ecclesiastical structure that would bring Ireland into line with the practices of the rest of the Church.

One Christian custom that the Church had difficulty in selling to the Irish was clerical celibacy. Apparently the Irish commitment to concubinage was so strong (and outlined in great detail in the customary law) that the Church had to be content, at least in the beginning, with bishops having only one wife. In later years, married men were ordained if they would promise not to live with their wives any longer. However, this regulation seems not to have been very effective, and later writers, like Columbanus, were willing to permit the married clerics to live with their families so long as they did not cohabit with their wives. One suspects that these regulations were not always honored.

By no means did all the higher clergy obey the laws of celibacy. Bishops and abbots had children, and many monasteries were passed from father to son. In addition, the abbots were also military and political leaders who engaged in battles with other monasteries, sacking and killing when they encountered opposition. One abbot-king, Feidilmid of Cashel (820–847), terrorized the countryside and killed rival abbots and kings with equal vigor. There is evidence that twenty-seven kings of Cashel ruled "under a crozier," although this may mean only that they were in holy orders and not necessarily that they were bishops.

The Church, then, transformed Ireland and at the same time Ireland transformed the Church. As Professor Hughes notes:

> The church had been founded as a religious force, and such it remained; but by the seventh century it had become an institution accommodated to secular law, and by the end of the eighth century certain churches were beginning to play a more direct and decisive part in secular politics. An ambitious monastic community, willing to fight for its own advantage, could also use its wealth to encourage learning and art; abbots who succeeded their fathers in office made efforts to maintain peace and order in society; they saw to it that the sacraments were performed, that Christianity was preached and hospitality provided.

The Irish Church was not merely different in structure from the rest of the Western Church; it had developed practices and customs which were bound to be offensive to Roman authorities and their advance agents in Britain and France. Married clergy, lay abbots, sons succeeding their fathers as abbots and bishops, offices held in plurality, constant and frequently bloody strife among monastic confederations—all this seemed to cry out for reform; and there were ambitious political leaders who were only too ready to use ecclesiastical reform as a pretext for aggression.

Irish monasticism and Irish liturgy had much in common with what we now call the Eastern Church. By our standards, and even by the relatively gentle standards of the Benedictines, monasticism was fiercely ascetic, and the liturgy was much more elaborate than the simple, reserved Roman rite. Scholars suggest that both the monasticism and the liturgy of Ireland came from Gaul of the third, fourth, and fifth centuries and that those traditions, effectively wiped out in Europe by barbarian invasions, survived in Ireland and in places in the British Isles and Spain remote enough to evade the barbarian invasion and later papal reform.

The Irish liturgy as contained in the *Stowe Missal,* for example, prays for the "most pious emperors," which suggests a time when there were two Roman Emperors; the prayer for the living in the *Stowe Missal* reminds one of the prayers of petition of the Eastern Church (which have now found their way back into the Western Church in the liturgical reform of the Second Vatican Council).

> the body of their elders
> and of all ministers,
> virgins and widows,
> fertility of the fruit of the earth,
> return of peace and the end of strife,
> kings, and the peace of the people,
> return of captives,
> forgiveness of our sins,
> repose of the dead,
> prosperity of our journey,
> the hierarchy,
> the Roman Empire,
> the Christian kings,
> erring and the sick

Irish spirituality was fierce; the body was not to be trusted, and penances and punishments were imposed. Fasting, confinement to the cell, and blows with the scourge are examples of penalties in St. Columbanus's *Rule.* Some monastic imperfections were punished with two hundred blows of the scourge, twenty-five at a time. The monk who showed up at Mass unshaven was to receive six blows.

The highest form of penance was self-exile or pilgrimage, and the most noble act of Irish monasticism was the vow of pilgrimage. The first great Irish missionaries, such as Columbanus and Columcille, were in fact not missionaries in the modern sense of the word. They took the vow of pilgrimage and left Ireland as a form of penance. Their work with the pagans in France and Germany was an unpremeditated result, not a goal, of the primarily penitential nature of their wandering. St. Brendan the Navigator was not an explorer like his successors from the north, who looked for new lands. He was a pilgrim venturing forth because of a vow of self-exile.

While there is no doubt that those pilgrim monks brought Christianity and civilization to many parts of Europe, it is also true that they did not fare well with the local citizenry. Anglo-Saxon St. Boniface complained about the nonconformism and individualism of the Irish clergy who worked side by side with him in the east Frankish kingdom. O'Sullivan describes the stormy career of St. Columbanus in Gaul:

> St. Columbanus's stay in Gaul was stormy, to say the least. His *Letters* and *Sermons* give evidence of a sharp denunciatory tongue that whiplashed the local episcopate, exposing their sins for all to see. His tone toward Pope Gregory, while respectful and conscious of the papal primacy, was at times equally sharp. The local bishops retaliated by criticizing his peculiar Irish tonsure which called for the front of the head being shaved. . . . But nowhere did St. Columbanus shine more than in his stand on the bad morality of the royal court, so much so that Queen Brunhilda ordered him to be expelled from the land in 610.

I have often wondered whether the ease with which the Irish missionaries still depart for the farthest points of the world may have some connection with the ancient tradition of the *peregrinatio pro Christo*—pilgrimage for Christ.

Irish monasticism, with its scourge, long hours of prayers, strict fasts, and hundreds of genuflections, strikes us as a bit bizarre and nonhuman. Yet, there was no lack of goodness and insight in the monasticism of the Irish. One of the ancient prayers indicates that the monastic spirituality was not without power and beauty.

> *May thou be my vision,*
> *O God of my heart;*
> *no one else in anything,*
> *but the king of the seven heavens.*

May thou be my meditation
by day and by night;
may it be thou I see
ever in my sleep.

May thou be my speech,
may thou be my understanding,
may thou be to me,
may I be to thee.

May thou be my father,
may I be thy son;
may thou be mine,
may I be thine.

May thou be my battle-shield,
may thou be my sword,
may thou be my honour,
may thou be my joy.

May thou be my protection,
may thou be my fortress;
may it be thou who will raise me
to the assembly of angels.

May thou be every good
to my body, to my soul;
may thou be my kingdom
in heaven and on earth.

May thou alone
be the special love of my heart;
may it be no one else
but the High King of Heaven.

Whether the peculiar forms of Irish monasticism were an importation of early Christianity (before the much more gentle style of Benedictine monasticism became common in Western Europe) or a reflection of Celtic culture is a question which, so far as I have been able to learn from scholars, has not yet been answered in any satisfactory way. Part of the difficulty, of course, is that both the monastic culture with its high-quality scholarship and art and the pre-Christian culture were practically obliterated by the Viking invasions of the ninth century. All that seems to have survived are a few old

churches now in ruins, some Celtic crosses, names and ruins of monasteries such as Clonmacnoise and Glendalough, and of course the
names and memories of the saints immortalized in parish churches in
all the large cities of America—Columcille, Columbanus, Killian,
Brendan, Brigid, Mel, Finbar, Kevin, and that well-known immigrant, Patrick.

Current scholarship presents a much more complex view of Irish
monastic life than the old penitential books. The monastery was a
school, an orphanage, a prison, a vast collective farm, a political and
ecclesiastical center, a place of prayer and penance. Clonmacnoise on
the Shannon with forty thousand habitants was the largest settlement
in the country. It's a small wonder it was sacked repeatedly by Irish
and Danish kings. Many of the "monks" were married men with
their families living on the land and working the monastic farm; the
abbots themselves were often married and passed on the inheritance
of the monastery to their offspring. There were also, of course, penitential monks for whom the books were written and who themselves
wrote and copied the books. The Irish viewpoint was that the pluralism of monastery life was the response to the religious need in many
different kinds of people. They were a scandal for the continentals
and the English, who had rather different views of the ecclesiastical
law.

The least of the scandalous practices is that called agapetism. In the
early Church there was a tendency for religious life to be "coeduca-
tional." Arguing that conversion in Christ Jesus had enabled them to
conquer the flesh and, in the words of St. Paul, that they were neither
male nor female but one in Christ Jesus, men and women lived lives
of religious community together, not only in the same religious monasteries but sometimes in the same dormitories and even in the same
beds. It hardly needs to be said that the practice was viewed with
great suspicion by many of the Church, and that splendid old cur-
mudgeon St. Jerome railed against it: no matter what anyone else
said, he *knew* what went on in those places. Most historians, however,
are not quite so suspicious. They are willing to concede that incredible as it may sound, most of the agapeti communities were indeed
platonic—in more than one sense of the word. Agapetism died out
well before the sixth century in most places where the Church pre-
dominated, but it continued to flourish in Ireland. Apparently there
were even monasteries in sixth-century Ireland that were presided
over by abbesses who were presumably selected by their colleagues.

The chroniclers tell us the story of the sainted Brendan the sailor and his colleague, the monk Scuthian. Brendan remonstrated with his colleague because the latter had developed the pious practice of sleeping at night between two beautiful virgins. Brendan apparently hinted to Scuthian that the two young women were probably no better than they ought to be, but Scuthian said that he engaged in this practice merely to prove how virtuous he was and what discipline he had over his flesh. Then he challenged the sainted sailor to prove his virtue the same way. Like many other Irishmen since then, the holy navigator was not one to turn away from a challenge, so he recruited two young women—how, the chroniclers do not tell us—and began to emulate the piety of his colleague. However, we are informed that he shortly abandoned the effort, for though he did not lose his virtue, he found the experiences most distracting and was unable to sleep at night.

Only in Ireland . . .

Whatever is to be said of the practices of Brendan, Scuthian, and their colleagues, and however interesting and even insightful the experiences may have been it did not represent a tradition that would survive to shape future forms of Irish Catholicism. More's the pity, perhaps.

It was not only agapetism that was destroyed by the Danish invasion. Dr. Brian O Cuiv describes the religious state of the country in the eleventh century:

We might suppose that with numerous religious houses throughout Ireland and the missionary movement under way again, the moral well-being of the people was assured. Unfortunately this was not so, for after the long centuries of the Viking wars and consequent upheavals, there was spiritual and moral laxity. Deeds of violence were frequent, even against priests and nuns and against church property. The Sacraments were neglected, there was a reluctance to pay tithes, and the marriage laws of the Church were disregarded. The laxity about marriage, it is true, may have been due to the brehon which differed from the rules of the Church in this regard. However, there was clearly a need for spiritual renewal, and with it reform of the Church itself, for part of the trouble lay in the organisation of the Church which was monastic rather than diocesan, a feature which resulted in a lack of priests engaged in pastoral work. Another characteristic of the Irish church was that there was hereditary succession to

certain Church benefices and that these were frequently held by laymen. Of course, to a people accustomed to the principle of hereditary
succession in other walks of life, including poetry, this would not have
seemed strange.

Hence when the only English pope, Adrian IV Breakspeare, decided to give Ireland to Henry II of England, there was perhaps some
legitimate purpose in his action. His Bull declares Henry's responsibility:

> . . . to extend the bounds of the Church, to proclaim to a rude and
> untaught people the truth of the Christian faith, and to root out
> nurseries of vice from the field of the Lord. . . . So we . . . are pleased
> and willing . . . that you shall enter that island and do therein what
> tends to the honour of God and the salvation of the people.

Pope Breakspeare's plan worked, of course, but hardly in the way
he intended, for the combination of the English invasion of Ireland
and later Henry's departure from the Roman Church guaranteed
that as far as the Irish Catholic was concerned, to be Irish and Catholic meant exactly the same thing.

The contemporary image of fervent and pious Irish orthodoxy
leads many to suppose that the Irish were always that way. However,
sober accounts of medieval and pre-Reformation Irish behavior present a very different picture. Divorce, concubinage, and incest (in the
sense of marrying within the forbidden degrees of kinship) were
widespread, particularly among the aristocracy. The brehon laws approved of divorce for a wife on the grounds of childlessness, ill treat-
ment, the absence of the husband from the country, criminal
conduct, accession to the clerical state, insanity, and incurable disease.
For a husband, divorce was justified also on the grounds of childlessness, constant stealing, abortion, child murder, and "general mis-
chief-making." Divorce by mutual consent was lawful, and
polygamy was not only tolerated but subject to complex regulations,
which dictated the compensation to be paid to a man for the violation of his secondary wives and also the duties and responsibilities of
the various degrees of wives. Whether a man was permitted to marry
his sister or his daughter is debatable, but he certainly was permitted
to marry his stepmother and to take as a concubine his brother's wife
while the brother was still alive. It was also possible for a man to live

in concubinage with two sisters simultaneously. Such practices persisted even into the fifteenth and sixteenth centuries. While the famous reform synod of Cashel in 1101 denounced clerical concubinage, it did not mention lay marriage customs, probably because so many of the laymen who were delegates to the synod were living according to the provisions of the brehon laws.

There were many married priests and bishops, the sacrament of Holy Orders was sold, confirmation was administered without charism (which led St. Bernard in France to conclude that the sacrament was not known in Ireland). "Corabs" and "erenagh"—quasiclerical lay abbots—appropriated Church lands and passed them on to their offspring. Illegitimacy was widespread (one contemporary observer guessed that only one-fifth of the births at the time were legitimate). Church services were irregular, slovenly, or often omitted. Communion was received only once a year; the Sunday Mass regulation was not honored; clandestine marriage was common. In some areas, children were not baptized. By the time of the Reformation, vocations had sadly declined and abbots had become little more than civil princes who exploited the people as much as their lay counterparts did. Religious education and training for the clergy were almost nonexistent. Gambling, banditry, perjury, violation of contracts, and tribal murder were widespread.

Hence, the worries of Pope Adrian that caused him to "give" Ireland to the English king were not altogether unjustified. Unfortunately, the English efforts at reform—which included attempts to impose both canon and common law as a substitute for the brehon laws—were doomed to be failures, since the Norman invasion created two societies in Ireland and added to the confusion instead of reducing disorder. From many points of view, Irish Catholicism ought to have been ripe for the Reformation.

In truth, many of the nobility and the hierarchy (including Archbishop Browne of Dublin) either went along with Henry VIII or at least tried to walk a tightrope between him and the pope. It was only in the time of Elizabeth I that the mass of the Irish people rejected the Reformation just as surely as the mass of the English people accepted it.

There were a number of reasons for the difference. Ireland had no intellectual dissidents such as Wycliffe; the "old Irish" developed a special loyalty to the pope because it was to him they turned for some kind of equality in the unfair competition with the Anglo-Norman clerics. The main reason for the firm identification of the Irish with Rome, however, was the Cromwellian genocide. As Corish puts it:

> The Cromwellian settlement made the "Irish" and "Catholic" synonymous: to be the one was automatically to be the other. It was of course the logical development of previous policy—the union of Catholics in Ireland was, from first to last, a Protestant achievement, not a Catholic one. The decision to which Irish history had been feeling its way for over a hundred years was now finally imposed by the sword of the Lord Protector. It was imposed effectively.

During the Cromwell years, when the papists were being driven to "hell or Connaught," most of the bishops were dead or in exile, and every priest was a hunted man with a price (five pounds) on his head. Concentration camps were set up for priests on the desolate Aran Islands. A large number were deported to the Barbadoes. Priests lived in caves on mountains and kept on the move in order to avoid spies and informers. They traveled at night or in disguise, said Mass by moonlight on "Mass rocks" or for small congregations in private homes. The sick were also visited at night, and communion was distributed furtively by priests wandering about disguised as peddlers or farmers.

The worst of the terror came to an end with the restoration of Charles II, but by then the issue was decided: Ireland was irrevocably Catholic, and its priests, the only successful resisters of the Cromwellian tyranny, were the acknowledged leaders of their hungry, miserable, persecuted people. If the Irish are so unquestionably loyal to their church, the reason is not hard to find: they were made loyal by English barbarism.

★   ★   ★

What did it mean to be Catholic? Again one must surmise, because there is not much scholarship on the subject. To be Catholic, of course, was to go to church, to receive the sacraments, and to pass on the symbols of faith to one's children; to rally around the parish priest, not only religiously but frequently politically, and to define oneself "Catholic" against the hated English Protestant; to go on pilgrimages, to say the rosary, to fast, to make vows, and to feel guilty about one's sinfulness.

But I think being Catholic also meant to have confidence in life.

Despite the Jansenism, the self-hatred, and the sexual puritanism, that confidence in life gave Irish Catholicism its greatest strength and also its most peculiar institution, the Irish wake.

The official Church was ambiguous about the wake. There were strains of paganism and much drunkenness and frequent dancing, and the Church was *very* suspicious of dancing. Still, the Church could hardly oppose the idea that death was not the end. Even in contemporary Irish-American Catholicism the wake is an extraordinary phenomenon, heartless and reassuring, melancholy and rejoicing, unbearably painful and stubbornly hopeful.

It would be easy to write off the wake as merely the symbolic hope for a better hereafter of an oppressed and miserable people who had precious little in this world, a kind of Celtic "pie in the sky." While there is unquestionably some element of that in the wake tradition, there is also, I think, a stubborn refusal to believe that death is the end, a refusal on which, of course, the Irish have no monopoly. Few people have ever asserted this conviction with so much stubbornness. Whatever can be said about repression of grief (and repression seems to be a characteristically Irish response), I have no doubt that refusal to accept death as the end is at the very core of the Irish religious commitment.

Emmet Larkin has made a very persuasive case that the intense level of religious devotion characteristic of the Irish on both sides of the Atlantic is a rather recent phenomenon, dating to the time after the Great Famine of 1847–1849. Part of the problem in the previous half century was a shortage of priests, with one priest for every 2,100 of the faithful in 1800, and one for every 3,000 four decades later. The Church, badly disorganized from the persecution years, was inundated by a population increase of almost 100 percent in a few decades. In addition, the clergy were often avaricious, contentious, and undisciplined, not infrequently given to heavy drinking, and on occasion even to adultery. There were not nearly enough churches or chapels, and perhaps no more than 40 percent of the population went to church each week. Finally, many of the clergy were still working in the casual, free-wheeling style of the persecution days. The hierarchy found it difficult to bring them into line, and its members were not infrequently dragged into court when they tried to exercise discipline.

According to Larkin, the effort of such reformers as the remarkable Cardinal Paul Cullen to modify the ecclesiastical style was aided considerably by the horrors of the Great Famine, which drove both priests and people back to religion. He suggests that the Great Famine was a final blow to the old Irish sense of identity. Despite the relative prosperity of the potato economy in the first four decades of the century and the relative success of the O'Connell political movement, the Irish were gradually being "Britonized" as they lost their culture, their language, and their way of life. In addition to striking terror into their hearts, the "devotional revolution" of the years after the Great Famine, according to Larkin, provided the Irish (and their American cousins) with a new symbolic language and a new cultural heritage around which a new Irish identity could focus.

★   ★   ★

The Catholicism of Irish Americans then is rooted in pre-Christian Celtic paganism; in the permissive pluralism of the monastic times; in the conflict with England; in the identification of the Church with Irish nationalism; and in the devotional reform of the post-Famine years. But in the United States, the complex heritage became more narrow than in Ireland. However, it developed one of the most remarkable institutions of American urban life—the neighborhood.

The Irish surely did not invent neighborhoods, and the Southern and Eastern Europeans who came afterward may invest even more importance in neighborhoods than do the Irish. Nonetheless, the urban neighborhood with its tight network of close relationships, its political and religious commitments unseparated and unseparable; the key institutions such as the parish church and schoolyard, the precinct captain's house or office, the pubs, the corner grocery store, the funeral home, and perhaps the local park, is more explicitly religious in the Irish-American tradition than in any other. Among Irish Americans, that particular part of the urban turf with which you are identified and in which live most of the people on whom you have a special claim and who have a special claim on you is virtually indistinguishable from the parish; when asked where they are from, Irish Catholics in many cities give not the community's name but the name of the parish—Christ the King, St. Barnabas, All Saints, Nativity, Little Flower, St. Sabina, and so forth. On closer examination it often turns out the name means indeed the whole neighborhood, but at the center of the neighborhood are the parish "plant" and especially the schoolyard, where the young people play basketball and volleyball. Despite the eager predictions by some Catholic writers that the parishes would diminish as Catholics moved to the suburbs, in fact the neighborhood parish (or the parish neighborhood) continues in the suburbs more by free conscious choice than by unselfconscious association.

My colleague William McCready has argued that for the Irish the neighborhood parish is little more than the western Ireland village community set down in the middle of a large city. In a brilliant address given at a summer institute in County Clare in 1976, McCready described his own well-to-do upper-middle-class parish on the southwest side of Chicago (in which his children are fourth generation on both sides) precisely as a western Ireland village which has taken on some of the trappings of America's affluent upper middle class but is still quintessentially a western Ireland phenomenon. The local Irish scholars agreed that what McCready described was a western Ireland parish. They were astonished that such an institution would survive among the well-to-do graduate-school-trained professional class on the southwest side of Chicago, for, as they insisted, the rural parish did not even survive in such Irish cities as Dublin and Cork.

However, the people who moved to Dublin or Cork may not have needed a neighborhood parish. The immigrants coming to the big cities of America needed neighborhood parish *entre ports* in order to survive in American society. Both the local churches and political organizations, each for reasons of their own (and sometimes the reasons were hard to separate), were only too happy to oblige by encouraging the development of a local Gemeinschaft (to which some people gave their loyalties much more completely than others).

Some of the immigrants and their offspring did not like the neighborhood parish and attacked it in their novels and biographies. James T. Farrell in earlier books was more savagely critical than he was in the later Eddie Ryan series about the neighborhood parish. However, in the Studs Lonigan trilogy there was a grudging fondness for St. Anselm's (the Chicago parish Farrell was describing) that even the young Farrell's anger could not completely eliminate. By the time he wrote his last novel—*The Death of Nora Ryan*—Farrell would return, despite himself, to the fringes of the transformed Irish Catholicism of his past, less grudging in his admiration and respect for the "old neighborhood." The old neighborhoods died. St. Anselm's, St. Lawrence, Our Lady of Peace, Holy Cross—the parishes in which Farrell's characters lived—have now become Chicago's black parishes (though with more than just a trace of the old neighborhood spirit being transmitted to the new parishoners).

As Farrell's classmates and nieces and nephews moved south to the fringes of the city and even into the suburbs, they continued to construct neighborhood parishes; not so much because they needed them to cushion the trauma of adjusting to a new world, but because they liked them and because they wanted their children to have the same relationships with neighbors and with parish priests that they had had. Part of the problem with fully appreciating the neighborhood parish, I think, is that most Irish Catholics who reflect on such things have assumed for a long time that everybody had a neighborhood and that at the center of everybody's neighborhood there was a parish church and of course a parish priest who at his best was very much a neighborhood Father Hesburgh. The more thoughtful of them have now discovered that most of the cities of the world have neither neighborhoods nor parishes, at least not in the Irish-American sense. Many are appalled, not quite able to understand why people don't do the sensible things in big cities and construct neighborhoods, and why the Church doesn't do the sensible thing and preside over the construction of neighborhoods and train or ordain the kinds of priests who build neighborhood parish communities. Fortunately for the Church and for the Irish Catholics themselves, they have rediscovered the importance of neighborhood communities before all such social structures cease to exist.

The importance of the priest in the parish in immigrant Catholicism in the United States had little or nothing to do with delivering the Catholic vote, censoring magazines, condemning the neighborhood theater for showing dirty movies, urging one's parishioners to have large families, or any of the other mythical hobgoblin activities that the nativists have depicted as the function of the parish priest. The parish was, on the contrary, a symbol of loyalty around which the immigrants and their children and grandchildren could rally in a society that was at first hostile and then not especially friendly. For many of us, it provided education, recreation, entertainment, friendships, and potential spouses. It was a place to belong.

A simple-minded analysis might argue that it was something the clergy forced upon us, particularly through the parochial school system. In fact, however, I suspect that the opposite was the case: the parochial school system was the result of Irish parochial loyalty rather than the cause.

The neighborhood parish—the mixture of precinct, politics, and religion is a classic example of cultural adaptation—is a western Ireland community set down in a large city. One could choose to stress the discontinuity—the American parish may be more affluent, more self-conscious, more defensive, and probably more democratic than its first cousin in County Clare; it is certainly more American.

The neighborhood parish didn't appear on a blank slate, however. Faced with the necessity of responding to challenges aimed at their religious, political, and social survival as Irish and Catholics, the immigrants relied on resources their cultural heritage made available to them. One can readily fault the immigrant neighborhood parish and its descendent in the professional-class suburbs for being parochial. It surely was and is culture-bound—like all time and place incarnations of religion. On the other hand, it did not appear as an arbitrary imposition of ecclesiastical authority on an amorphous and undifferentiated immigrant mass.

What else were the immigrants to do but fall back on the cultural resources available to them, religious and political? At its worst the neighborhood parish was and is insufferably parochial. At its best, it was and is a remarkable humanizing force in urban life. At its very best it is magic. If the older Irish Catholic intelligentsia still patronize it and condemn it, then they merely reveal the power of their own self-hatred.

★   ★   ★

Although some of the old relaxed permissiveness of the Irish seems to be reasserting itself—and the decline of nativist bigotry and prejudice, the success of Irish Catholics in American life, and the loosening of the bonds of ecclesiastical discipline by the Second Vatican Council might have modified the style of immigrant Irish Catholics—loyalty to the Church does not seem to be suffering.

In the wake of the birth control encyclical there has been a decline in certain Catholic religious practices affecting all American Catholics. The decline still leaves the Irish more devout than other Catholic ethnic groups. Fifty-eight percent of them went to Mass every week in 1974 (as compared to 50 percent of other Catholics); 38 percent received communion every week (as compared to 24 percent of the non-Irish); 50 percent would strongly approve of religious vocation for a nun in their family, and 58 percent would be enthusiastic about a priest in their family (as compared to 49 percent of other Catho-

lics); 40 percent have read a spiritual book in the last year (as compared to 31 percent of other Catholics); and the typical Irish Catholic
belongs to 1.1 religious organizations (as compared to .87 for other
Catholics). According to a composite "Catholicity" scale, differences
between Irish Catholics and other Catholics in their religious devotion have, if anything, slightly increased since 1963.

On the other hand, the Irish have lost all of their distinctiveness
from other Catholics in attitudes toward sexual morality. Only 17
percent disapprove of birth control and only 28 percent disapprove of
divorce. Only 50 percent disapprove of premarital sex. A mere 13
percent (as compared to 49 percent a decade ago) think that one
should have as many children as possible, and only 35 percent as
compared to 63 percent think the Church has authority on birth
control techniques. Actual disapproval of birth control among Irish
Catholics fell from 63 percent in 1963 to 17 percent in 1974. But only
12 percent of those who were raised as Irish Catholics in the United
States are no longer Catholics as compared to 17 percent of other
Catholic ethnic groups—a very slight increase in the past decade and a
half. The Irish then are less devout than they were but are still more
devout than other Catholics. They may have rejected the Church's
sexual morality, but they have not broken with the Church in deed.

The Irish were disproportionately involved in the modest late-
1970s religious revival that led to an increase in the Catholic rate of
weekly (or nearly weekly) church attendance. In the mid–seventies,
51 percent of the Irish Catholics and 43 percent of other Catholics
attended church weekly. By the end of the decade, however, this had
gone up five percentage points for the other Catholics and ten percentage points for Irish Catholics. Most of the increase was accounted
for by a drift back to the Church by men and women in their thirties.

Those who expected the Irish to stop being Catholic after the
Second Vatican Council are doomed to the same disappointment as
those who a century ago thought that Americanization would lead
the Irish away from their papal superstitions. The transitions from
the Old World to the New World, from slum to suburb, and from
the Reformation to the ecumenical age have left the Irish as Catholic
as they ever were.

Not only is their religious behavior distinctive, so is their basic
religious world view. Professor William McCready has developed a
series of vignettes to measure religion as "meaning system," a response
to the mysteries and tragedies of life. Interviewees are asked to react

to such situations as the birth of a handicapped child, the death of a parent, the contraction of an incurable disease. There are three basic patterns of response: anger, optimism, and hope. Anger emphasizes evil in the situation; optimism minimizes the evil and sees only good ("it will all work out," and "God will take care of it," and "we have no right to question God's goodness"); hope sets a middle course, eliminating neither evil nor good but giving the marginal advantage to good. The Irish in several different studies have scored highest on hope and low on anger, while Jews, on the other hand, have scored high on anger and low on hope, and Italian Catholics somewhere between the two. The Irish advantage in hopefulness also continues undiminished in the adolescent generation. The great-grandchildren of the immigrants continue to be both Irish and Catholic.

Irish Catholics are more certain than other Americans that life is not chance, that there is purpose in human existence, that love is at the heart of the universe, and that prayers are heard. Curiously enough—or perhaps not so curiously given the twist and a turn of the Irish mind—they are less certain (32 percent as compared to 40 percent) that they personally can find the ultimate meaning in life. Nevertheless, Irish Catholics are 29 points higher on a religious "certainty" scale than blacks, 37 points higher than Italian Catholics, and 125 points higher on the certainty scale than American Jews.

Closer than anyone else to the Jews on political, racial, libertarian, and feminist liberalism, the Irish Catholics are farthest away from them in religious certainty, adding perhaps to the ambiguity of the relationship between these two powerful and successful urban American ethnic groups. Politically, they have more in common with each other than either has with other groups. Religiously, they have less in common with each other than either has with other groups.

To what extent does the Irish preference for Catholic schools (their average number of years of attendance is 6.8 as compared to 5.5 years for Poles, 4.7 for Germans, and 2.5 for Italians) contribute to their higher levels of religious devotion? On the "Catholicity" scale, for example, the Irish score is 37 standardized points above the Italians, while the Irish contribute about two and a half dollars more per thousand dollars of their annual income to the Church than do the Italians.

Even after one has taken into account parental religiousness and the religiousness of spouse, the different levels of Catholic education make a contribution of their own to Irish religiousness. Even after family devotion is taken into account, Catholic schools account for 57 cents per thousand dollars of income in the different contribution rates of Irish and Italian Catholics—substantially more than the 22 cents accounted for by the spouse's religiousness. The evidence seems to indicate that the schools pay for themselves through the increased revenue in adult life from those who went to such schools. It would appear that this is particularly true of the Irish. Catholic schools do not account for all of their higher levels of religious devotion, but they make a solid and important contribution to an explanation.

Hopeful, confident, devout, defining religious activity narrowly and religious influence broadly, somewhat less given to prayer, loyal to the Church but no longer accepting its sex morality—the religion of the Irish Catholics may be unfathomable to others (particularly when the others are Jewish) but is totally unexceptional to them. To previous layers of experience—immigrant defensiveness, post-Famine devotion, anti-British nationalism, pluralistic permissiveness, pagan defiance of death—they have added yet another level of Irish Catholicism, one that is distinctively American: survival of the pilgrimage from poverty to affluence.

Irish Catholicism, both from the Old Country and the New World, has, like all human religious forms, its limitations and inadequacies. As in most religious forms, the past is not always what is needed in the present, but it does not follow therefore that for all its stubbornness, its narrowness, its Jansenism, and its authoritarianism, immigrant Irish Catholicism did not respond to the challenges it faced in the light of its own definitions. On the contrary, those various religious forms that are seeking to replace it would be fortunate to do as well.

NINE

Irish Politics

THERE ARE SOME SUBJECTS ABOUT WHICH OBJECTIVE AND RATIONAL discussion seems impossible—abortion, feminism, the existence of God, child rearing, and the Cook County regular Democratic organization. I have on other occasions tried to discuss the last subject objectively and found myself written about by such Chicagoans as Studs Terkel and Mike Royko as the "house intellectual" of the Daley organization, even though at that time I had never met the mayor or any of the major officials of the organization. The machine of course does not need, did not have, and does not have a "house intellectual." Insofar as anyone plays the role at all, it would be University of Illinois Professor Milton Rakove, whose two books, *Don't Make No Waves, Don't Back No Losers* and *We Don't Want Nobody, Nobody Sent,* along with Eugene Kennedy's *Himself,* are the best descriptions available of the Daley years in Chicago.

Many educated people all over the world, however, have a strong emotional need to believe that Richard Daley was a corrupt tyrant, ruling with absolute dictatorial power over an oppressed and downtrodden city; exploiting if not murdering blacks and Hispanics, and keeping the rest of the city in bondage. I was given this portrait of Chicago political life once in Dublin by a political scientist who, when pressed for evidence, cited an article he had read in *Time* magazine. In New York and Washington and Harvard and Berkeley, reputable political scientists will make the same case, citing *Boss*, the work of that most objective scholar, Mike Royko.

Under such circumstances, any discussion of Chicago politics which deviates from the stereotype is immediately denounced out of hand as being biased or false. Eugene Kennedy's *Himself*, for example, a brilliant portrait of Daley, was dismissed by many reviewers on the a priori argument that since it was not totally hostile to Daley, it had to be an error.

Humans need their ink blots and scapegoats, and no great deal of harm is done by stereotyping the late mayor and Chicago politics. It certainly did not bother him much, nor did it seem to offend most Chicagoans, when *The New York Times* correspondent in Chicago equated Daley's home neighborhood, Bridgeport, with "Back of the Yards" and described it as being west of the stockyards (in fact, Bridgeport is northeast of the yards, and "Back of the Yards"—"Canaryville"—is east, not west of the yards). The only problem created by the caricature of Chicago politics is that it interferes with understanding and intelligent discussion. It makes it impossible for anyone who tries to explain how Chicago politics works to be heard, for immediately such a person is written off as defending the Democratic organization or sanctifying the mayor, and is at once put on the defensive with such questions as, "But what about the Chicago public schools?" One may patiently say that the Chicago public schools are probably pretty bad, but that they are no worse than other urban public school systems, and perhaps a little better. But by this time the victim of the conventional wisdom has gone on to another charge.

Despite my attempts to explain to the world of the academy and the mass media how the organization works, the mayor viewed me with grave suspicion, remarking often to a mutual friend (Raymond Simon, his sometime corporation counsel), "Did you see what *your* friend wrote the other day?" It was only in the last year of his life, when he read a book of my meditations on the prayer of St. Patrick, that the mayor became sympathetic. Once he called me on the telephone and said, "Father, I read your book on St. Patrick with great emphasis [sic], and it proves what a wonderful priest you are. That is what counts, Father, that you are a good priest." He went on with an invitation for me to speak at a Chicago Irish gathering.

In Daley's world, priests were for priesthood and not especially for journalism or scholarship. Even though he went to church every morning, he held himself aloof from the political influence of clergymen and of bishops. There was no love lost between him and Chicago's madcap Cardinal John Cody (they did not publicly feud as have Daley's successor, "Calamity" Jane Byrne, and the cardinal). While he was a close personal friend of Cletus O'Donnell, an auxiliary bishop of Chicago until Cody's arrival and then exiled to Madison, Wisconsin, Daley was wary of clerical politicians like Cody. Once he was harassed before a Chicago television camera by a young priest who was criticizing a new city council ordinance. Patiently the mayor let the young clergyman rave on. Then, in a brief break in the priest's harangue, Daley said, "Did you read the ordinance, Father?" The priest did not answer him but continued his attack. Going in for the kill, the mayor said again, somewhat more insistently, "Did you read the ordinance, Father?" "I read a summary of it," said the young cleric lamely, and returned once more to his attack. Daley gave him a few more sentences: "What kind of a priest are you?" he said. "You come in here and you attack me over the ordinance and you haven't even read it." He turned on his heel and walked away, leaving the TV cameramen to mop up the remnants of the unfortunate priest.

The first point to be kept in mind by anyone interested in understanding Chicago Irish politics is that the organization is, as Professor Rakove has repeatedly observed, a loosely structured decentralized network of relationships based on a combination of loyalty, mutual interest, heredity, friendship, intimidation, ambition, dedication, and greed. No one "controls" the organization in the sense of being able to give absolute orders without consultation and then expect these orders to be obeyed. Calamity Jane tried to run the organization that way during her first year in office and then discovered that she didn't control it at all. In fact, it took two terms in office before Daley could have been said to have brought the organization under his domination, and then his control was severely limited by the need to persuade various factions to "go along" with policies and candidate choices they did not like.

Control of the organization means the ability to build a broad consensus among a large number of factions and groups and opposing constituencies; the ability to assume very considerable power to enforce and impose one's will—but that power isn't nearly enough, as Jane Byrne was quick to learn. Eugene Kennedy's portrait of Daley, in which the mayor is described as an Irish chieftain governing through a complex system of clan loyalty, is fundamentally accurate, however much East Coast reviewers may have ridiculed it. Whether such an approach to modern urban government is wise or not may well be a matter of opinion, though the citizenry of Chicago found out after Daley's death what happens when responsible coalitions cease to operate.

One can argue endlessly about whether Chicago was in fact under Daley a "city that worked." It worked well enough, however, to suit most Chicagoans. In his last hurrah race, Daley won more than 70 percent of the vote: 80 percent of the black vote, 75 percent of the Polish vote, and 70 percent of the Jewish vote (against a Jewish candidate). The lopsided victories of Daley's later years have always been annoying to the Roykos, the Terkels, and the literary critics of the organization, who would mutter when faced with these lopsided victories about "vote fraud" and "the patronage army" (meaning Democratic job holders), trying to persuade you that a man could pile up three-quarters of the votes in the election by a combination of fraud and political patronage. It was doubtful that they ever took the argument seriously themselves, for Daley was enormously popular with the ordinary people of Chicago, including—and one might say especially—the blacks, despite the hostility of Lake Shore limousine liberals, reformers, and journalists of the Royko/Terkel ilk.

Like all political leaders, Daley made mistakes. He lost his temper too often; in the sixties he did not understand the importance of television (though he quickly learned); he was never able to organize the suburban Democrats, many of whom were loyal organization members before they moved and others of whom were the offspring of organization members; he did not understand the sixties genera-tion of young people (many of whom could have belonged in the organization rather than fighting against it); he may have tolerated more corruption from others than was necessary—though this is ar-guable (and no one who knows the facts has ever argued that he personally was corrupt); and he may also have tolerated cronies like Fire Marshall Quinn, who had no business in public office; he also might legitimately be criticized for not arranging a more orderly succession and for not having succeeded before he died in encourag-ing a generation of potential leaders younger than him but above forty to stay in Chicago's political life.

Yet any honest assessment of Richard Daley as mayor of Chicago must concede, as did his sometime rival/sometime ally Adlai Stevenson III, that Richard Daley was the best municipal adminstrator in America—precisely because he combined administrative and financial skills (which always astonished cocky graduate students, who thought they could trip him up in the rare interviews he gave them) with extraordinary and very Irish political abilities.

Daley was not an outgoing, charming, song-and-dance type of Irish political leader like Jimmy Walker of New York or Frank Curley of Boston. On the contrary, he was an intensely private man, shy and reserved, protective of his family life, and would relax only when surrounded by his close friends. The colleagues, associates, friends, and enemies who described him in *We Don't Want Nobody, Nobody Sent* all agree about his administrative abilities, his shyness, his long memory for enemies, his loyalty to his friends, and his quick flashes of anger. They also agree that his rise to power was unexpected. If other men had not died suddenly or withdrawn from politics, Daley would never have ended up as "boss." Royko and others do their best to hint that there was something dark and mysterious and conspiratorial about Daley's "luck." However, there was nothing mysterious involved; he happened to be in the right place at the right time, which, as anyone in politics knows, is at least half the battle. Precisely because he was shy, reserved, and even somewhat taciturn, Daley would not have been marked by many in his own time as a likely heir to the chaos of Chicago organization politics, much less as somebody who would, over a period of twenty years, impose some order on that chaos. Even in his younger days, no one doubted his administrative and fiscal abilities (skills proven as finance director under Governor Adlai Stevenson). But those kinds of abilities had not normally been required in the gladhanding, wheeling-dealing world of Chicago Irish politics. Daley's peer and ally, though not close friend, Alderman Tom Keene, fit the role model of a Chicago Irish politician much better than Daley did. According to legend, they worked out an agreement in which Daley would have the power and Keene would make the money. While that does seem to be what happened, it is most unlikely that the two men ever articulated such an arrangement between them. They were far too clever politicians to arrange anything like that.

It is fashionable to say that Daley was the last of the old political bosses, though one might say with equal truth that he was the first of the new political bosses, because he combined his skillfulness in organization politics with administrative and fiscal abilities that his pre-

decessors either lacked or didn't consider important. Eugene Kennedy
is correct when he says that Daley was an Irish political chieftain, a
leader of the clans. But he was clan ruler who could read a budget
and understand every line item, and the latter skill was finally as
important to his success in Chicago—if not more important than—as
were his Irish political abilities of coalition-forming and consensus-
creating. Daley won over most of the people of Chicago. He was not
successful with the journalists and the writers and most of the intellectuals, though in truth he cared very little about such people. More
importantly, he was not able to appeal, particularly after 1968, to the
growing lakefront limousine liberal constituency; and most important of all, he never did get the hang of winning over suburban
voters, save when almost by chance he proposed a candidate they
found acceptable.

Interestingly enough, his son, Richard M. Daley ("young Rich"),
was able to assemble just such a coalition in his successful run for the
Democratic State Attorney nomination in 1980 against the candidate
chosen by Calamity Jane. It is too early to say, but it is altogether
possible that Richard M. Daley will be yet another version of the
"last of the Irish political bosses." In Chicago the question is not
whether Richard M. Daley or someone else will play the role; for as
long as one needs coalition builders, there are almost certainly going
to be Irishmen around who are ready to take on the task.

If not the last, however, Richard J. Daley was surely the most
successful of the Irish political leaders. He was not typical in many
respects; less outgoing, more honest, and more competent than most.
Daley still had the basic Irish political skill of coalition-building; a
skill which, try as they might, not even his worst enemies can effectively deny him. You may not appreciate the skill. You may believe
that the purpose of politics is to separate the sheep from the goats, the
right from the left, the liberals from the conservatives, but you must
at least concede that Richard Daley was a master at blurring such
distinctions and drawing people together instead of setting them at
odds with each another. Some might even go so far as to believe that
there are not nearly enough men in public life with precisely those
kinds of political skills.*

---

* Those who know more about the inner workings of Chicago politics than I say that
Daley's wisest political move was to marry a woman who was smarter and more politically
insightful than he. It is even asserted that his son followed the same pattern. Whether these
whispers be true or not of those two Irish politicians, it has been my observation that the
most successful Irish politicians do indeed marry politically brilliant women—a large supply

★   ★   ★

Professor Edward Shils of the University of Chicago used to begin one of his courses with a joke about an Irishman who was washed up on a desert island. The natives found him crawling up the beach. "Is there a government here?" the Irishman asked. "There is," said the natives. The Irishman grabbed a rock, struggled to his feet, and threw the rock toward the palm trees. "Then I'm agin it," he shouted. Everyone laughed, of course. No one pointed out to him that the last time the Irish engaged in aggressive war was when Neill of the nine hostages raided England in the early fifth century and brought back a number of Irish slaves, including a teenage boy named Patrick. Nor did anyone observe that the violence and the bloodshed which has marked Irish history was in fact Irish blood shed at the hand of foreign invaders. Nor did anyone dare to comment that wherever the Irish have migrated in the world they have practiced politics not of violence but of consensus, compromise, and coalition-building. One learned early to laugh at Professor Shils and not to argue with him. The stereotype of the violent political revolutionary means too much to too many people for one to permit it to be challenged.

★   ★   ★

Of all the stereotypes about the Irish, the one least likely to survive the test of empirical evidence is the one about their politics. The Irish, we are told, were successful in American politics because they knew the English language. In fact, the early Irish immigrants spoke Irish rather than English as their first language and many of them spoke no English at all. Their political success was rather the result of a combination of the political skills they learned in Ireland and the social structures of the American cities into which they moved.

The Irish, we are further told, are corrupt in politics, taking to it, as one writer in *The New Republic* suggested a number of years ago, their deficient Irish Catholic morality. However, there is no evidence that city governments run by the Irish in the nineteenth century were any more corrupt than those run by others. Tammany Hall was WASP, not Irish, in its origin; nor is there any evidence that the notorious Irish political machines in the twentieth century—Hague's

---

of whom can be found in the Irish communities of Chicago and elsewhere. Someday, perhaps, these women will seek political office on their own and then we will all be in trouble!

in Jersey, Prendergast's in Kansas City, Curley's in Boston, and the perennial Cook County organization in Chicago—were any more corrupt than those run by WASPs that came before them or by other ethnic groups—black included—that coexist with them. There have been Irish Catholic reform governors, like Dunne in Illinois and Smith in New York, and Irish Catholic reform mayors, like Dever in Chicago. To suggest the Irish developed corrupt politics in America shows as deficient a sense of history as to attribute organized crime to the Italians. Both institutions were developed long before the ethnic immigrants arrived and are as American as cherry pie.

It is further argued that Irish Catholic politics are reactionary, conservative, and nonideological. The historical and sociological evidence to refute the charge of Irish conservatism is overwhelming. As we shall see in this chapter, the Irish approach to politics is indeed pragmatic and consensual: it is concerned with winning elections, and it is based on the premise that you can accomplish nothing if you lose elections. To most Irish politicians, the moral victory is no victory at all, perhaps because in their heritage is the memory of so many defeats.

Finally, it is said that Irish political influence is waning in America. As the Irish become affluent and move to the suburbs, it is said, they are being replaced as mayors of the great cities. Daley was, after all, succeeded by a Croatian, wasn't he? And what happened to the Croatian?

In the introduction to the new edition of *Beyond the Melting Pot,* Daniel P. Moynihan laments the passing of the Irish political power in New York—a passionate and moving lament pronounced before Hugh Carey became governor of New York and before Moynihan himself decamped to the august halls of the United States Senate.

★   ★   ★

In some ways the most offensive part of the mythology of Irish political success is the mindless repetition of the cliché that their command of the English language is the principal reason for that success. Even if it were not true that many of the immigrants who came before 1870 did not speak English or did not speak it well, this explanation ignores the fact that the native-born American spoke English too, at least as well as the Irish. Yet in the competition to see who was going to gain political control of the big cities that were being filled with immigrants, the Irish won easily.

This suggests that they had other advantages over the native-born Americans, most notably political skills. Professor Emmet Larkin argues that the Irish immigrants had already been trained at the Daniel O'Connell school of politics. They knew very well how to make the most of a situation in which they were forced to labor under a tremendous handicap and in the face of great prejudice. Daniel O'Connell himself, according to Larkin, was both a western Ireland clan chieftain and a Whig "magnete" in a rotten borough parliament. Combining the clan loyalty of western Ireland with the parliamentary skills required in a corrupt parliament, O'Connell had won notable improvement in conditions for Irish Catholics, mostly by training his followers in the exercise of these skills. The Irish therefore arrived in the United States at the right time and with the right political skills and were able to organize themselves and other urban ethnic groups. They took power away from the native-born Americans who had dominated those cities and had indeed developed their own form of corrupt politics, including Tammany Hall.

From the Irish point of view, "reform" was merely an attempt on the part of native-born Protestants to take what they had lost to the Irish in a fair fight. Laments of reformers like Jane Addams in Chicago merely amused the Irish. The native-born reformers were at least as corrupt as the Irish and, in addition, they were hypocrites. All they were interested in were jobs for their own people, which meant taking back the jobs which the Irish had won in the polling place. That this analysis was not completely unfounded is demonstrated by Douglas B. Shaw in "The Making of an Immigrant City: Ethnic and Cultural Conflict in Jersey City, New Jersey, 1850–1887." As early as 1853 in Jersey City, the Hudson County Bible Society had warned that unless measures were taken, "the foreign element which is so rapidly flowing into the country is destined at no distant day to exert an immense if not controlling influence in our county affairs, both politically and religiously."

Between 1860 and 1870, Irish immigrants managed to seize most of the elective offices and to challenge the native-born leadership of Jersey City. The nativists responded by literally abolishing local government in Jersey City. Legislative commissions were imposed on the city, but their members proved to be incompetent, corrupt, and dishonest. Indeed, some of them were even convicted and sentenced to (very light) jail sentences. Only then, when democracy returned to Jersey City, did the Irish assume more or less permanent power in the city's politics. The corruption of later Irish bosses in Jersey City was scandalous. Needless to say, they were merely continuing a tradition of corruption that had been set by their native-born predecessors.

The Irish aproach to politics was for the most part pragmatic: it meant jobs and power. It was also an endlessly fascinating game. Just as they were not about to yield power once again to the native-borns whom they had replaced, so the Irish were not especially eager to be replaced by those who came after them. Using their considerable political skills and their strategic position, the Irish managed to maintain control of the politics of many large American municipalities well into the second half of the twentieth century, though, as Thomas Anderson points out in his *Tammany Hall and the New Immigrants: The Progressive Years,* the Irish in New York were flexible and pragmatic when it came to admitting to power the Jewish and Italian immigrants who came to New York City after them. Jews and Italians were something less than full-fledged partners and something more than token members of Tammany. Ultimately the New York Irish failed in this attempt to maintain power by coopting the groups that came after them but only, it would seem, because Jewish politicians were themselves too skillful to be coopted for very long.

In other cities, the Irish had little trouble integrating into their political machines Italians, Poles, and later even blacks. Indeed, as the black political scientist Matthew Holden has remarked, "In Chicago the Irish direct the music for a delicate minuet and the Poles and the blacks dance with one another." The Irish have continued their political control, gained initially by force of numbers and strategic positions, by developing skills as power brokers among the other cultures.

★   ★   ★

Irish politics were and are a variegated phenomenon. Some Irish politicians were merely greedy, others were motivated partly by a desire to improve conditions of their own people and to settle scores with the native-born Protestants, and still others, notably Edward Dunne in Illinois and Alfred Smith in New York, were political liberals committed to social and economic reform and to the ideals of the progressive era. John D. Beunker has shown with careful precision in a number of articles that men like Dunne, Smith, David I. Walsh, Thomas Walsh, Martin Glenn, and Joe Tumulty were solidly in the progressive camp on issues such as labor, welfare, regulation of utilities, initiative, and referendum, and they even supported Woodrow

Wilson for reelection in 1916 despite grave reservations about Wilson's attitude toward Ireland. Beunker remarks about Illinois's Governor Dunne, "Taken as a whole, Dunne's utterances and actions identify him as a governor whose devotion to the welfare state and his sympathy for the industrial worker at least matched that of any contemporary reformer. It seems fair to say that his concern for labor and welfare probably outstripped that of the average native progressive, felt little attachment to the alien wage earner and sometimes evidenced little sympathy for his plight."

There were of course dishonest Irish politicians. There were also Irish politicians whose only concern was electoral victory and the power it brought them. But there were also progressive, liberal, and reform-minded politicians who are rarely mentioned in any of the sweeping critical generalizations made about corrupt Irish Catholic political morality. From the very beginning, the native-borns have practiced a double standard when judging the morality of Irish politicians and they, and now many of their Jewish allies, continue to practice that double standard. Irish politicians are to be judged on the basis of the worst among them and the other politicians are to be judged on the basis of the best among them—the "reformers."

Reform politics ultimately does not work because it is incapable of keeping touch with the complexities of urban problems. Political organizations, on the other hand, are more likely to work because machine politicians, bent on preserving their own jobs and being elected, are much more likely to be in touch with the personal needs of a majority of the electorate than are the principal ideological reformers. John Lindsay was a disaster for New York City in the most recent and spectacular display of the failure of reform. Daley, so cordially despised by the reformers, kept Chicago running rather smoothly. His successors promptly got themselves thrown out of office when they failed to do what Daley always did—plow the streets during a winter snowstorm.

Chicago critics like Mike Royko used to say the city worked if you were white and if you were middle class. It worked for a lot of the blacks and the poor, too, but no city worked very well for these people. Royko and company loved to blame Daley for the state of the Chicago public school system, ignoring the fact that he had little political power over the schools and that Chicago's public schools were no worse than the public schools of other cities. What Daley did in Chicago was to provide the minimum in public services—garbage collection, snow plowing, police and fire protection—free of strike, which a majority of American urban dwellers consider absolutely essential. To the reformers it did not seem very much, but it was more than the reformers were ever able to do when they obtained political power in cities like New York.

Professor Jack Douglas, in analyzing critical differences between Chicago and New York in their dealings with municipal unions, shows how John Lindsay, riding to power on a wave of self-righteous reform, set out to break the power of the municipal unions and ended up, after disastrous defeats, with a policy of caving in almost immediately to every demand the unions made. Indeed, Mayor Lindsay astonished the union leadership with the speed of his surrender and his willingness to concede to even the demands they had not made seriously. Lindsay, in other words, turned the municipal unions into adversaries, lost every battle with them, and drove the city to the brink of bankruptcy.

Daley, on the other hand, coopted the union leadership by making them part of the city government. When the unions came to the city with their wage demands, they were in effect making demands on their own political organization. So great was the mutual trust that had been established that most of the agreements Daley made with the unions were based on verbal agreements and handshakes. The reformers thought that these "deals" were corrupt, but Chicago got away with paying much less to its union employees than did New York City and hence remained financially solvent when New York became virtually insolvent. At the present writing, it would appear that Daley's successors do not have his skills and that Chicago is faced with the same fate that has befallen New York and Cleveland and other American cities whose leadership have lost the political power to hold together the complex array of political, economic, social, religious, racial, and nationality diversity at work in a large city.

For the reformers and their ideological supporters, what counts is that one be against "patronage" and take the right stand on critical issues. For them, it really does matter what the mayor of a city thinks about abortion or the death penalty even if he has neither statutory power nor statutory responsibility in either of these questions. But to the pragmatic professional Irish politician, all that matters is that you're able to get the job done. He is told by his WASP or Jewish critic that he's corrupt and merely interested in power. He is forced to reply that as far as he can see, the reformers want power too and that when they do get it, they use it as ruthlessly as he uses it, and not nearly so skillfully or effectively.

Much of what has been called reform is in fact exactly what it seemed to the Irish Catholics in Jersey City a century ago—an attempt to drive the Irish out of the political power they seized from their "betters." This is not the place to launch defenses of either Richard J. Daley or Daniel P. Moynihan. Much of the liberal and reform assault on these two men (as well as that on John F. Kennedy when he was a living politician instead of a dead martyr) is based on the fact that they were Irish, that "everyone knew" the Irish were immoral, corrupt, and dishonest politicians. The unfair attacks on Daley and Moynihan in the liberal press in the last decade simply would not have been tolerated if the targets were not Irish.

The Irish are the most politically active of American ethnic groups. They are more likely to campaign, to contribute money to politics, to vote, to join civic organizations, to contact a political leader. Even when one takes educational attainment into account, the Irish still are the most politically active group in American society.

Professor Terry N. Clark, in an analysis of the Irish political ethic, has observed in his study of 51 cities that the proportion of Irish in a city leads to an increase in expenditures but a decline of political reform; an increase in a mayor's authority; an increase in responsiveness to the lower socioeconomic groups (reformers ignore it, but Clark found that in reform-dominated cities there is less responsiveness to the lower socioeconomic groups). The Irish, according to Clark, also hold more political offices in urban areas than other American ethnic groups. The higher expenditures in Irish-dominated cities, according to Clark, are not the result of the Irish demanding more governmental services but rather an Irish-dominated urban government providing more services and more jobs.

> The system consists of three basic actors who aspire to three distinct resources, each controlled by the next: candidates seek votes, voters seek favors, political campaigners seek government jobs. As each actor obtains his desired resource, he helps the others achieve theirs, and thus keeps the patronage system operating. Such a patronage system may be part of most empirical political systems . . . in some American cities it is of central importance. Patronage systems have been developed and manned by Irish political leaders for decades; the Irish have

been particularly active as candidates and political campaigners, and as a consequence, have often held jobs in city government.*

Reformers turn purple when they read such lines, but Professor Clark—himself not Irish—continues matter-of-factly.

Response to such demands is not without costs. Jobs may be created arbitrarily and may be filled with more attention to competence in politics than in the government job. Such "featherbedding" and "special" favors can raise the costs of government. But patronage in no way necessitates corruption or illegal activities. Irresponsible leaders may emerge, but regular elections constrain their uses of the public purse.

If some Americans vehemently denounce patronage, others support it. But most supporters just do it, without talking about it. Our broader concern is not to argue in the abstract for or against non-ideological particularism and governance by patronage. Rather we simply record that these appeal to some citizens if not to others. In considering local government in particular, a position of ethical relativism with mutual respect (cultural pluralism?) is more viable than in national affairs: dissatisfied citizens can change cities and suburbs far more readily than their passports.

Patronage is not about to disappear from the face of the earth. Rather than condemning it naively, more careful analysis of its relations to effective performance is in order. Legal structures of most governments were established long ago, and are not frequently redrawn. The demands placed on our urban leaders, however, have constantly increased. A mayor who must face repeated demonstrations and strikes by (honest and nonpartisan?) city administrators has difficulty just surviving. We cannot reasonably expect urban leaders to resolve basic policy issues without giving them tools to work with.**

A number of commentators in American political life, most notably Edward Banfield, James Q. Wilson, and Martin Meyerson, have glorified even more than Terry Clark the political achievements of urban ethnic governmental style. Ultimately, the issue of the Irish in

---

* Terry N. Clark, "The Irish Ethic and the Spirit of Patronage," *Ethnicity*, Vol. 2, No. 4 (December 1975), p. 344.
** Ibid., pp. 344–345.

politics is comparable to that of racial intermarriage a couple of decades ago. It is not a subject about which it is safe to talk for very long. It touches off deep resonances in the preconscious and the unconscious of both Irish Catholics and other Americans. It is an issue that has emerged from the bitter racial and religious tensions that have been part of our city life for more than a century.

Very few people are ready to be rational on the subject. Writers like Meyerson, Wilson, and Banfield (and Robert Dahl from Yale) are arguing against an implicit bias that infects much of American political science and is still dominant among the nation's cultural elite. A still younger and even more ideological generation of political scientists has turned against the so-called "pluralists" with little in the way to support its arguments other than passionate "concern." It is not any more likely now, however, that an objective stand be taken on the pragmatic, patronage-oriented, coalition-building, informal Irish political style than it was a century ago, when an English visitor to Boston suggested that the final solution to America's political problems would be to have "every Irishman kill a nigger and then be hung for it." All one can reasonably expect is that when Irish Catholic young people go out to the universities they be skeptical about what they hear in their politial science and history classes about "machine" politicians.

They should also be skeptical about what they will be told on the subject of Irish racism and conservatism. If no final judgment can yet be made on the Irish contribution to urban ethnic politics, there is definitive evidence available on Irish political and racial attitudes, and indeed it is possible to trace changes in the racial attitudes through the years.

Daley was accused repeatedly by his enemies of being a racist and a conservative, even though there was ample evidence that the Cook County organization provided proportionately more jobs for blacks than any other employer in Cook County and that blacks had more representation in government elective and appointed offices in Chicago than in other cities in the country. Daley's racism was so much a foregone conclusion among limousine liberals and their favorite journalists that it never really had to be proved, though Mike Royko hinted darkly that Daley was responsible for the 1968 race riots (without a shred of evidence of course). The only argument that could ever be made to prove that Daley was a racist was the contention that there were no blacks in his neighborhood of Bridgeport.

In fact, there are and have been blacks in the Bridgeport neighborhood for a long time, and the neighborhood is about 20 percent Hispanic (and there are Hispanics and blacks in the Catholic parochial schools in Bridgeport). Daley's enemies were never deterred by the facts.

By conservative one meant that Daley was not an ideological liberal. It must be conceded that he was surely not that. However, he was a pragmatic New Deal Democrat, committed to providing jobs, housing, and urban improvement. If to be a liberal you have to take the approved stands on marijuana, quotas, busing, and abortion, Daley was not a liberal. But neither are most other Americans. However, like the rest of the Irish-American population, Daley's claim to being part of the traditional American liberal heritage was persuasive (though, characteristically, he never felt a need to make any such claims).

The NORC racial integration scale measures attitudes toward integrated schools, integrated social life, integrated neighborhoods, interracial marriage, and black militancy. Even when comparisons are limited to the north, where Catholics are concentrated, the Irish have been more sympathetic to integration than both their coreligionists and all Protestants throughout the 1970s. Indeed, the gap between Irish Catholics and all the other groups (except Italian Catholics) seems to have *widened* during the seventies. The Irish sympathy for integration is higher than that of the other gentile groups (though behind that of Jews), and the Irish "advantage" in prointegration attitudes has increased rather than decreased in recent years.

These racial attitudes of the Irish are not necessarily the result of their living in safe suburban enclaves. Eighteen percent of Irish Catholics live on the same block as blacks, and 20 percent of them live within three blocks of blacks (as compared to 12 percent and 14 percent respectively for other Americans). Two-fifths of Irish Catholics, in other words, live in racially integrated neighborhoods and about the same number have no objection to their children attending mostly black schools (so long as the schools are safe), and 89 percent say they would vote for a black president—twice as many as American Protestants willing to vote for a Catholic president in 1958.

It is not only on racial matters that the Irish are on the liberal end of the political continuum; 62 percent of them describe themselves as Democrats, 30 percent as liberals. Fifty-three percent voted for

Hubert Humphrey and 39 percent for George McGovern. The Irish are more likely than most other ethnic groups to oppose the death penalty, to approve the legalization of marijuana, and to support gun control. They are also consistently more tolerant than other Americans of the rights of atheists, Communists, and homosexuals to lecture publicly, to teach in state universities, and to have their books displayed in public libraries. Only Jewish Americans have higher scores on measures of liberalism. If both the political and civil-liberties items are combined into a single measure, Irish Catholics are once again the highest on liberalism of any gentile group in America and also the strongest supporters of civil liberties. Nor is this higher liberalism and libertarianism merely the function of education; indeed, it persists even when education is taken into account. We have already seen in other chapters that the Irish are the strongest gentile supporters of feminism among all ethnic groups, so on multi-item measures of political liberalism, feminism, support for racial integration, and civil liberties, Irish Catholics are, even when their superior educational achievement is taken into account, more liberal than any group in the society save Jews. If it is the standard of Jewish liberalism by which Irish Catholics are to be judged conservative, then everybody else is even more conservative. If, on the other hand, it is the national average which is to be the dividing line between the left and the right, Irish Catholics have a strong, indeed irrefutable, claim on the title of the most liberal gentile Americans.

That this claim will seem to many readers so counterintuitive as to be absurd is perhaps the best indicator of the difficulty of communicating on the subject of the American Irish. We come from a revolutionary political tradition; we are involved at the top levels in such radical organizations as the United Mine Workers of America (the famous "Black John" Mitchell), the Knights of Labor (Terrence Powderly), the American Railroad Union, the Haymarket riot, and the Automobile Workers and the United Steel Workers in their formative years, and even in the Molly Maguires. We have consistently voted for the liberal Democratic candidates. Many of our political leaders were themselves progressive and liberal Democrats. We were denied the presidency in 1928 and almost denied it in 1960 (winning by only 110,000 votes) and are still viewed with contempt and disdain as politicians by many Americans. Despite our past history of radical and liberal involvement, and despite incontrovertible evidence of our present liberalism, we are still written off as conservalives—even by such a perceptive observer as Terry Clark. The social scientist faced with such factual obstacles to mythological evidence, which he thinks ought to be unquestioned, has no choice but to shrug his shoulders. There are some convictions so deeply rooted in personality needs that overwhelming evidence simply cannot shake them. When "everyone knows" that the Irish are "conservative," the evidence that they have been and are more liberal than other Americans is unacceptable.

But then the Irish are unacceptable, always have been, and are likely always to be. At the end of his *I'd Do It Again,* James Michael Curley says proudly that he met Ralph Lowell at the Harvard Club one night and Lowell said, "How do you do, Governor?" Curley adds, "It is a far cry from the days when the Back Bay Hatfields fought the Roxbury McCoys. In those days one Brahmin said, 'Curley might have been president if he'd been one of us.' And another made the whimsical statement that Jim Curley is the best orator in the country; too bad he's Irish. All that is changed now . . . the Lowells and the Cabots speak to the Curleys."

Maybe in Boston that's important; out on the shores of Lake Michigan, we find it hard to understand in Curley's sense of achievement whether they speak to us or not.

Despite Edward Shils, the Irish are actually substantially less violent than are many other American groups, according to measures of violent behavior such as fighting. They may not be accepted or acceptable, but in elections they are still masters of urban politics, and still the most active and probably the most skillful politicians in the country. Probably they will only become acceptable when they prefer to lose more than they do to win and when the joy in moral victories is preferred to the concrete rewards of real victories—though a moral victory never got anyone a job, never changed a power structure, never made anyone any money, never had any impact on society.

T E N

Irish Drinking

Various travelers to the Celtic lands—Strabo, Gerald of Canterbury, Geoffrey Keating, and wandering Victorian Englishmen coming to stare at the natives—have all commented on the Irish proclivity for that which is delicately called "the creature." Drinking has been frequently said to be the "curse of the Irish race," as if the Irish were the only people in the world who drink or who have serious drinking problems. Heavy drinking, in the minds of the Irish Americans, and other Americans as well, is an integral part of Irish Catholic culture and, indeed, the reason for the lack of Irish success in the United States. It is also both the cause of the failure of Irish family life and the result of the rigors of that family life.

The drunken Irish male abounds in fiction and in folklore and in the alcohol research of social science. If there is one issue on which the myth and the research evidence ought to converge, it ought to be on the subject of Irish Catholic drinking.

Or so it seems.

But the matter is somewhat more complicated. Of the nine Common Market countries, the Republic of Ireland is sixth in its per capita alcohol consumption, eighth in its per capita consumption of spirits, and ninth in its per capita consumption of wine. There are, in other words, five Common Market countries where the per capita liquor consumption is higher than that of Ireland.

Furthermore, while the American Irish are more likely to drink (91 percent) than English Protestants (61 percent), most of this difference is attributable to the rural and Southern background of many English Protestants. In four large metropolitan areas studied intensively by NORC, there is little difference between English Protestants and Irish Catholics in drinking rates, in the amount of alcohol consumed in a year, and in serious drinking problems. Furthermore, there is considerable evidence that other ethnic groups—blacks, Poles, and Slovenes, for example—have at least as serious a drinking problem in their cultural heritage as do Irish Catholics.

How, then, has it come about that the Irish have a special reputation for being heavy drinkers?

There are two answers—one pertaining to the perspective of the early alcohol research literature, and the other to the historical myth about Ireland.

Early alcohol research began at Yale University in New Haven, Connecticut. The Yale scholars ventured forth into the outside world and encountered three ethnic groups: Italians, Jews, and Irish. Drinking rates among the Italians and Jews were high, but their problem-drinking and alcoholism rates were quite low, whereas the alcoholism and problem-drinking rates among the Irish were extremely high by comparison. Therefore, with that fine display of objectivity and balance which marks Yale social research, the scholars concluded that the Irish subculture was deviant, that the Irish family life which produced such acute alcohol problems was a hard, cold, almost inhuman cultural environment—marked especially, be it noted, by sexual repression. If one wishes to read bigotry that is totally unself-conscious, one should peruse the literature of Irish Catholic drinking in the United States. Any scholar who would dare attribute, let us say, the problems of blacks (including problem drinking) to black cultural deviance would be bitterly denounced as a racist who is blaming the "victim."

It seems to have occurred to none of the alcohol scholars that there are other people in the United States besides Irish, Italians, and Jews; that there are many problem drinkers who are not Irish; and that the deviant or variant subcultures are the Jewish and Italian ones, not the Irish. The important intellectual question is not why the Irish are so prone to problem drinking, but why the Italians and the Jews are so little prone to it. One of the reasons why this seemingly obvious set of questions never occurred to the alcohol scholars is that they began their research with the American myth about the Irishman as a heavy drinker and found no need to question the accuracy of the myth.

The origins of the myth and the fact of Irish Catholic drinking in America have been confronted with dazzling brilliance by Professor Richard Stivers in his remarkable book, *The Hair of the Dog*. Stivers notes that an epidemic of heavy drinking swept the British Isles in the early 1700s after the invention of gin in France and its import to England and Ireland. Before the arrival of gin, the upper classes consumed brandy and the lower classes downed mead, ale, and stout. It took a lot of stout and a fair amount of brandy to produce the same effect that gin could achieve very quickly. Gin consumption quickly became part of the daily life of the early industrial working class. To prove that one was a "man," and to prove one's personal worth, one demonstrated that one could consume every bit as much gin as anyone else. In fact, initiation to the usage of gin became part of the ritual introduction to factory life to kill the pain of long, hard, and monotonous work and also to help keep the new industrial working class (and the proletarian class in Ireland) docile and unrevolutionary.

As industrial technology became more complex, however, it was no longer in the interest of a capitalist nation to have a labor force that was dazed with gin through most of the working day. The temperance movement launched by the Methodists in England and the total abstinence movements pushed by the Catholic Church in Ireland were strongly reinforced by the "better" classes on each island. The combination of religious devotion and capitalist greed was remarkably effective, particularly after 1830 and especially among nonconformist working men in England. Whatever the ancestral practices may have been, Father Theobald's total abstinence movement was extraordinarily successful in the prosperous Ireland of the first half of the last century; it is estimated that more than half of the people in Ireland were abstainers before the Great Famine. The drinking revolution introduced by gin, in other words, had been effectively contained.

The Great Famine wiped out the total abstinence movement along with the many other aspects of Irish life it destroyed. As an organization, the Pioneers (as the abstainers are called) continued to exist, and indeed they still have a considerable impact on Irish life, especially on the Irish clergy. But abstinence from drink did not regain its place as a dominant theme in the Irish culture, and the temperance movement did not have anywhere near the influence it continued to have among English and American Protestants. Thus when the Prohibition Amendment to the American Constitution was passed, Irish Catholics and English Protestants were on opposite sides of the debate and neither knew the historical event which had caused the split.

In the bleak culture of survival which emerged in western Ireland after the Great Famine, with marriage postponed until one was well into one's thirties and immigration to America the only choice for those who would not inherit the family farm or marry and inherit one, for those who were ambitious and aggressive, drinking became recreation and an escape. It is fashionable to blame the Church for the late age at which the nineteenth and twentieth century Irish married, though in fact, as Robert Kennedy has demonstrated, the Church was bitterly opposed to late marriage, in part because the parish clergy, not being blind, could see the relationship between postponed marriage and heavy drinking. It was economic necessity that imposed the mid-nineteenth-century demographic revolution on Ireland and brought with it a return to heavy drinking as a means to killing the pain.

The village pub became the recreational center of the western Ireland community, partly because there simply was no place else to go. The narrowness, rigidity, and pseudomasculinity of male groups permeated pub life. One's masculinity was established by one's ability to consume prodigious amounts of liquor and not show its effects. Those who could not hold their liquor were treated with contempt; those who would not drink were viewed with suspicion. Heavy drinking and alcoholism spread through post-Famine Ireland like an infectious disease. The English, who caused the problem by the economic and governmental policies that almost destroyed Ireland during the Great Famine, used the epidemic as an explanation for Irish poverty and as proof of Irish inferiority.

In emphasizing the cultural inferiority which leads to Irish drinking, the American alcohol researchers did not hesitate to point to the origin of the drinking in nineteenth-century Ireland. None of them, however, has bothered to explain why it started or to investigate the political and economic dynamics that produced the drinking. Better to explain Irish drinking as the result of Catholic sexual repression than as the result of English political repression.

This picture of the heavy-drinking Irish awaited the Irish immigrants in America. They were perceived as living up to the stereotype—as of course every group with a stereotype is perceived, since the stereotype is a self-fulfilling prophecy. "Paddy" was depicted in American cartoons as a gorillalike personage with a stovepipe hat (a shamrock stuck in the hatband), a shillelagh in one hand and a beer mug in the other. It is a foregone conclusion among the "better" people in America that Irish Catholic drinking precluded the possibility of the Irish "race" ever achieving success in America or ever becoming "real Americans."

Stivers carefully demonstrates how the negative stereotype was transformed by the Irish Americans into a positive stereotype—a process which goes on in every group that is stereotyped. Paddy the brutal, violent drunk became Paddy the carefree, happy, comic, singing drunk ("We may drink," the Irish Americans responded to the nativist stereotype, "but we can hold our liquor, and we're happy, good-natured drunks"). Professor Stivers (who is neither Irish nor Catholic, by the way) argues that Irish Catholic Americans are heavy drinkers because the stereotype imposed on them by native American bigotry demands that they drink. The Irish Americans drink a lot, he contends, because they are expected to drink a lot; indeed, they drink more than their cousins in Ireland, because their Irish cousins do not have to live up to a stereotype. It does not matter that the stereotype of the happy drunk is propagated by such Irish Catholic writers as Joe O'Flaherty, Pete Hamill, and Jimmy Breslin; it is still a stereotype, and a vicious one, even though these authors take its accuracy for granted.

In *The Hair of the Dog,* Stivers is calm and dispassionate until its final two pages, when he explodes in anger at what the drinking stereotype has done to Irish Catholics in America.

More important was the difference in the cultural contexts and existential meaning of hard drinking between Ireland and Irish America. In Ireland hard drinking was cultural remission, a release from sexual puritanism and the great sacrifice in restraint that a stem-family farm economy entailed. Hard drinking was a cultural demand, and status accrued to those who could hold their own and thus keep hard drinking from the label of church-condemned drunkenness. Hard drinking as an integral part of male identity was moral in that it acted to preserve a stem-family economy.

In America, on the other hand, hard drinking has been removed from its original context and ceased to be a cultural remission. Now it was a control in Irish-American culture. As a sacrament in the re-

ligion of Irish American nationalism, it differentiated the Irish from
other ethnic groups. It became a spiritual value, symbolizing Irish
group identity. It implied that the more one drank the more Irish one
became. Drink in Ireland did not fundamentally symbolize one's
Irishness or one's Catholicism and thus was not ultimately religious.
In America the religion of nationalism superseded that of Catholicism,
though they were still united in the minds of the Irish. But the
growing dichotomy between the private and public spheres of life and
the growing importance of the public at the expense of the private
meant that Irish nationalism—the improved status and advancement
of the Irish-American—was dominant. Therefore the saloon as the
point at which ward politics and the lure of the street were most
intertwined was more a church than it had been in Ireland. Hard
drinking ceased to be modified by the stigma of drunkenness, as it had
in Ireland. In Ireland the drunk was ambivalently regarded as the
good man with a failing—but he was still a sinner. In America in the
give-and-take of ward politics and in saloon and street life, the drunk
was no longer a sinner/saint; he had been transformed into a complete
saint, the professional Irish inebriate.

In Ireland there was greater insulation from the English stereotype
of the Irishman as drunkard because Catholic Ireland had little desire
to be assimilated by the English. But in America, the great desire of
the Irish to be accepted by native Americans, coupled with the impos-
sibility of remaining authentically Irish, meant that they were
doomed to become a caricature—the only terms on which native
Americans would accept them.

One must remember that these comments come from a writer
who is neither Catholic nor Irish and who began his exploration of
Irish American drinking with no particular prejudices or precon-
ditions.

Not having studied at Yale University, of course, Professor Stivers
was not concerned with explaining why the Irish are culturally deviant to Jews and Italians. If one only hears of his thesis, it seems easy
to dismiss. When I read it in his introduction to *The Hair of the Dog*, I
did not believe he could persuade me of its truth. In fact, however, his
full argument is subtle, sophisticated, and powerfully persuasive. In
addition, it is the only explanation ever attempted that can account
for the singular phenomenon that Irish Americans drink substantially
more than the Irish in Ireland. The happy Irish-American drunk has
been imposed on the Irish Catholic culture in the United States every
bit as much as the "Stepin Fetchit" stereotype has been imposed on

the black culture. Their drinking behavior has not prevented the Irish from becoming the most gentle ethnic group in America (and perhaps now the most affluent of gentile American ethnic groups). One wonders what they might have done, however, if they had not been burdened with both the historical disaster of the Great Famine, which reintroduced a heavy drinking subculture to Ireland, and the American stereotype of the Irish drunkard, which reinforced that subculture in the United States.

It is not my intention in this chapter to deny that there is a drinking problem among the American Irish, but the typical Irish American is no more alcoholic than the typical black is a criminal, the typical Italian is a Mafia don, and the typical Jew is a ruthless businessman. All my uncles on both sides were alcoholics, or at least serious problem drinkers; my mother and father did not drink; my sisters and I are only cautious consumers of "the creature" (wine only, thank you). One cannot be a priest very long in an Irish Catholic parish and not be aware that the toll problem drinking takes on our subculture is most assuredly not a laughing matter. Nor do I propose to deny that family personality variables are a fact in Irish American problem drinking. The truth can be summarized, I think, in three propositions:

1. The Irish are not the only ethnic group in America with a drinking problem; indeed, among those who drink, there seems to be little difference between English and Irish drinkers.

2. While there are family and personality factors at work, the available evidence accounts for most of the Irish drinking problem in historical and cultural terms, compatible with Stivers's theses.

3. Therefore, the negative stereotype of the brutal Irish drunk and its mirror image, the positive stereotype of the happy Irish drunk, are unjust stereotypes—which have been imposed on American Irish by the native culture—for which there has not only been no reparation, but not even an apology.

Three different explanations for drinking problems are advanced from the alcohol research literature: cultural, historical, and psychological. The psychological explanation, most skillfully articulated by David McClellan in his book *The Drinking Man,* asserts that the problem drinker is a person who has high need for power, a need rooted in his experience of growing up in an unloving and unsupportive family environment, and a low sense of esteem or no sense of personal efficacy. The problem drinker becomes dependent on the dream world that his drinking creates where his "need for power" is temporarily met.

The cultural explanation, devised originally to account for Irish "inferiority" to Italians and Jews, borrows heavily from the psychological explanation but adds a description of aspects of Irish life other than the family environment which also account for problem drinking. The Italians, we are told, treat drink as a food. Wine is something to be consumed as part of a meal; one does not drink it to get drunk, it is merely an accompaniment to the food. The Jews think of wine as something sacred and sacramental; it has ritual significance in their religion and must be treated with respect and reverence. To lose personal control through the abuse of this sacred beverage is both inappropriate to and unworthy of a Jew. To the Irish, on the other hand, drink has neither eating nor religious purposes but recreational ones. Irish drinking is an aspect of Irish gregariousness. Being drunk is a form of entertainment.

The historical explanation, one on which Stivers relies for the most part, says that the Irish Americans drink a lot and have drinking problems because such modes of behavior have been passed down to them by their ancestors. If one takes it for granted, for example, that one serves a drink to anyone who comes into the house, there must be an historical explanation of how such a custom got started, especially because it occurs in families where there are no personality problems of the sort which lead to McClellan's paradigm of the problem drinker and no custom of celebrating gregariousness by getting drunk. One does not have to reject either the contribution to problem drinking of the Irish need for gregariousness or the Irish family structure (though I would note in passing that McClellan's research, based as it is on those in institutions for alcoholics, does not address itself to the question of why most Irish are not alcoholics); one must merely ask to what extent cultural and personality variables contribute to an explanation of Irish problem drinking. It still remains an historical question of how these personality and cultural forces came into being.

It simply will not do to blame the whole matter on the sexual repressiveness of the Catholic Church. The Italians are also a Catholic people and they also, despite a brave show to the contrary, have, according to recent research, enormous problems of sexual repression. The French, too, are a Catholic people, and they have hardly if ever

been accused of sexual repressiveness. Alcoholism and alcohol consumption are far more serious problems in France than they are in
Ireland. Unlike England and Ireland, France never had a total abstinence movement. It is the merit of Stivers's work that he demonstrates the historical origin of contemporary American Irish Catholic
drinking problems in the savage blow struck to Irish culture by the
Great Famine and the aggravation of the problem by the negative
stereotype of the violent Irish drunk.

The empirical evidence, as we shall see, supports Stivers's argument. While there are powerful family and personality dynamics at
work in Irish problem drinking, one need not fall back on such
explanations (and on even more dubious and racist explanations of
the genetic transmission of alcoholism among the Irish) to account
for the differences among the Irish, the Italians, and the Jews in
drinking and problem drinking.

The national survey data collected by NORC in the mid-1960s
show that at that time the Irish were the most likely of any American
ethnic group to drink, to drink more than twice a week, and to
consume two or three or more drinks at a single sitting. However,
Slavic respondents were more likely than the Irish to say that alcoholic beverages made a party more enjoyable, and English Protestants
were more likely, among those who drank, to score high on the
drinking-problem scale, and English Protestants and Slavic respondents were more likely than the Irish to score high on a serious
drinking-problem scale. While the number of respondents in each
ethnic group was quite small in this national survey, the study still
raised a serious question about the myth of Irish drinking and indicated that Slavs and English Protestants (once the latter began to
drink) had at least as serious a drinking problem as did the Irish.

In the mid-1970s, with a substantial grant from the National
Institute for Alcohol Abuse and Alcoholism, NORC returned to the
question of ethnic drinking, concentrating for theoretical reasons on
four groups—Irish, Swedes, Italians, and Jews (with an English comparison group)—and sampling these five groups in four major American cities—Minneapolis, Chicago, Boston, and New York. The focus
was on alcohol's socialization—transmission of attitudes and behav-
iors across generation lines—so the respondents in the survey were
adolescents and their parents. In addition, retrospective data were
collected about the parents of the adult respondents so that there
were data on three generations—grandparents, parents, and adolescent
children.

In both the parental and grandparental generations, the Irish were heavy drinkers with serious drinking problems. However, Italian, Swedish, and English women consumed more alcohol than did Irish women, and there were only marginal differences between Italian men and Irish and English men. Irish men were also the most likely to score high on the problem-drinking scale, but there was no appreciable difference between them and English men. Similarly, while Irish adolescent males were moderately heavy drinkers, they did not drink nearly as much as English adolescent males, nor were they as likely to have drinking problems as were English adolescent males.

There is clearly an Irish drinking subculture that exists across all three generations, a culture involving both heavy drinking and serious drinking problems. That subculture, particularly for men, is strikingly different from the Italian and Jewish drinking subcultures, but it is not very different from urban English drinking behavior. Indeed, the notable difference that exists between the English and Irish drinking on a national level—two-thirds as many English Protestants as Irish Catholic Americans—vanishes in the city, where English Protestant and Irish Catholic drinking rates are virtually the same.

Who has ever heard a joke about an English drunk?

Having established the diversity of ethnic drinking subcultures, the NORC research then had to turn to the quest for an explanation. A nine-variable model was developed taking into account the drinking of one's father and mother; whether there was a drinking problem in the family when one was growing up; parental approval of drinking; power and support in the family structure; one's personal sense of efficacy; one's spouse's drinking behavior; and the drinking environment in which one lived (friends and neighbors). It was possible to account for all the differences between the Irish and the Jews in the amount of alcohol consumed a year by merely taking into account mother's drinking, father's drinking, spouse's drinking, friends' drinking, and whether Jews were Orthodox or Conservative in affiliation. In other words, a pure socialization, without any need to resort to either genetic or psychological explanations, accounted for all the differences in drink consumption between the Irish and the Jews. The Irish drink more than the Jews because their mothers drink more, their fathers drink more, their spouses drink more, their friends drink more, and because they do not have the Jewish ritual tradition of respect for alcohol as sacred. However, Reform and unaffiliated Jews from heavy-drinking families are every bit as likely to have serious drinking problems as their Irish counterparts.

There is little difference in the amount of alcohol consumed by Irish and Jewish adolescents, and most of the difference in alcohol consumption between Irish and Italian adolescents could be accounted for by parents' and friends' drinking. The same factors account for the variance in alcohol consumption among adult males in these groups.

In urban American society there are quite distinctive drinking subcultures that are effectively transmitted from grandparents to parents to children, subcultures that are sustained by what one might broadly call environmental influences—the drinking of parents, spouses, friends, and, in the case of Jews, the influence of religious tradition. Not only are the outcomes of drinking socialization different, the processes of socialization are different. Some factors are considerably more important in some groups than they are in others. A wife's drinking, for example, is influential in the total alcohol consumption of all groups but the Italians, and a mother's drinking is influential for all men except those who are Jewish. When it comes to problem drinking, the behavior of wives and mothers has very little effect on Irish men, and the support and efficacy factors are important influences at work for the Irish and the Jews, but less so for the other groups. A father's drinking, particularly when it turns to problem drinking, leads to a drinking problem for Irish women but not for other ethnic women. The problem drinking of Irish men, in other words, is not affected by how much their mothers drank, but the drinking of Irish women is influenced by how much their fathers drank and by whether their fathers had a drinking problem. Both these phenomena are unique to the Irish collectivity.

Another way of considering different socialization processes for the different groups is to divide drinking influences into four separate categories—family of origin, present family and friends, the amount of liquor consumed, and the family structure/personality socialization. Fourteen percent of Irish problem drinking is explained by the family of origin as compared to 19 percent of Italian problem drinking and 10 percent of Jewish problem drinking. When one adds the drinking of one's present family (wife) and friends, this accounts for 17 percent of the variance in Irish drinking, 32 percent of the variance in Italian drinking, and 15 percent of the variance in Jewish drinking. Adding the amount of alcohol consumed per year to the explanation, one can account for one-third of the variance in Irish drinking, half of the variance in Italian drinking, and one-fifth of the variance in Jewish drinking. Finally, when one considers only structure and per-

sonal efficacy, one adds only 2 percentage points to the explanation of
variance in Italian drinking, 13 percentage points to the explanation
of Irish drinking, and 15 percentage points to the explanation of
Jewish drinking.

Family and personality then are not distinctive factors in accounting for the problem drinking behavior of Italians (or Swedes or
English). They are important in accounting for the problem drinking
of Irish men and Jewish men. McClellan was correct in his assertion
that being raised in an authoritarian family and having a low sense of
personal efficacy are strong predictors of problem drinking for Irish
men; the same forces also work in the Jewish culture—though there
are many fewer problem drinkers among Jews. These dynamics do
not seem to be very important in Swedish or English or Italian drinking subcultures. You need not, in other words, appeal to family
structure and personality to explain the differences between the Irish
and problem drinking and problem drinking among some other
groups. The Irish are more likely to be problem drinkers because they
come from a subculture milieu in which there is extremely heavy
drinking (though no more heavy than that among urban English
Protestants). However, family relationships and personality factors
are more likely to affect a given Irish problem drinker than they are a
Swedish, or an Italian, or a Jewish problem drinker.

It remains only to be said that these distinctive drinking subcultures are not notably changed by education, by generation in the
United States, by subjective ethnic identification, by the proportion
of one's own ethnic group in one's neighborhood, or even, for the
Irish and Jews at any rate, by ethnic intermarriage. If you have one
Irish parent or one Jewish parent, you are likely to absorb their
distinctive drinking subculture (there were only three cases in the
NORC study of Jewish/Irish intermarriages, so we cannot be sure
who would "win" in the drinking subculture contest between the
two groups, though one would be ill-advised to bet against the Irish
only because their drinking behavior is closer to the national norm
than is that of the Jews).

There is then a distinctive Irish Catholic drinking subculture, especially among males. Personality and family structure do indeed have
an impact on Irish problem drinking that is different from the impact
that these factors have on the drinking of other ethnic groups. In
urban America, the drinking and drinking problems of Irish Catholics are little different from those of English Protestants; as a matter of
fact, more English Protestant adolescent males have drinking prob-

lems than Irish Catholic adolescent males. Most of the differences
between the Irish on the one hand and the Italians and the Jews on
the other in both drinking and problem drinking can be accounted
for by environmental factors without any need to appeal to their
personality or genetic differences. The Irish drink more because their
parents, families, and friends drink more, because their religion does
not put a check on their drinking whereas ritualistic Judaism affects
the drinking of the more devout Jews. The Irish are more likely to
have serious drinking problems than Jews or Italians, but they're
more likely to come from families where there were serious drinking
problems (which seems to be especially true for Irish women). The
most fundamental questions then are, Why do the Irish drink more
than either the Jews or the Italians, and Why are they more likely to
come from families that have drinking problems. Such questions necessarily transcend the limits of psychology and sociology and become
historical. Stivers's ingenious answers seem to be the only ones that
adequately fit the data. Irish Catholic Americans drink more than
Italian Catholic Americans and Jewish Americans because neither of
the two latter groups has been through a culture-destroying historical trauma like the Great Famine nor have they been burdened with
the stereotype of the angry, violent drunk. In large American cities,
however, where the temperance movement seems to have waned,
English Protestant problem drinking is roughly comparable to Irish
Catholic problem drinking. There are, I repeat, no jokes about English drunks.

There does not seem to be any reason to believe that problem
drinking among the Irish will go away. Drinking subcultures have
remarkable durability. They are passed on from generation to generation less by conscious intent (though in the Jewish family sobriety
and control are undoubtedly emphasized) than they are by unself-
conscious example and imitation. Once a group gets locked into a
given subcultural pattern, in other words, there is an inertial power in
the pattern that survives for generation after generation without the
need for conscious thought. Heavy drinking and problem drinking
are a distinctive part of Irish American life, but Irish Americans are
not the only heavy or problem drinkers, and their distinctive drinking patterns are part of the burden of a long history of oppression and
caricature that they must carry with them.

ELEVEN

Irish-American Writers

IRISH CATHOLIC FICTION WRITING IN THE UNITED STATES HAS PRO-duced a Greater Trinity, a Lesser Trinity, and a whole clutch of aspirants from among whom has emerged a New Trinity. One can search in vain among the whole lot of them, however, for a sympathetic and yet critical depiction of Irish Catholic life in the United States, though the Greater Trinitarian James T. Farrell in his old age and the "now generation" Elizabeth Cullinhan come closest to such understanding from the inside, the length and the breadth, and the height and the depth of American Irish Catholicism. Among the others, self-hatred and selling out to the enemy seem, as usual, to have gotten in the way.

In the Greater Trinity, F. Scott Fitzgerald ignored his Irish heritage (though, as William Shannon points out, there are traces of Irish lyricism in his work), John O'Hara did his snobbish best to escape from it, and James T. Farrell in his early years bitterly attacked it.

The Lesser Trinity is more explicitly Irish. Defying Harvard and the East Coast literary establishments, the late Edwin O'Connor managed to write two best sellers and won one National Book Award (for *The Edge of Sadness, not* for *The Last Hurrah*). His novels were unabashed celebrations not only of the Irish but, heaven save us, of the Boston Irish. Flannery O'Connor is Southern in her perspective, not Irish, though surely the most Catholic of all the Irish-American writers; and J. F. Powers writes with wry sympathy about the Catholic clergy, most of whom are Irish (though his most famous priest, Father Urban, is not).

One can almost program a computer to do an Irish novel from the "younger generation." It is peopled with corrupt politicians, dishonest and sex-crazed policemen, crooked construction contractors who belong to the Knights of Columbus, pious clergy who support the contractors, politicians, and policemen, castrating mothers, alcoholic fathers, sex-starved women, intellectuals battling for freedom from the Church, and an occasional crusading reformer, either Protestant or Jewish. In novels in which the hero triumphs over his environment, he normally breaks with his Irish Catholic past and becomes a reformer or a university professor. In novels in which the environment triumphs, the hero yields to his Irish Catholic tradition and settles down to be a crooked lawyer or a crooked politician or a crooked policeman. More recently, Kennedy-like millionaires, Notre Dame graduates who belong to the John Birch Society, and an occasional Irish Catholic general who wants to drop the atomic bomb on some hamlet in Southeast Asia may be added to the story.

If this sounds like a synopsis of John Gregory Dunne's *True Confessions,* the reason is that *True Confessions* is not only a caricature of Irish Catholicism but a caricature of all of the other caricatures of Irish Catholicism. It is as though Mr. Dunne sat down to read such novels from the past as Joseph Dinneen's *Ward Eight,* Thomas Fleming's *All Good Men,* and Harry Sylvester's *Moon Gaffney,* as well as the contemporary caricatures of Irish Catholicism by Jimmy Breslin *(World Without End, Amen)* and Tom McHale *(Farragan's Retreat, Principato),* and to observe carefully the Irish Catholic characters in books by Norman Mailer and Taylor Caldwell—and from all of these derived the quintessential contemporary American literary stereotype of the Irish Catholic. *True Confessions,* it goes without saying, was an enormous literary success.

Contemporary Irish Catholic writers like Dunne and McHale do not ignore their Irish Catholic backgrounds, as did Fitzgerald, or run from it to the WASP establishment, as did John O'Hara. If a caricature can be considered a step up from denial on the self-hatred scale, then perhaps there is progress in attitude, if not in literary ability, from John O'Hara to John Gregory Dunne. Cynicism, one supposes, is also an improvement on snobbishness. The Irish have always admired the man who exploits the oppressors more than the one who sells out to them.

There are also a few contemporary Catholic writers, like Elizabeth Cullinhan, who are actually sympathetic to their own heritage. Ms. Cullinhan is moderately sympathetic in her *House of Gold* and unreservedly sympathetic in her brilliant collection of short stories, *Yellow Roses.* It did not sell very well but is nonetheless made up of stories which appeared in *The New Yorker*—no mean literary achievement for someone who writes with increasing sympathy for Long Island Irish Catholicism. There are enormous differences between James T. Farrell's south side of Chicago and Elizabeth Cullinhan's Long Island—and I am enough of a Chicagoan to prefer the former if push comes to shove. Yet, it seems to me that Ms. Cullinhan and Farrell, in his Ryan series, are among the very few Irish Catholic writers who are disposed to be sympathetic to their heritage. The flaws and faults of the Irish are surely visible in both *Yellow Roses* and *The Death of Nora Ryan,* but the characters are not caricatures and there is nothing in either book that panders to the literary elite's stereotype of the American Irishman—as does, let us say, Jimmy Breslin's *World Without End, Amen.* The balance between wry dispassion and sensitivity and objectivity that is easily found in a dozen Jewish writers, like Bellow and Malamud for example, seems to be much more difficult for the Irish Catholic storyteller to achieve.

To oversimplify a vast and complex literary tradition, Irish writers tend to be lyrical, mystical, grotesque, hopeful, innocent, and deeply sympathetic with nature. Contemporary Irish poets like Seamus Heaney, Brandan Connelly, and John Montague demonstrate all of these characteristics at the same time. The innocence, lyricism, and mysticism seem to me to be the important characteristics (though the grotesque black humor one finds in the sagas of ancient times and in the short stories of Sean O'Faillon and the novels of Tom McHale in the present is also important). By lyrical I mean in this context a songlike melodious quality in which the very rhythm and sound of the words catch up the reader (whatever his other attributes, for example, one could not say that James T. Farrell was lyrical, and one would have to say that both Eugene O'Neill and F. Scott Fitzgerald were). By mystical I mean a feeling of unity that the writer senses and wants the reader to sense between himself or herself and the rest of the universe, human and nonhuman (and in particular in the Irish

tradition, the nonhuman universe). By innocent, I mean the conviction that however terrible things may seem, they are not ultimately
terrible and may indeed ultimately be comic. William Halsey, in his
recent intellectual history of American Catholicism,* argues that this
last quality was taken away from American life in general in the
1920s and 1930s but survived among Catholics into the 1960s, when
it expired there too.

I think Halsey is simply wrong and that he has not looked at the
right American Catholic thinkers and writers—like David Tracy in
the theological and philosophical world, perhaps, and a whole younger generation of Catholic social scientists such as Mary Hanna,
Teresa Sullivan and William McCready.

I would propose a New Trinity of American Irish Catholic writers, not yet as famous and perhaps never to be as famous as Farrell or
Edwin O'Connor, but far more Irish than writers like John Gregory
Dunne and indeed in a way more Irish than many of the fiction
writers currently practicing on the Emerald Isle itself (though no one
could be more Irish than Montague or Heaney or the dazzlingly
brilliant contemporary playwright Brian Friel). My New Trinity is
made up of short story writer Elizabeth Cullinhan, poet and theologian John Shea, and novelist and playwright John R. Powers.

The most beautiful of Cullinhan's short stories, "The Crime of
God," in *Yellow Roses,* is a classic of Irish writing: sweepingly lyrical
in its prose, profoundly mystical both in its subject matter and its
style and, for all Ms. Cullinhan's New York sophistication, breath-
takingly innocent. A disillusioned and saddened young woman at her
summer home in Long Island sees a Picasso face on an ordinary
working man who is performing labor around the house, and in a
breathtaking moment of revelation, she becomes aware of God's
goodness and God's love as revealed in that gratuitous, unnecessary,
but spectacularly attractive face. It is a moment of grace, a moment of
revelation, a limit experience, a rumor of angels, an overwhelming
hint of an explanation, a secret touch of the Spirit. Doubtless, other
writers besides the Irish have recorded such moments, but in a sweeping change from gloom to ecstasy achieved by a pilgrimage through
the commonplace, Cullinhan writes and sees with profoundly Irish
innocence. As long as the American Irish can produce such short
stories, the Irish literary heritage is alive and well.

---

* *The Survival of American Innocence.* Notre Dame, Ind.: Notre Dame University Press,
1980.

John R. Powers makes a third generation of writers who celebrate or lament the Irish on the south side of Chicago. Finley Peter Dunne wrote of Bridgeport; James T. Farrell wrote of the southeast side of Chicago a quarter of a century later; and now Powers writes of the southwestern fringes (Mount Greenwood, St. Christina's parish) yet another quarter of a century and more after Farrell (mysteriously and, according to him, unintentionally, the hero of one of his books bears the same name as the hero of the later Farrell volumes—Eddie Ryan). In his first novel, *The Last Catholic in America*, and to some extent in his second, *Do Patent Leather Shoes Really Reflect Up?*, Powers is not unlike Farrell. His anger at the Catholic heritage is less bitter and his vision of spiritual poverty is less dark. Farrell is innocent of a comic sense, and Powers's genius lies precisely in his comic sense. Yet there is anger in *The Last Catholic in America* and even more anger in *Do Patent Leather Shoes Really Reflect Up?* However, the musical drama version of *Patent Leather Shoes* is gentle and mellow, nostalgic, affectionate, sensitive, and retrospective on the "old church." Indeed in one scene, in which the second grade of St. Christina's prepares for the May Crowning and sings "Bring Flowers of the Rarest," the audience spontaneously joins in the refrain "Oh Mary, we crown thee with blossoms today/Queen of the Angels, Queen of the May." According to Powers, this happens almost at every performance. I taxed him with becoming nostalgic, and his wife—an Italian American, who hence has a unique perspective for evaluating the modified dualism of the Irish—responded with an expressive shrug, "Oh, John wrote the novel during his agnostic phase."

Powers's third book, *The Unoriginal Sinner and the Ice Cream God*, goes beyond anger and beyond nostalgia and arrives paradoxically enough at innocence. The Ice Cream God, who slips notes to the lonely, confused, and unhappy young hero, is a God of joy and hope and surprise, not a God on which the Irish by any means have a monopoly, but one which, in their better moments, they know very well.

Where Powers, currently the most promising young Irish Catholic writer, will go next remains to be seen. His conversation style is still that of someone from the neighborhood, his Ph.D. having academicized it not a bit. Indeed, he says that he finished the doctorate (from Northwestern University) so that he could advertise the fact that he was a Ph.D. on the back flap of the book; then when it came to the publication of the *Ice Cream God*, he deliberately left his academic credential off the dust jacket. (Something like another Irish Catholic

Ph.D. I know, who hangs his doctorate in his bathroom.) Powers is
working at present on his fourth novel, very slowly, he insists, because he writes slowly despite the vividness of his prose. He has
already achieved the mysticism and the innocence of the Irish Catholic tradition and began (with his marvelous song of praise to the
Swank Roller Rink at 111th and Western in Chicago) with the Irish
sense of the grotesque. Like John Shea, the third of the New Trinity,
Powers has little concern for the "critical" audience but writes what
he knows about and feels for the people he knows. He is too much of
a street person to be at ease with or care about the culture of the
upper academy. Unlike his contemporary Tom McHale, who has
abandoned his affiliation with his origins, religious and communal,
Powers seems to have sunk even deeper into his heritage and tradition.

John Shea, priest, theologian, and poet, is as much a product of the
west side of Chicago as John Powers is of the south side, and is
profoundly skeptical of the world of the professional academy, if not
more so than Powers. A Catholic theologian with enormous impact
on Protestants, indeed perhaps more on Protestants than on Catholics, Shea belongs to none of the professional theological organizations
and does not attend their meetings. What he thinks of them is clearly
explained in one of his comic poems:

A THEOLOGIAN AT PRAYER

O
(that is the vocative
of a cosmic disclosure)
Thou
who cannot become
and It,
Being in whom
all beings participate,
Absolute Future
who masters every present,
Origin and Destiny
of every concrescing actuality
whose Primordial Nature
cannot change
and whose Consequent Nature
cannot sit still,

Unknowable Mystery
who knows us,
Transcendent Third
in every duo,
please help me get tenure.

Shea's "narrative theology" is aimed less at the professional techni-
cal theologian and more at the parish priest and the educated lay
person (though in his brilliant dissertation on Protestant theologian
Langdon Gilkey, Shea more than established his claim on the union
card even if he doesn't want to collect the card). His most recent
theological work, *Stories of Faith,* contains three final chapters that are
written in biblical verse, the sort which brings awe and respect from
nontechnical readers and contempt from many professional theolo-
gians. The popularity of his work will also assure that many of the
professionals will not take him seriously, a fact which will trouble
Shea not in the slightest. He is, nevertheless, rated among the most
perceptive students of theology in the United States and is perhaps
the most original and most creative American Catholic theological
voice of our times, notwithstanding the philosophical theologian
David Tracy, a unique American contributor to the Catholic theological world.

But it is in his poetry, lyrical, mystical, sometimes grotesque, often
comic and profoundly innocent, that Shea's unique Irish American
Catholic genius is to be found. He disdains academicized poetry of
the little magazines as much as he disdains the academicized theology
of the professional theological journals. His verse is, however, by no
means always transparent:

A PRAYER FOR A FRIEND

Whose wit decreed
that electricity would live
between the fingers of friends
and every second question be
why do people trip
and every first
where did the sky come from?
The same who said
that dreams would chase waking men
and love catch them.

I am sure this poem means something wonderful, but I am hard put to say what precisely it means. And Shea himself conceded that he did not want to try to interpret it.

Nevertheless, his poetry is extremely popular, his two books having sold tens of thousands of copies, even though he defies the norms of professional poetry and his poetry is usually anything but opaque. As, for example, in his "The Prayer of Someone Who Has Been There Before":

After the last time—
 when I finally turned from flight
 and from somewhere came the strength
  to go back—
I rummaged the ruins,
 a refugee picking through bombed belongings
  for what surely was destroyed
and began again.
 I grew my new life
  thick and rough
 with an alarm system on the heart
 and an escape hatch in the head.
It was as spontaneous
as a military campaign.
 I loved in small amounts
  like a sick man sipping whiskey.
Each day was lived within its limits.
Each moment swallowed quickly.
 It was not all—our embracement of life
  but neither was it the hunched
   and jabbing stance of the boxer.
There was a courtesy and a sort-of caring.
 It was not bad.

 Now this.
 This thing.   *This feeling*
  this unbidden intrusion
   which had no part to play
  but played it anyway.
All those things scrupulously screened out
want in.
 And I can sense it coming,
  a second coming,
   a second shattering

Someone   Something
is at me once more,
mocking my defenses,
wrenching my soul.
God damn it!

Is it you again, Lord?

Shea's vision is above all mystical; he sees a God who comes back pounding once again on the door of human life demanding admission. This vision is to be seen in both his theological and poetic work and will doubtless appear in the fiction he plans eventually to write—fiction which I tell him will have 370 pages of blackness save for a space between two paragraphs in the penultimate page in which there will be a dazzling flash of light, the explosion of hope streaking across the sky from the east even unto the west, which led John in the Book of Revelations to his final explosion of faith and hope, "Come Lord Jesus."

Cullinhan, Powers, and Shea are all quintessentially Irish, especially in their mysticism and innocence. Unlike many earlier Irish Catholic writers, they have made their peace with the institutional Church, if indeed they ever had any trouble with it. In Shea's case in particular there is little trace of anger at the ecclesiastical institution which, on the west side of Chicago in his day, hardly seemed worth getting angry at anyway. Shea, like any mystic, saves his anger for God:

A Prayer of Anger

No hymn of praise today.
No hand-clapping alleluia
for the All-Good God
and his marvellous handiwork
Lord,
a child has been born bad.
He gangles and twitches and shames
the undiscovered galaxies of your creation
Why could not the hands that strung the stars
dip into that womb to bless and heal?
Please no voice from Job's Whirlwind
saying how dare I.
I dare
Yet I know no answer comes

save that tears dry up, skin knits,
and humans love broken things.
But to You who are always making pacts
You have my word on this—
on the final day of fire
after You have stripped me
(if there is breath left)
I will subpoena You to the stand
in the court of human pain.

But in his most recent book, *Stories of Faith*, Shea goes beyond anger to a dance which surely could be executed to the music of an Irish reel. A theology book, *Stories of Faith* ends with three chapters written in biblical verse that can be called poetic short stories. The final verses of the last story, "The Storyteller of God," are some of the finest words of Irish poetry ever written in America:

Now the sun,
which Ecclesiastes says always rises,
broke the night of fierce debate
but no rooster greeted it.
Instead
a stone the size of twelve men
moved like a mountain on its way to the sea
and on the fresh wind of morning
came the Son of Man,
his shroud a wedding garment,
his feet between earth and air in dance.
Death, Sin, and Fate poured rhetoric
into the stirring air about them
but the silent Son of God only danced
to music beyond their words.
He whirled around Death
and with each turn
Death himself grew old
till with a last, unbelievable look
he saw no more.
Then wordless
Christ spun around the words of Sin
till a stammer started, sound choked,
and finally there was only a mouth
without a voice.

Next Fate heard the risen footsteps
and frost formed on his tongue.
As Christ lept before him,
he froze in mid-syllable,
iced by the warmth of God.
Now
there was only the morning
and the dancing man of the broken tomb.
The story says
he dances still.
That is why
down to this day
we lean over the beds of our babies
and in the seconds before sleep
tell the story of the undying dancing man
so the dream of Jesus will carry them to dawn.

From Shea's mystical lyricism it is a long way down to *True Confessions* and *Farragan's Retreat.*

Ridicule of Irish Catholicism sells. *True Confessions* became a best seller while *Yellow Roses* and *The Death of Nora Ryan* will never go into paperback editions. Edwin O'Conner was succeeded in Boston not by someone who would offer a more subtle celebration of the Boston Irish but by George V. Higgins, whose Eddy Coyle becomes the typical Boston Irishman.

One cannot of course demand that a novelist be a sociologist (and sociologists become novelists at their own risk), but there is, I think, a critical difference between the somber melancholic realism of the early Farrell and the slick, glib self-ridicule of John Gregory Dunne. The people in *Studs Lonigan* are the sort about whom an Irish Catholic can say, "I know them all well," whereas the people in *True Confessions* are of the sort about whom most Irish Catholic readers would say, "I never met anybody like that." I am not suggesting that Farrell is to be admired because he presents a flattering portrait of the Irish in America and Dunne be condemned because he presents an unflattering portrait. Both, indeed, have very unflattering descriptions of Irish Catholic life. But of Dunne one says, "That is not the way it is," whereas of Farrell one must say, "That is not the whole story, but that is the way it is."

The younger Farrell was angry at the atmosphere of spiritual poverty in which he grew up, but his anger did not destroy his sympathy. John Gregory Dunne and Tom McHale don't seem to be angry at all, but they have very little sympathy. Farrell was interested in social criticism; the others are interested in ridicule.

An interesting indicator of whether a contemporary Irish American self-portrait is designed for ridicule or sympathy is the attitude of the portrait on the social and religious changes in Irish Catholicism during the last two decades. There are rich Catholics in the writings of Dunne and McHale but no Catholic intellectuals; there are priests and nuns, but both authors show very little awareness of the changes in the Church since the Second Vatican Council. Elizabeth Cullinhan, on the other hand, has room in her work for the beginnings of an Irish Catholic literary and intellectual elite and makes very skillful use in the tapestries of her stories of the Second Vatican Council's effects on Irish Catholicism. The implicit theme of many of the stories in *Yellow Roses* is the difference between the old-fashioned pieties of the parental generation and the mixture of belief and nonbelief that torments both the clergy and the laity in the younger generation. Mysteriously, but I think convincingly and accurately, Ms. Cullinhan seems to think that the faith of the younger generation is more authentic than the faith of its predecessors; she implies that it is harder to believe when many of the old supports are swept away but that the faith that does survive may be stronger and richer. One can find no trace of such insights in the writings of Dunne or McHale, mostly because neither of these writers is especially interested in what is really happening to the Irish Catholic Church in the United States or to those who in one way or another are trying to remain committed to its world view. When your goal is self-ridicule, such issues are not pertinent.

I am not suggesting that anyone who sets out to write about the Irish in America in our age need be sensitive to the changes occurring in the Catholic Church—though the comic as well as the tragic potential in such changes are enormous. But I am saying that when novelists write explicitly about the Catholic Church, as does Tom McHale, they at least should be accurate as to what the Irish Catholic Church in America is like these days and not serve up a faintly modernized 1930s version of Irish Catholicism. The point is not that one must be "balanced" about the Church, or that one ought not to be critical about the Church, but rather that one simply ought not to be totally false about the present reality of the Catholic Church in

America In my own attempts at fiction, there are, heaven knows, unattractive churchpersons and their Catholicism is something less than perfect, but I do my best to make the absence of attractiveness and perfection moderately consistent with the real world instead of creating what is essentially a Disneyland version of contemporary Catholicism.

I do not object to Eugene O'Neill's anguished descriptions of Irish Catholic family life any more than I object to Farrell's angry description of the spiritual poverty that destroyed Studs Lonigan. There are, God knows, many things in contemporary Irish Catholicism which ought to stir up anguish that one does not find in writers like McHale and Breslin and Dunne. Indeed, there is much that is ridiculous in contemporary Irish Catholicism—diocesan senates, pastoral councils of priests and laity, for example. But, if one is to write a novel of ridicule, at least one ought to ridicule absurdities which actually exist rather than absurdities which no longer exist—if they ever did.

Or to put the matter somewhat differently, *Hogan's Goat* is a description of corrupt Irish politics in New York, Edwin O'Connor's *Last Hurrah* is perhaps a one-sided celebration of Irish politics in Boston. No one has thought of writing fiction about Chicago Irish politics (unless you happen to think, as I do, that Mike Royko's *Boss* is mostly a work of fiction). That there are no novels about Chicago politics, to say nothing of novels that are both critical and sympathetic, is utterly mind-boggling. Yet, clearly no Irish Catholic writer has thought the subject worth fictional analysis; even if one should attempt such a novel, it would almost certainly not see the light of publication unless it were a simple-minded assault on the evils of the organization and the goodness of "reform" or "independence."

Let me try to make my point with a comparison. Philip Roth has written savage satires of the American Jewish culture, but they are effective precisely because there is enough verisimilitude in them to make them plausible. One does not turn to Philip Roth for a sociological presentation of American Jewish life, but one turns for a rather bitter satire of some dimensions of that life, just as one turns to Woody Allen for a more mellow and sensitive satire. But in *True Confessions* and *Farragan's Retreat* one doesn't find satire at all because one doesn't find verisimilitude. Such novels will appeal as satire to those whose prejudices and stereotypes lead them to believe they know what Irish Catholics are really like.

An Irish Catholic version of *Portnoy's Complaint* would be hilariously funny; maybe we could bring Eugene O'Neill back from the dead to do it. But the cops in *World Without End, Amen* or *True Confessions* are not funny at all. Portnoy is a lunatic; the cops of Dunne and Breslin are merely ink blots served up for WASP and Jewish prejudice.

The Irish Catholicism that is presented in this book (affluent, intellectual, acquiring self-confidence, stuck with its own Irishness whether it likes it or not, learning to laugh at itself at the same time it laughs at everything else) is a rich lode to be mined by the imaginative writer. Despite its richness, however, this mine does not yet seem "commercial." Only the very young among Irish Catholic writers seem even to be aware of the existence of this richness. The suburban WASPs in the short stories of Updike and Cheever are hilarious, pathetic, and somehow still admirable. I simply cannot see why the far more colorful, more manic, more amusing and, perhaps in some ways, more glorious suburban Irish should be so uninteresting to the writers, the publishers, and the readers of imaginative literature.

Doubtless part of the problem is the residual self-hatred of Irish Catholic writers. Another part of the problem is the stereotypes on which the editors, publishers, book reviewers, and book readers still depend (even if many of them happen to be Irish Catholic). Bigotry which would be unacceptable about blacks or Jews or Hispanics or native Americans is still eminently acceptable about the Irish. However, at the risk of sounding something like William Shannon and blaming the Irish for their own victimization, we must bear a good deal of responsibility for ourselves. Not merely because we have accepted self-hatred for so long but also, and perhaps more importantly, because in our desperate quest for acceptability in and respect from American society, we made it impossible for many of our writers to practice their trade and not be alienated.

Writers always risk some alienation from the communities about which they write. For a number of decades in the history of American Irish Catholicism only those with the most alienated personalities to begin with would think about being writers. If you wrote about the Irish Catholic community, it was assumed that you were hostile to it and that you had betrayed community responsibility. If Jim Farrell, John O'Hara, and F. Scott Fitzgerald left the community, it was in part because there was no room for them in the Irish Catholicism of their young adulthoods. The ancient Celtic art of telling tales and singing songs was negatively reinforced until very recently in the Irish Catholic community. No parents wanted to raise their sons to be novelists or their daughters to be poets, and everyone was suspicious of the parish priest who wrote books—without of course experiencing the slightest need to read his books!

During the Augustin Bea symposium at Harvard in 1963 (when that astute Roman cardinal came to the stage at Sander's Theatre in Harvard to signal the end of the counterreformation), I spent a spare hour and a half with a young man from our parish who was a student at Harvard University. Every available space in his room was filled with English literature—poetry, drama, and novels. And he showed me his short stories, read me his poetry, spoke about the plays and novels that he would like to write. I asked him, I think not unreasonably, why he was majoring in biochemistry with this enormous literary interest. He shrugged his shoulders, "The old man is paying the bills and he wants me to go to medical school," he replied.

His whole generation, coming of age between 1955 and 1965 and now between their mid-thirties and mid-forties, was subjected to the same pressures and sanctions. You might leave outlines for novels in the glove compartment of your car or scribble poems on the commuter train, but you really didn't think seriously about publishing them, much less devoting a lifetime to such activities. You had "serious" responsibilities which had to take precedence over such frivolity.

Even though I am a writer, I am not persuaded that writing is inherently superior to law, medicine, business, dentistry, politics, or any other profession. But the Irish, with a long tradition of literature in America, have produced relatively few and mostly alienated writers while they have produced a superabundance of other professionals. There is no reason why someone should have to be a writer just because he has literary talents, but neither is there any reason why he should feel obliged not to be a writer or think that poetry or fiction or playwriting interferes with serious, respectable work.

On the south side of Chicago all of this is changing. Before he died, they had receptions in Beverly when Jimmy Farrell came to town. The writer down the street is admired almost as much as the professor down the street. If a priest-writer happened to show up in the parish, people might read his books!

A classmate of the young man at Harvard persisted in her literary ambition, despite powerful negative sanctions from family and community. Now, she is the chairman of her parish liturgy committee and agrees after only mild persuasion to the reading of some of her material at Sunday Mass.

In this chapter it has been necessary to rely on personal opinion (sometimes perhaps highly idiosyncratic personal opinion) more than statistical data, but the thesis of the chapter is the same as that of the rest of the book:

1. Stereotypes which persist in the United States about Irish Catholics simply are not compatible with the truth.

2. To a considerable extent, Irish Catholics have contributed to the stereotype because of their self-hatred and because of their search for acceptance and respectability, which have been the all-consuming goals in our American pilgrimage.

3. Things are changing, though. John Gregory Dunne made it to the mass-market paperback and Elizabeth Cullinhan did not. John R. Powers did—and Powers represents the future and Dunne the past.

T W E L V E

What Next?

THE THESIS OF THIS BOOK—THAT THE IRISH ARE WEALTHY, POWERFUL, and still Irish—is utterly unremarkable. If someone would observe that American Jews or American blacks or American Hispanics or native Americans were profoundly influenced by their cultural heritage and historic past, no one would be at all surprised. If a writer should then go on to suggest that many members of these communities were interested in preserving that historical heritage, there would presumably be applause from critics and reviewers and readers. Finally, if the writer should suggest or even demand that the rest of the society facilitate the preservation of such heritages, very few would dare to disagree. But to make even the first assertion about the Irish is asking for trouble. "Everyone knows" that the Irish have assimilated, and if they haven't, they ought to. Any demand to work for the preservation of Irish culture is un-American and "divisive."

Indeed, it is probably un-American and divisive even to write a book which offers evidence of a distinctive Irish Catholic subculture within the larger American culture. Perhaps the editor of *Commentary* will even warn me again of the dangers of "ethnicity" and not see any irony at all in such a stand in the pages of his magazine.

I will confess to a certain annoyance: I am perfectly prepared to cheer for the preservation of the black or the Hispanic or the Jewish cultural traditions. Why aren't the inheritors of those traditions or Anglo-Saxon Protestants, who are sympathetic to them, prepared to cheer for the survival of my tradition? I can only conclude that they think the black or Jewish or Hispanic heritages are worth preserving and mine isn't. I wonder why.

It has always been, of course, an assumption that some groups had to assimilate and others didn't have to. In the beginning, the Irish were one of the groups targeted for assimilation. All right-thinking Americans know that the Irish should assimilate and assume that most of them have. It is terribly disturbing when someone suggests that maybe they haven't assimilated completely and maybe they ought not to. There is, you may notice, a double standard.

At a more general level the discussion of "ethnicity" and "cultural pluralism," distinctions established by this double standard, are important: scholarly research which describes, analyzes, and explains the persistence of the approved subcultures is to be applauded, for it explains why that which everybody knows is true is in fact true. On the other hand, research which describes, analyzes, and explains the persistence of an unfashionable subculture is divisive, biased, and probably immoral. Once one can grasp the niceties of that distinction, one is able to make the approved comment on the so-called "ethnic revival."

To discuss black or Jewish distinctiveness is not part of the ethnic revival at all. To discuss Irish or Italian distinctiveness is part of the ethnic revival. Such discussion must be viewed with grave suspicion as a regression to particularism, trivialism, and primitivism.

Got it?

Hence, this volume is a study not in the survival of diversity among ethnic groups in American society—because no one seriously believes that such diversity has been eliminated and no one seriously suggests that it ought to be eliminated; rather, this book represents a study of the survival of objectionable distinctiveness and raises the scary possibility that all kinds of other objectionable distinctive groups might have also survived.

I have established, I think, that Irish Catholic religion, politics, family structure, personality, political style, drinking behavior, and world view are different from those of other Americans. The differences are measured by different mean scores on behavioral and attitudinal scales. Around the differences, of course, there are standard deviations which overlap. Some Italians are political activists, and some Irish are politically inactive. Some Irish drink not at all, and there are Jewish alcoholics. Subcultural diversity does not mean that all the members of one group are different from all the members of another group, but rather that there are different averages and, hence, different tendencies and propensities. The Irish in the European Economic Community, for example, are much more likely to be feminists than are the Germans. That does not mean that the two European cultures are totally different from one another. Rather, they are partially different and partially similar.

It is beyond the scope of the present volume to ask whether subcultural diversity inside the United States may be greater than crosscultural diversity between the United States and other countries. However, in an analysis that Norman Nie and I are presently undertaking, we do establish that there is more diversity in political participation styles among American ethnic groups than there is among the various nations that Professor Nic and Professor Sidney Verba studied in their monumental crossnational political-behavior research. It would appear that there may be more differences in political participation between Irish Americans and Italian Americans than there is between the Irish and the Italians in Europe; however, it is not necessary for the thesis of this book that subcultural diversity in the United States in some respects be greater than subcultural diversity within the EEC. It is merely necessary that there be subcultural diversity in the United States, that it be linked with the historical heritages of the various groups, and that it show durability and persistence despite higher educational levels and increasing numbers of generations in the United States.

The Irish are different. They are different in ways that are predictable from or can be easily linked to their cultural inheritance, and these differences show remarkable persistence and durability despite education, generation, moving away from ethnic neighborhoods, decline of self-conscious ethnicity, and even ethnic intermarriage. Furthermore, I think my colleagues and I have established through our "socialization" model (described in the chapter on Irish drinking) an explanation of the process through which subcultural diversities persist. One does not absorb considerable residues of the Irish past in a classroom or by reading magazines or books or newspapers, or even by keeping Old World customs or eating Old World foods. One learns one's cultural inheritance—religious, political, familial—in the context of early childhood experiences, modeling appropriate behavior patterns not so much on what parents say as on what parents do.

Some social scientists, carefully pondering an enormous amount of evidence that has been assembled in the last decade on the persistence of subcultural diversity in America, are willing to concede that there is indeed a good deal more "ethnicity" in American society than they had thought. Nevertheless, say such observers (as for example, Professor Herbert Gans), all of this is going to go away eventually anyhow. Only it is just going to take longer than we thought it was. Comments like that (particularly from such distinguished scholars as Professor Gans) cause me to go back and look at my tables again to see whether they have discovered something I missed. But, for the life of me, I can't find evidence of the assimilationist trends they seem to see. If the Irish, the most affluent of gentile ethnic groups and the one that has been here the longest (with the possible exception of the Germans), do still have distinctive mean scores on measures of world view, family structure, personality, political style, drinking behavior, attitudes toward the role of women, and many of these differences do not seem to be wiped out even by ethnic intermarriage, what grounds does anybody have to say that the homogenization process is going on, only somewhat more slowly?

If one argues that the Irish have indeed been assimilated and merely means that most of us speak without brogues, eat with knives and forks, no longer live in shanties, and wear underwear most of the time, then, fine, the Irish have been assimilated. If they mean that whatever cultural distinctiveness still persists among the American Irish is no threat to larger national unity, then I am not prepared to disagree, though I don't think Irish distinctiveness was a threat to the national unity in 1860 either. Still, I find myself wondering why the issue of divisive Irish distinctiveness concerns those who are quite unconcerned by the possibility of divisive Jewish or black distinctiveness.

My problem is that I keep forgetting about the double standard.

There are two particularly obnoxious aspects to this book, either one of which could provide scholars like Harvard's Professor Orlando Patterson with more than enough motivation to dismiss my data as being the result of "pro-ethnic bias." First of all, I contend that while the Irish are different, they are not different in the direction that the stereotypes dictate they ought to be. Pro-integration, pro–civil liberties, pro-feminism, sexually tolerant, with no more serious drinking problems than urban English Protestants, my description of the American Irish is counterintuitive—even when, as in their religion of hopefulness, their feminism, and their political style, they represent continuity rather than discontinuity with their own past.

Secondly and perhaps even more offensively, I contend, on the basis of overwhelming evidence, that despite their distinctiveness the Irish have been successful in America; or if you prefer, that despite their success they have remained different (at the risk of being repetitious, not completely different but still on the average different). We were given our choice upon arrival: we could either be different or successful, but not both. We were urged to be successful and to give up our distinctiveness as a prelude to success. We tried to take the advice and couldn't quite pull it off. We continued to be different and were successful anyhow.

In research which William McCready, Gary Byram, and I are presently working on, we have discovered there is a negative relationship between number of children in the family and economic success for all the groups we are studying (Japanese, Korean, Irish, Jews, blacks, and white Protestants). The more siblings one has, the less likely one is to be successful. Large Irish family size was indeed, as predicted by our betters, an obstacle to success. So we kept right on having large families, but we became successful, too. We are the most affluent gentile ethnic group in America, despite the size of our families, and would have been even more affluent if we had curtailed family size as we were told to do. We insisted on having our cake and eating it too.

This book, in other words, denies the validity of the choice with which the Irish immigrants were confronted: stop being Irish or fail. Despite ourselves, we didn't stop being Irish and we didn't fail either. To demonstrate this finding with overwhelming statistical evidence is subversive, seditious, divisive, disloyal, and probably un-American. If the Irish can be different and still be good Americans, then so can anyone else.

Consider the conclusions of other books on the Irish Americans. Marjorie R. Fallows concludes her book with the assertion that the "Irish American experience will serve as a model for other ethnic groups of how gradual assimilation can occur." Ms. Fallows has available much of the data from the NORC research on which this book is based. I cannot for the life of me see how she concludes that the Irish are a model for gradual assimilation. Again, I look over my tables to be sure they still say what I thought they said: the Irish are, if anything, a model of how a group can become enormously successful in America and still remain distinctive. How distinctive? As distinctive as the Jews or the blacks? In some ways, less distinctive than those two groups; in some ways, as distinctive; and in some ways, even more distinctive. But surely, not a model of "gradual assimilation" any more than the blacks or the Jews are models of "gradual assimilation."

John B. Duff, in his *The Irish in the United States,* contends that "the Irish purchase acceptance by paying the price of conformity. They got along when they accepted the traditional American values of work, progress, success or respectability." All that is clear is that in the Ireland they left behind, English oppression made it impossible for their work to lead to progress, success, or respectability (and the progress and success in the contemporary Republic of Ireland would indicate that the Irish are by no means an unambitious people). The Irish may indeed have tried to pay the price of conformity, but it didn't win for them acceptance, and as it turned out, they never were very good at conforming.

Lawrence McCaffrey, in his *Irish Diaspora in America,* observes that "although it is probably too late to matter, Irish Americans should ask whether the price of assimilation and demand of ethnic identity has been too high." The Irish, he tells us, made the trip from the old city neighborhoods to the suburbs, which turns out to be a pilgrimage from someplace to noplace. But, alas, it is too late to save them, even though they have given up a great deal for very little. McCaffrey, like Duff and Fallows, accepts the choice imposed by the nativists: stop being Irish or fail. Since the Irish have clearly not failed, they must have ceased at being Irish. With all due respect, I must assert that Professor McCaffrey, vigorous critic of assimilationism that he is, yielded to the assimilationists too much by accepting their definition of the problem and their view of the issue.

William Shannon, in *The American Irish,* concludes, as does Duff, with a description of the Kennedys as "archetypes of the American Irish." "Fundamentally, the Irish have been a people outside of the business system and have never fully been reconciled to its values. At the lower levels, they have been obsessed with the security of civil service jobs because they have been more impressed by the failures and vicissitudes of capitalism than by its opportunities and rewards. At the higher levels, this same alienation reappears as an aristocratic disdain for mere money making." Once more you see the dilemma; either success or Irishness, but not both—not unless you are somebody special like the aristocratic Kennedys (Shannon feels John Kennedy epitomized the Irish attitudes when he said of politics, "It beats chasing a dollar").

Maybe, but for a people who have not accepted the values of the business system, who have been obsessed with security, and who have disdained mere money making, the Irish Americans seem to have made a lot of it. Maybe the reason is that the bucks often come more quickly when you really don't chase them.

But these four books—each in its own way admirable and making important contributions to the understanding of the American Irish—accept the assimilationist dilemma. Shannon, like the Pat Moynihan of *Beyond the Melting Pot*, sees the Irish as unsuccessful because too much of the Irish cultural residue has survived. McCaffrey, Duff, and Fallows, faced with the insurmountable NORC data, have to abandon the failure part of the choice and conclude that the Irish have stopped being Irish.

I said pretty much the same thing in *That Most Distressful Nation*. "And so the WASPs won. Seduced by the bright glitter of respectability and egged on by the mothers, the Irish had become just like everyone else, and the parades on St. Patrick's Day are monuments to the lost possibilities of which few people in the suburbs are aware."

I really didn't mean it; I went on to quote a poem by a young Irish American which was profoundly and passionately Celtic and ended my book with the words, "So maybe the Irish haven't been tamed at all." I didn't have the data in 1972 that I have now and didn't perceive then nearly as clearly as I do now how strong was the cultural residue or what were the dynamics by which it was kept strong and is likely to continue to be kept strong. In the early 1970s, I was half persuaded that the Irish had accepted the choice the nativists had imposed upon them and opted for success at the price of giving up much of their heritage. I have learned through the research of the last seven years that we did indeed accept the choice, we did indeed opt for success, and we did indeed try to stop being Irish. And succeed we did—at everything else but giving up Irishness. That persisted despite our efforts, precisely because we grew up in families where the Irish cultural heritage was passed on, even if nobody tried to do so and even if most everybody did his best not to pass it on.

And yet I wonder why so many American scholars have been so

willing to accept the idea that the Irish had to choose one of two options when there was so much evidence all around them, and, in the case of Irish-American scholars, even inside them. Being affluent and being Irish were quite compatible and indeed, on occasion, gloriously compatible.

Perhaps the price of questioning the conventional assimilationist, even only in our minds, was too high.

What then for the future of the American Irish?

1. On the basis of the evidence available to us, the Irish-American subculture is likely to persist indefinitely. The Irish Catholic Americans will continue to be different in their religion, their family life, their political style, their world view, their drinking behavior, and their personalities. Any assertion to the contrary must be made in the teeth of overwhelmingly convincing data and taken as a sign of profound assimilationist faith.

2. The Irish will continue to be affluent and probably become even more affluent as they settle down securely amidst the upper crusts of the middle class with a firm foothold in the nation's economic and political, if not intellectual and artistic, elites.

3. There almost certainly will be a return to higher levels of self-conscious Irish identification. Irish adolescents are already more likely than their parents to say that their ethnic background is important to them. The "new pluralism" of the 1960s has survived for more than a decade now, and despite periodic predictions that it was on the wane, it seems to be as strong as ever. If black pride is legitimate, then so is Irish pride; and while not all Irish Americans, or even a majority of them, are likely to be culturally self-conscious, an increasing number are almost certain to be.

4. Self-hatred has had it. The newly emergent Irish intellectuals and artistic intelligentsia simply are not going to play that game anymore and probably could not do so even if they wanted to. Ashamed of being Irish? Forget it, my friends. That's over.

5. My colleague J. David Greenstone suggests that the Irish are going to be artistically, intellectually, and politically the Jews of the "end of the century." He may exaggerate. Any prediction about these matters goes far beyond the available evidence. Yet I am as convinced as Professor Greenstone that there is going to be a flowering of Irish-American cultural life.

6. Since anti-Irish nativism is not going to go away, it seems to me to be very likely that Irish "militancy" will increase. I don't expect to see a revival of the Fenians or the Clan Na Gael, but I think it will be impossible for the younger Irish intelligentsia to stomach the anti-Irish nativism that still dominates the universities, the mass media, the large foundations, and much of the federal bureaucracy. Nor do I think that we will be able to pretend, as do many Irish editors and journalists, that the bigotry isn't there. Until recently, you could control an angry Irishman by appealing to his self-hatred; with the self-hatred gone, such appeals can be dangerous. The first couple of generations of Irish Americans to make it to the national elites took contempt for the Irish as a matter of course, and when they didn't embrace it or ignore it, they were at least silent about it. More recently, the Irish have grown up without learning about the hatred or about the need for self-hatred. So when they encounter contempt, stereotyping, prejudice, and bigotry, they are first astonished and then dismayed and then—at the risk of being autobiographical—furious. The days of the "tame cat" Irish of the intellectual world are over, and you have been given a fair warning about it.

This book then is a celebration both of the success and the survival of the Irish: a celebration of the end of self-hatred, and a celebration for the beginning of the ultimate confrontation between the Irish and the nativist enemy.

But in this happy ecumenical age one must not end on a hostile note. Surely one of the most important traits of the Irish heritage is lyricism. Alas, our lives for the last couple of centuries in both Old Ireland or Great Ireland have not been very lyrical. Yet the poetic imagination survived, even on the south side of Chicago. Perhaps, I should add, especially on the south side of Chicago, where an Irish mother sings a lullaby to a tow-haired, leprechaun-eyed, boychild named Liam.

I shall not to you give, my son, a heritage of
splintered dreams
that slushed down the sink with stale beer and
squeezed out tears of pain
for all the years that might have been if I had
lived

instead of killing dead my heart and ours, bit by
                    bit,
with breaking rage and chunks of sorrow,
passion which guilt turned sour and then,
                    misunderstanding
took my soul and crashed it in the night.
I shall not go desperate dying into life.
The enemy that dare to take the sea's surge from our eyes
I shall defy and drag to hell and back and shake the
                    skull of suicide
which says the gift will be ungiven and the hope denied.
No, for we shall sing, my son, and eat the sweets of
                    victory.
Lie peaceful down your head
This hunger will not be quieted, nor ever fully fed
Not before we hold the stars and until then,
we'll go a'brawling and wooing life
there're fights to be fought and battles won
But never in the name of life direct our own undoing
Nor allow while we breathe that Life should be undone!

Oh yes, my friends, there are still a few of us around!

Index